# THE POLITICS OF RITUAL
# AND REMEMBRANCE
## Laos since 1975

# THE POLITICS OF RITUAL
# AND REMEMBRANCE
## LAOS SINCE 1975

BY

## GRANT EVANS

UNIVERSITY OF HAWAI'I PRESS
HONOLULU

Published in North America by
University of Hawai'i Press
2840 Kolowalu Street
Honolulu, Hawai'i 96822

First Published in Thailand by
Silkworm Books
P.O. Box 76, Chiang Mai 50000

Printed in Thailand

**Library of Congress Cataloguing-in-Publication Data**
Evans, Grant 1948-
The politics of ritual and remembrance : Laos since 1975/Grant Evans.
p.     cm.
Includes bibliographical references and index.
ISBN 0-8248-2054-1
1.  Laos—History—1975-      I. Title.
DS555.84.E94      1998
949.404'2—dc21          97-43294
CIP

Set in Palatino 10 pt. by Silk Type.

In memory of

CLAUDE VINCENT

Claude Vincent was shot down with five others near Kasy on the road between Vientiane and Luang Prabang on 11 September 1996. The death of a friend is a chilling reminder of the fragility of our existence. So it is against the waves of forgetfulness that threaten to engulf us all that I offer this small epitaph to his memory. Claude knew more about Laos than most people and I would have loved to hear his views on what I have written in the pages below. No doubt he would have had his disagreements, but unlike many others, they would have been worth listening to.

# ACKNOWLEDGMENTS

First I would like to thank all the Lao who over many years have contributed to my "souvenirs" of their culture and society. It has been their "insider" dialogue with this "outsider" which has produced this book which seemed to spring almost fully formed from my mind over a few hectic months in 1996.

Less anonymously, I would like to thank Charles F. Keyes, now one of the godfathers of Tai studies (in the avuncular rather than *chao poh* sense), for his careful comments on the the text. I have learnt a great deal from him over the years as will be evident in the pages that follow.

I am also indebted to Ing-Britt Trankell for her meticulous reading of the text, during which (apparently) she paced the floor debating point for point with my ghost. Independent of my own research her thoughts on Luang Prabang have paralleled mine in striking ways thereby, perhaps, adding an intersubjective authenticity to both our arguments. I can only invite readers to *tri-angulate* this relationship by buying her book when it appears.

The photographs which illustrate the text are all taken by the author. The exceptions are individually acknowledged.

# CONTENTS

The destruction of the past, or rather of the social mechanisms that link one's contemporary experience to that of earlier generations, is one of the most characteristic and eerie phenomena of the late twentieth century. Most young men and women at the century's end grow up in a sort of permanent present lacking any organic relation to the public past of the times they live in.

—Eric Hobsbawm, *The Age of Extremes*

Left: Kaysone Phomvihane (1988). Below: Bust of Kaysone inside the Vientiane Municipal headquarters. The plaque reads: "Kaysone Phomvihane is in our thoughts whenever we carry out our duty." Note the base of stylized lotus petals.

Stupa to the unknown soldier at the end of the That Luang parade ground.

That Luang, the Grand or Royal Stupa in Vientiane, with a statue of King Setthatirath.

National Day parade, 1985. Note the old laurel being carried at the front depicting the hammer and sickle. Behind that are posters of Marx and Lenin, and then posters of Kaysone, Nouhak, Souphanouvong and Phoumi; the rest of the politburo are out of sight.

Minority women's "militia" at the 1985 parade. In the background are banners exhorting people to build socialism, and posters of the party leaders.

Billboards from the early days of the revolution.

Young novices wait for offerings from the laity during the That Luang festival.

A billboard for the 1995 National Day celebrations, sponsored by Pepsi Cola. The slogan reads: "To Build and Expand the People's Democratic Regime Under the Leadership of the Party is the Way to Prosperity."

A young Lao woman pays hommage to the Buddha at the That Luang festival.

Left: Young novices study on the porch of Vat May in Luang Prabang.
Right: Poster detail depicting Lao monks' support for the revolution.

Katay Don
Sasorith's
statue being
inaugurated
by then
education
minister,
Boun Om, in
Pakse in 1962.
(M. Sasorith)

A banner made of old RLG notes with the picture of King Sisavang Vong spirals down from the ceiling of a *vat* in Luang Nam Tha.

A *nang tiam* dancing.

Souphanouvong (front center) posing with officials in Luang Prabang during the coalition government in 1974. A large picture of the king stands in the background.

Prince Boun Oum's abandoned "palace" in Pakse before it was taken over and made into a hotel by a Thai company.

King Chulalongkorn, the centerpiece of an altar in Laos, flanked by Prince Phetsarath.

Thai Princess Sirindhorn makes offerings to Lao monks at Vat Xieng Thong in 1990. (KPL)

Pictures of King Sisavang Vatthana and Crown Prince Vong Savang, alongside King Chulalongkorn.

Calendar carrying the image of King Sisavang Vong, produced by Lao refugees in America. Some copies found their way to Laos.

Vat Phu in Champassak.

Statue of King Sisavang Vong at That Luang Dai in 1993. In 1994 it disappeared.

Above left: LPDR stamps are grouped at left, and RLG stamps at right.
Left: Early Pathet Lao "Liberation kip."
Above: Both sides of the old RLG five-kip note. The side featuring the former king, Sisavang Vong, is "unmentionable."

xxi

Left: The Prabang procession leaves the palace, led by the *thevada muang*, Phou Ngeu Nga Ngeu, the lion Singkheo Singkham, and the monks.
Right: In the past the Prabang was carried by *kha*, but now they are Lao dressed in the traditional tunic.

Foreign Minister Somsavath Lengsavad (third from left), stands on the palace steps with the *chao muang* of Luang Prabang, before the Prabang parade.

The so-called *"kabouan son pao,"* the minorities section of the *nang sangkhan* parade.

Minority "beauties" in the *nang sangkhan* parade. Front left to right: Black Tai, Hmong, Yao. Immediately behind them: Yao, Khamu.

Poster depicting minority solidarity with the revolution. Sam Neua, 1988.

# COMMUNISM REMEMBERED

W E live in a new era. It follows the disintegration of communism as a historical project after the collapse of the Soviet Union in 1990. In the Far East, however, communist regimes did not collapse, they mutated into "post-socialist" regimes. Why the term "post-socialism?" For Laos I have argued that while it is economically and socially capitalist by almost any social scientific criteria (Evans 1995), I prefer for now to use the term "post-socialist" to describe the regime because of the political continuity between the revolutionary and post-socialist phases. Most obviously, the Lao People's Revolutionary Party (LPRP) which came to power in 2 December 1975 promising to build a communist society is still in power, and the name it gave to the state, the Lao People's Democratic Republic (LPDR), remains unchanged, as does one of its key symbols, the national flag. During the LPDR's twentieth anniversary year, 1995, we witnessed intensified political ritual marking the fortieth anniversary of the founding of the LPRP, the seventy-fifth birthday anniversary of the late party leader Kaysone Phomvihane, and also a greater emphasis than has been usual since the collapse of communism on the Marxist-Leninist roots of the LPRP and on socialism with "Lao characteristics." This rhetoric however, is common among the remaining post-socialist regimes in Asia, and it is a sign of Laos's close relationship with the People's Republic of China

1

and its long-standing relationship with the Socialist Republic of Vietnam. Yet, it is important to understand that among these states "socialism" no longer represents an economic program, or a program of social and cultural transformation. Instead, it is a device of political rhetoric which proclaims, both externally and internally, that the one-party state has no intention of allowing liberal-democratic reforms. The LPRP continues to insist on its exclusive, leading role and crushes signs of political dissidence. Prime Minister Khamtay Siphandone made this quite clear during his December 1995 address on the occasion of the birthday anniversary of Kaysone: "We must," he said, "uphold the socialist ideology and goal. We must increase unity within the Party, and oppose the multi-party concept . . ." (*Vientiane Times (VT)* 15-21/12/95) Earlier, in March, during the party's fortieth anniversary he said, "The Party is also the sole party whom the people trust. All slanders and attempts designed to undermine the leadership role of the Party are regarded as contradictory to the historical reality and the national interest . . ." (*VT* 24-30/3/95).

Laos was always a poor arena for any socialist experimentation. It has a population of around four and a half million scattered over a surface area two-thirds the size of Vietnam, a large part of which is mountainous and not easily accessible. This population is ethnically diverse (perhaps sixty percent could be characterized as ethnically Lao), and poor in terms of the demands of modern economies. Most people are rice-growing peasants, though there are several small cities stretched out along the Mekong River from the north to the south of the country, with the capital Vientiane having a population of around half a million. Infrastructure is poor, although large aid projects are in the process of changing this and Laos is fast moving from being what used to be called a land-locked buffer-state to being a crossroads state in the mainland Southeast Asian region. Had it not been for the Vietnam War which engulfed the "sideshows" of Laos and Cambodia, a socialist seizure of power would never have had

vietnam
caused

2

occurred in Laos. And some say it should never have occurred.[1]

The so-called communist states which remain in the late twentieth century are not so different, in broad outline, from the developmental states that emerged in the Third World in the post–World War II period. Many of these were one-party states espousing some allegedly indigenous form of socialism. As Peter Worsley wrote: "Every party with any pretentions to power . . . preached some form of socialism." (1964:117) Most, however, in fact developed into varieties of state-capitalism or colonels' capitalism, with deeply entrenched political oligarchies. In the recent period we have seen some attempts to roll back bloated state sectors created by these regimes, and in some cases to liberalize the political system. In mainland Southeast Asia, Burma remains an example of colonel's capitalism, while Thailand has moved towards liberalization in many spheres. Political instability in Laos caused by the war in Vietnam in the 1950s and 1960s led to civil war, and ensured that attempts to create a liberal-democratic state collapsed and that no vigorous developmental state could be put in place there until after the communist revolution in 1975.

The main difference between authoritarian capitalist states and communist states is the totalitarian pretensions of the latter (Evans 1990a:182). That is, they attempt to organize and transform all of human behavior in the service of a higher goal, such as creating a "new socialist man."[2] This aim, however, has eluded even the most powerful states, let alone Laos, but it guided the actions and rhetoric of cadres after the revolution. These millennial pretensions have now been abandoned in Laos. In the following pages, therefore, through an exploration of rituals, symbols and rhetoric, I wish to trace

1. The simple facts of the matter are that the Pathet Lao would not have come to power in 1975 without the long-term assistance of North Vietnam's own "Secret Army" in Laos of approximately 70,000 men in the closing stages of the war. We await revisionist histories of the war in Laos.

2. For an extended critique of the concept of "socialist man," see Evans (1990a: Chapter 1).

the trajectory of this millennial moment in recent Lao history from the heady revolutionary days of late 1975 to the sober realities of the present.

# IDENTITY@LAO.NET

T HE advent of the information super highway has made all of us more aware than ever of the importance of knowledge and information in the modern world. Yet some governments in Asia have seen the explosion of information as a threat and have made moves to censor the Internet. In Singapore, for example, government officials "surf the net" looking for a catch. Just how successful they will be is not yet clear.[1] Satellite television which can now reach into the remotest regions of any country has also been a headache for those wishing to manage minds. Influence over the means of mass communications is an important aspect of the exercise of power, and totalitarian governments in the twentieth century have attempted to control all information inside their borders. Some have been more successful than others. While North Korea is the last, moribund example of this form of government, other states which were once communist, such as China, Vietnam and Laos, sometimes still respond to old reflexes with sudden crackdowns on "spiritually polluting" information, whether it be fashion magazines or music. These

1. According to Agence France Press (24/3/96) Vietnam is seeking advice from Singapore about how to build a "firewall" against politically dangerous information on the Net. The *South China Morning Post* (27/11/ 96) in the article "Fear of anti-state propaganda sparks Internet crackdown" reports on attempts by authorities in Vientiane to stop people accessing the Internet through Thailand. In 1997 Laos still had no Internet server.

latter regimes are now best described as authoritarian, which roughly means that while they do not try to control all information and activities in their societies, they do make strenuous attempts to control particular sorts of information, especially politically sensitive information. This means that certain topics are not able to be discussed publicly, and discourses about the past, present and future are monopolized by regimes which also attempt to control memory and the construction of it.

In his book *How Societies Remember*, Paul Connerton argues that "our experience of the present very largely depends on our knowledge of the past"(1989:2). New regimes, like the LPDR at the end of 1975, set out to reconstruct the past through repression and reinterpretation, in order to create a different present. Yet, despite the massive means of coercion at the disposal of modern states, this project is an extremely difficult one to accomplish. In Laos we saw the spectacle of books and memorabilia from the old regime being burned by soldiers. Anticipating trouble, others burned books or old photographs, depleting the sources of stored memory in a country with a preciously small historical archive anyway (fortunately, many people hid them away in the bottom of draws or cupboards). Some with surnames belonging to "leading reactionaries" changed them or ceased to use them—in a historically perverse reversal to an earlier time when Lao did not use surnames. The other technique was to dispatch thousands of members of the old regime to "concentration camps," to "seminar" as it is called in Laos. Their families stayed behind and endured a milder "reeducation" through forms of ritual refiguring and propaganda. The blatantly coercive and vengeful nature of the camps appear to have made few converts, and finally as the regime began to soften, these people returned home only aware of the coercive weight of the new state but not convinced of its legitimacy. Many of these returnees followed the thousands upon thousands of Lao who had streamed across the Mekong to become refugees. In France, America, Australia, they formed a pool of counter-memory, or as the

LPRP saw it, a pool of counter-revolutionary memory, and contact with these *pattikan* (reactionaries) was strictly monitored. But as reforms have been introduced into Laos, and as the LPDR has opened up to the capitalist world, so interchange with this counter-memory has been inevitable. Many refugees have returned to Laos to visit or invest in businesses. Some have returned to stay. Social order requires shared memories, but this has become increasingly problematic in Laos. As Connerton argues: "It is an implicit rule that the participants in any social order must presuppose a shared memory. To the extent that their memories of a society's past diverge, to that extent its members can share neither experiences nor assumptions" (1989:3). There are many people in Laos today who retain positive memories of the old regime. For the people who fought for the Pathet Lao in the mountains for many years and who never really lived under the Royal Lao Government (RLG), their only memory of it is war and propaganda about the "feudal" or "neo-colonial" Vientiane government. Even today some of these people become extremely uncomfortable when one tries to initiate a discussion about the old regime. Yet there are signs that such discussions now take place, at least at private parties and under the influence of alcohol (which perhaps makes everything deniable), without anyone getting arrested.

There are, however, two other groups who need consideration. They are the young people who have grown up entirely within the LPDR, or entirely in exile. The former, who comprise over fifty percent of the population, have only known socialism and "post-socialism." They know little or nothing about the RLG, and while they show little *angst* concerning their identity as Lao, the reorientation of Laos towards Bangkok and beyond has opened up a dream world of modernity for the youth of at least the main cities, and for some it has meant a rejection of Laos's economic and cultural "backwardness," and the failed socialist experiment is equated with this. The appearance of young rebels on fast motorbikes in the main cities in recent years has caused something of a moral panic among their parents and there is talk of the collapse of "traditional Lao values"(Evans 1994). Most of these rebels are in fact the sons and daughters of the LPRP leadership who have only known elite lifestyles and city life. While the old revolutionaries maintain their grip on state power, they are increasingly unable to control the venality of their families or channel the desires of their children. The disaffection of youth has impressed on the government its need for new symbols of legitimation.

As for the young in exile, theirs is a fantasy Laos, a place most have never seen or experienced. They have grown up as young Americans or Australians or French hearing about Laos from their parents who possibly romanticize the old Laos and demonize the new. With the apparent growing importance of ethnic identity in the modern world, especially in places like America, some of these young Lao now search for their roots by surfing the Internet—"to resource yourself and to relink yourself emotionally and spiritually to the land where you are born," as one surfer put it. The search takes many forms. "Does anyone have a picture of the old royal flag ie. white elephant on red?" one plaintive message asked (1/2/96). In early February 1996 I monitored a billboard which posted an intense debate that suddenly erupted over whether a pamphlet being produced in the US should use the term "Lao" or "Laotian" to refer to people from Laos. As one contributor tried to explain, Lao would refer to the "ethnic majority of Laos" while Laotian "refers to all 'citizens' of Laos." For this he was swiftly attacked. "To me, calling Lao people 'Laotian' is an insult . . . a term imposed on us in times of our subjugation; therefore, if we continue to use that term, we're more or less intellectually enslaved." He went on to say that "Laotian" does not include other ethnic groups, and advises Hmong to "distinguish themselves" by using "Lao Hmong or Hmong Lao." He continues: "I painfully acknowledge that it is the fate of our country that she falls so low for the last two hundred years that other ethnic groups residing in Laos come to think of themselves differently" (3/2/96). This latter point was quickly confirmed in a reply from a Hmong who saw the idea of "Lao Hmong" as "insulting."

"Hmong is Hmong always and forever. . . . I will always be a Hmong wherever I live—in Laos, China, France, or Thailand. I cannot afford to be 'half' American or 'half' Lao and 'half' Hmong as the terms 'Hmong Lao' or 'Hmong American' suggest" (4/2/96). Thus this search for roots soon found itself ensnared in the major debates plaguing our time—ethnicity, nationality and nationalism. Some adopted a very liberal American solution, saying it is a matter of "personal choice," while others opted for a kind of Buddhist universalism. Inevitably, perhaps, a sweetly innocent question on language followed: "I know that in China, there are many dialects from many regions. But all of the people of China use one CENTRAL language . . . What about the people of Laos?? Do we have a central language?? Do all the ethnic groups in Laos have to learn one central language when they attend school?? Do the Lao people have one form of written and spoken medium to communicate?" (12/2/96) An older person replied (12/2/96) and talked about the standardization of writing and grammar under the RLG, but this quickly degenerated into an attack on the "Sam Neua's party invention" (i.e. the LPRP) of new words based on northern dialects, which drew a reply complaining about this person's representation of dialects (13/2/96). Language, identity and nationalism have always been thorny issues, as participants in this exchange soon discovered. A final contributor turned their attention back to the problems of the Lao diaspora and global cultural change: "If 'English' became the 'official' language of the United States (or the world—given the technologies driven by the English language, e.g. Windows 95, Cyberspace, etc.—non-English speakers have to learn English in order to be able to use the technology), what will happen to 'Lao' as an ethnic language in America (or in the world)?" (13/2/96). Having opened a Pandora's box full of problems, the debate ended abruptly and inconclusively here. After briefly staring into the abyss of the future, with its imponderables of identity, language, globalization and so on, these surfers took themselves back to shallower waters.

9

But for them the problem of "who are the Lao" remains, and further billboards have posed a variety of naive questions about Lao history. On the other hand, for the young in Laos the problem is barely articulated because, unlike their overseas confrères, they are surrounded by the everyday practices of being Lao. Nevertheless, their increasing interaction with the wider world in various forms has made them increasingly aware of their Lao-ness.

*[handwritten margin note: not problem for young Lao]*

As we shall see, however, it is in fact the Lao state which is experiencing a serious existential crisis.

It has become almost a cliché of modern writing about Laos to assert that somehow it is not a "real" nation-state. Veteran commentator on Lao politics, Arthur Dommen, says of Laos that it is more a conglomeration of "tribes" than a people (1971:17). Jean Lateguy in his novel *The Bronze Drums* has one of his characters say: "The French are preventing them [the Vietnamese] from gobbling up Laos. Laos is a paradise, as I told you in Paris. Only, like paradise, Laos doesn't exist; it's a figment of the imagination of a few French administrators" (1967:147). Journalistic commentary repeats these ideas. Behind many of these statements lies the idea of 'natural' nations rather than historical ones. This *ideological* view of the nation which demands a lineage that stretches far back into the mists of time, not surprisingly, has many advocates within Laos. The Lao prime minister of the mid-1950s, Katay Don Sasorith, strenuously asserted the ancient unity of the Lao despite the fact that the country was divided into several principalities at the time of the French takeover:

> From oldest antiquity to the present day we have said in our everyday language:
>
> *Sua Sat Lao*, meaning Laotian origin and race;
>
> *Sat Lao*, meaning the Laotian Nation;
>
> *Muong Lao*, meaning the Laotian country;
>
> *Pathet Lao*, meaning the Laotian State.
>
> . . . It is clear, therefore, that even when *Muong* Luang Prabang, *Muong* Vientiane, and *Muong* Champassak had each a separate existence, *Muong* Lao nonetheless

10

remained *Muong* Lao. For Lan-Xang, unlike many other
empires past and present, but like present day Laos,
lumped together within the limits of its territory a
number of populations that were extremely homogenous.
If we leave out a few ethnological Minorities (Khas,
Meos, etc. . . .) that are scattered here and there, generally
in the heights, the whole of *Muong* Lao spoke the same
language, honoured the same genii, cultivated the same
religion and had the same usages and customs. The same
can not be said either of any of the ancient empires, nor
of India or of the Great China of the present day.
(1959:29-30)

Katay also berates the French for not restoring "the
Confederacy in favour of one of the ruling Laotian kings of
the moment . . ." (ibid:31). Leaving aside Katay's contentious
assertion concerning the minorities (who are always a
problem for ethnically based views of the nation), we can see
here one strong discourse on the ancient unity of the Lao—in
the face of its obvious disunity.

All modern nations create such discourses, with the
important difference that some historical stories are more
immediately plausible than others. All modern Lao political
movements have asserted the unity of Laos and attempted to
create plausible histories. These are still in the process of
creation, and the writing of history in contemporary Laos has
been extremely problematic, yoked as it has been to the
political demands of the present, for it too has had to come to
grips with the disunity of Laos in the recent civil war.

Katay Don Sasorith's discourse was elaborated following
the creation of the modern state of Laos through French
concessions to Lao sovereignty from 1946 to 1954 when Laos
gained international recognition as an independent state. This
discourse was centered on the king and Buddhism, and this
same framework was verbally shared by the opposition
Pathet Lao for much of the period prior to 1975. The
important difference was that in the latter's discourse
"feudalists" and "imperialists" featured as those who had

thwarted the full flowering of Lao nationalism. After 1975, two central features of this pre-1975 discourse were discontinued—the king "abdicated," and Buddhism was no longer the state religion. But as Laos has traveled from socialism to post-socialism one can see the reemergence of older patterns of action and thought. A new past is being remembered in the present, and it is one of the purposes of the following essay to try to trace this process.

Connerton writes about how commemorative ceremonies act to establish continuity with the past, one way a society remembers. For this reason we shall look at several commemorative ceremonies in Laos to try to understand how Lao society remembers. But Connerton also points to the many less conscious ways a society remembers, through gestures, acts and bodily performance, and so we shall look at these too because the socialist state in Laos also tried to modify them.

The importance of symbolism for revolutionary political and social change and the reconstruction of the past can be seen in the fact that some of the first decrees passed by revolutionary regimes concern symbolism, and this was true in Laos. In early December 1975 a series of resolutions were adopted by the National Assembly concerning language, the national anthem and the national flag.[2] It was decided: "(1) to use the Lao language as language of popular and administrative use; and (2) to cease using royal language for daily record and correspondence except when necessary as in

2. The detailed attention paid to symbolism can be seen in the description of the now superceded national laurel crest on its adoption in January 1976: "The gear wheel, symbolizing industry; paddy ears and paddy field, symbolizing agriculture forestry and mining; flash of lightning symbolizing national prosperity and wealth; golden star, symbolizing the bright, prosperous and vigorous future of the LPDR led by the LPRP in advancing towards socialism, which is the destiny all Lao people must strive to achieve; the hammer symbolizing the proletariat; the sickle, symbolizing the working peasants who comprise the majority of the Lao people; and the hammer and sickle, symbolizing the alliance of workers and peasants led by the LPRP, serving as the base for the solidarity of all nationalities, tribes and strata in the struggle to defend and build the country" (*SWB* 26/1/76).

poetry or other forms of literature" (*SWB* 9/12/75).[3] Soon after, there was an attack on the use of foreign languages and "some officials' slavish worship of other countries" (*SWB* 20/2/76). The abolition of "royal language" saw the attempt at an egalitarian reform of the language and so honorifics, like *sadet* (prince) or *tan* (sir), were pushed aside by the ubiquitous use of *sahay* (comrade). Later in July 1976 Phoumi Vongvichit gave lectures on Lao grammar and modifications in the Lao script.[4] These linguistic shifts were most apparent among bureaucrats and in cities, but were often ignored by the peasants.

A new national anthem was also adopted, but significantly the music of the old anthem written by Thongdy Sounthone Vichit in 1943 was retained thereby maintaining a phonic continuity. References to Buddhism in the old anthem and to a singular Lao race were replaced by references to all the Lao ethnic groups,[5] but otherwise the new anthem was typical of the genre, and both anthems expressed strong nationalist sentiments. Having abolished the monarchy on 2 December 1975, the flag of the royal government, a three-headed white elephant standing on a five-step pedestal, under a nine-tiered white parasol against a red background, could no longer be retained, and the flag referred to earlier of two horizontal red stripes flanking the blue background to a white moon was adopted as it "has long been the symbol of the Lao national salvation struggle" (*SWB* 9/12/75).[6] It is significant that the

3. *SWB* = BBC *Summary of World Broadcasts*, Far East.

4. Recall the contentious nature of these reforms in the discussion conducted over the Internet. The reforms were first set out in a book on grammar published by Phoumi in Sam Neua in 1967: ໄວຍະກອນລາວ, ພະແນກ ສຶກສາສຸບກາງ, ຊຳເຫນືອ, ວັນທີ 22 ມີນາ, 1967.

5. Both anthems are reproduced in Duangsai Louangpasi's, *Short History of Laos* (1995:77-78) in Lao.

6. Interestingly, the creator of this flag during the independent Issara government in 1945, General Tham, said he had been influenced by the design of the Thai flag at the time, just as he and his Lao Issara comrades had been influenced by the establishment of a constitutional monarchy in Thailand by the military in 1932. (Interview with the author in Vientiane, February 1996.) Another Issara participant, Maha Sila Viravong, published a

Pathet Lao, unlike their comrades in Vietnam and Cambodia, did not rename the streets of the main cities. While at times making dramatic breaks with the past, such as the abolition of the monarchy, the Lao communists sometimes had to adjust themselves to existing realities—on one occasion with amusing results. In May 1976, realizing they could not produce new stamps in time, an order went out to say that the old stamps could continue in use: "However, the word 'kingdom' must be crossed out on the stamps, and only the word 'Laos' should remain" (*SWB* 1/5/76). However, there were other more dramatic public attempts to obliterate the past. In July ceremonial burnings of the old kip notes—"a remnant of the old, rotten regime"—took place and they were replaced by the Liberation Kip.[7]

Thus, through gesture after gesture the new regime distanced itself from the old regime, and then embarked on modifying old rituals and symbols and creating new ones.

---

pamphlet on the history of the Lao flag (1975a. In Lao). In it he explains how Thailand in the late nineteenth century became increasingly conscious of the need for a national flag. It therefore produced a red flag with a single elephant in its center. The Lao in Luang Prabang adapted this and produced a red flag with a three-headed elephant (he disputes the idea that it represented the unification of the three principalities of Luang Prabang, Vientiane and Champassak, an idea perpetuated by Thongsa Sayavong-khamdy in a recent pamphlet produced for the Ministry of Information and Culture "Guide to the Royal Palace, Luang Prabang" (n.d.). During the Thai participation in World War I they saw the need for a new flag and adapted the French tri-color. Maha Sila, however, does not acknowledge the influence of the Thai flag on the Issara flag. He simply says that the three-headed elephant flag only represented the king of Luang Prabang and therefore Laos needed a "national flag." In fact, the three-headed elephant flag of Luang Prabang became the national flag with the creation of a nationwide constitutional monarchy in 1947. Subsequently the Neo Lao Hak Sat appropriated the Issara flag as their own. For another account of the creation of the modern Thai flag, see Vella (1978:137-40).

7. The new notes were much less attractive than the old RLG notes. They were small and poorly printed, compared to the colorful and beautifully designed old notes. One could speculate that the less glamorous notes under the communist regime also reflected a symbolic downgrading of money in the new order.

# NATIONAL DAY

NEW nations and revolutionary regimes all require rituals of legitimation, thus one of their first acts is to reorganize the ritual calendar.[1] According to Lao communist historiography Laos first achieved its independence from France in late 1945 when the Lao Issara government declared independence and ruled for six months before being forced to flee into exile by French troops. The Pathet Lao claim they are the true heirs of this movement, and thus not until 2 December 1975 did Laos once again achieve "true" independence.[2] "That great event," said Kaysone in his tenth anniversary speech, "gloriously ended the national democratic revolution in our country, completely terminated the yoke of the cruel and depraved rule of the feudalists and colonialists, and opened a new era—the era of independence, freedom and socialism—for our nation" (SWB 5/12/85). The Royal Lao Government, which had achieved full independence from France in October 1953, had celebrated

1. The control of time and with it the sense of destiny pre-dates modern revolutionary regimes. New dynasties in China would issue their own calendars. Also see Chandler (1996:168) for disputes in Cambodia in the 1940s over attempts by the French to replace the Buddhist calendar with the Gregorian calendar.

2. A good history of the Issara movement remains to be written. For one account by a participant, see Maha Sila Viravong (1975b. In Lao). Jean Deuve (1992) is the fullest account to date but is slanted towards French sources.

Independence Day on 19 July and Constitution Day on 11 May. Both of these celebrations were swept away. No longer a Buddhist state, the LPDR did not recognize holidays associated with Buddhist festivals. May Day, however, was retained and expanded as a day for celebrating "socialist internationalism."

For the first two years of its existence the LPDR felt embattled and threatened by outside forces and internal *pattikan* forces. National Day rallies presided over by the top leadership, therefore, were held in the compound of the National Defense Ministry. By 1977 a white stupa to the "unknown soldier" for the revolution's war dead had been built at the far end of the parade ground constructed in front of the main stupa in Vientiane, That Luang, and so began the annual wreath laying at this monument.[3] In 1978 and 1979 the celebrations moved out onto the That Luang parade ground. Stringent security precautions surrounded the leadership, especially Kaysone, who by this time had already survived three assassination attempts, and he was absent during these years, leaving the key role to Phoumi Vongvichit.

Time is imbued with significance by us all and punctuated and divided up to mark the march of "progress," "the revolution," "Five Year Plans" or whatever. And so decades and half-decades become "naturally" significant moments. Nineteen eighty, therefore, saw the first big National Day celebration by the LPDR. At this time the regime had encountered extreme economic problems and was calling for "thrift," and security problems continued to plague it: "Each province is prohibited from staging a massive military parade because such an act is considered to be extravagant, reveals our strength and is unsafe" (*SWB* 18/11/80). A grand rally presided over by the main party leaders, however, was held in Vientiane with a full parade by the Lao People's Liberation Army. The following year cadres were informed that the Central Committee had decided "that a grand celebration of

3. Stupas to the "unknown soldier" were constructed in the capitals of every province.

the occasion will be organised at the national level once every five years" (*SWB* 25/11/81); therefore "this year's celebration will be brief and simple . . . There will not be large-scale rallies, demonstration, parades or banquets; only tea, soft drinks, cakes and tobacco may be served" (ibid).

On the tenth anniversary in 1985 the party and state decided "to organise a grand, joyous, extensive, and massive celebration of the 2 December historical day throughout the country" (*SWB* 18/11/85). And it was celebrated in high Stalinist style for at the time of the tenth anniversary of the revolution the world still looked and felt differently. Only ten years later, by the time of the twentieth anniversary in 1995, so much had already changed. As Eric Hobsbawm (1994:5) remarks: "in the late 1980s and the early 1990s an era in world history ended and a new one began."

But in 1985 the ritual was still full-blown communist triumphalism. President Souphanouvong and Prime Minister Kaysone Phomvihane were flanked on the main viewing stand by the head of Vietnam's Communist Party, Le Duan, and president of the People's Republic of Kampuchea, Heng Samrin. Today, only the latter is still alive. In his address Kaysone stressed the "special relationship" between the three states of Indochina. Yet a Cold War pall hung over the region, and the Cambodian problem remained to be settled.

As I reported at the time: "For weeks security in the capital has been tight, and an identity check of the inhabitants of this city of 377,000 is rumoured to have netted from 400 to 10,000 people, said to have then been trucked out of the city. Typically, no one really knows the facts. Feelings of paranoia were not helped two weeks ago when a Thai merchant chose to pay back a debtor by planting a bomb which killed one person and injured three others, all innocent bystanders. The incident quickly led to other rumours of bombings" by *pattikan* (*The Age* 3/12/85).[4] Public buildings in the city had

4. The following account is largely based on a paper I gave to a workshop on "Power and Everyday Resistance" held at the Australian National University in July 1986. Later, James C. Scott (1990) used this paper for some very insightful comments on the celebration.

been repainted for the occasion, and the loudspeaker system throughout the whole capital had been rerigged to broadcast propaganda from Lao radio throughout the day, everyday, beginning at 6 A.M. The state's presence was inescapable.[5]

The parade was held at the That Luang parade ground, and the viewing stand of the party leaders stood where the new People's Assembly would be built. The "masses" were instructed to arrive in the early hours of the morning (4 A.M.), several hours before the dignitaries. "The bizarre starting time of 6 A.M. reflects the peasant norms of the country. The parade was all over by 9 A.M.—just when most people in Australia are beginning to work" (ibid). The opening speeches by Souphanouvong and Kaysone went on for over an hour to the long-assembled and dutiful crowd, who increasingly leaned on the poles of their placards carrying the portraits of the seven-member politburo, as well as occasional ones of Marx, Lenin and Ho Chi Minh, and more rarely Engels. Others leaned on their poles with Lao national flags or banners with slogans.

The march past began with goose-stepping military, police and policewomen, followed by male and female workers dressed in sky-blue boilersuits (Laos's non-existent proletariat), then a minority women's militia and then motorcycle police and military. They were followed by tanks, and as the heavy hardware rolled past, Mig jets thundered over the parade ground. Then came the veterans, the scouts with their red scarves who stooped and saluted the dais, followed by

5. The loudspeaker systems were one of the first things installed by the new regime, and were considered to be "an important factor in the propaganda work aimed at improving the material and moral life of our fraternal people" (SWB 25/1/76). While the system occasionally fell into disrepair, and there were rumors that in residential areas people deliberately sabotaged it by cutting the wires leading to loudspeakers, it was fully repaired and expanded for the 1985 celebrations. In the years that followed, however, sections of this system once again slowly broke down and were not replaced. Now, only in some small sections of Vientiane does this public address system continue to function. One reason the system has become defunct is that with the new prosperity most people now have radios or TVs of their own. In provincial towns, however, especially around the market, the loudspeaker system still blares out its message to passersby.

Lao women dancers and the Lao Women's Union. Finally a string of floats from the various ministries, including three elephants as part of the forestry section, all exhibiting themes of national development. "The mood relaxed and I counted some twenty bands playing from the back of these floats, while other Lao walked and danced alongside waving real or paper flowers, and on one occasion little red books of Lenin in Lao" (ibid).

Where were "the people?" for there were no unofficial spontaneous spectators at this parade. In fact, the celebration underlined the ideology of the totalitarian state in that only those people who fell within the purview of its structure constituted "the people" in the Lao People's Democratic Republic. The parade was an affair for the government, its cadres and employees, and the foreign community of diplomats, aid workers, etc. It was the theater of power being acted out by the institutions of power to the members of those institutions. It presented images of national and political unity and demonstrated to those present and absent who was in control. In the evening the elite attended a dinner and then watched didactic revolutionary theater. The state media quickly broadcast and published accounts of the event.

Scott saw this whole ritual as an attempt by the state to "suggest to the participants that they are a legitimate part of a larger fraternity of communist states with the control, discipline, purpose, and might which that implies. The ceremony serves to link them to Marx and Lenin and to Marxist-Leninist states in much the same way the celebration of any provincial mass links its celebrants to Christ and the apostles and to Rome" (1990:59). And further: "the parade is an effective idealisation of the desired relation between the central Committee and the society it aspires to direct." (ibid:61)

For the next few years "simple and straightforward" celebrations were called for, and only 1990 saw the organization of a "grand rally." Held at the time communism was collapsing in Europe, it exhibited none of the sweeping confidence that derived from being part of a larger imagined world.

*no more cel.*

In 1995 the National Day ceremony was no less state-centered—as one *samloh* driver explained to me, "It's just for the leaders"—but its form had changed dramatically. The five-year program of grand celebrations had been quietly forgotten. There was no parade; there was simply a large meeting of cadres and foreign invitees in the National People's Assembly, addressed by Prime Minister Khamtay Siphandone. It began at 8 A.M. and was over by 10 A.M. That Luang square was sealed-off by police and largely deserted except for the limousines which would speed up Lane Xang Avenue and deposit their dignitaries at the steps of the assembly. Some loudspeakers still in operation around the capital broadcast the proceedings to a public now speeding past on motorbikes and in cars, oblivious to the formal celebrations and Khamtay's droning voice.

There was no longer a larger ritual complex in the communist world to imitate. The state over the intervening years had retreated economically and politically to become an increasingly grey and bureaucratized apparatus. Enquiries in the days before the "celebrations" revealed that there would simply be a "meeting," and the explanation for the scaled-down celebrations which had gained currency was that with the new economic policies the government wanted to save the money larger celebrations would cost. In the two days leading up to 2 December, the leaders of the municipality, and then the leaders of the party and government had laid wreaths at the white stupa for the unknown soldier. These were all highly formal state ritual occasions.

One important change since 1985 has been the rapid growth in private television ownership,[6] and that evening viewers could see a summary of the day's celebrations, the evening reception held by the country's leaders, and the now

6. Lao national television began broadcasting on 1 December 1987, and then only two programs a week in black and white. In opening the station Political Bureau member Sisomphone Lovansai said that the station "should firmly adhere to principles of the Party, state and manifest the combatant, popular nature along with beautiful and pure national heritage" (*SWB* 5/12/83). It could not compete with the variety offered by Thai television, and still badly trails it.

rather stylistically incongruous revolutionary opera played to the state elite and cadres after the reception. The majority of people in Vientiane, however, watch Thai television "because it's more interesting,"[7] and so it is unclear just how many people even saw this much of the National Day celebrations. One telling change in presentation between 1985 and 1995 was the fact that these television highlights were interspersed with advertisements for Johnny Walker Whisky, Toyota, and various banks and hotels, all of whom had composed national day poems which praised the party and the government for leading the country to prosperity and development.

Indeed, the large billboard posters around the capital had also been sponsored by local companies, such as Beer Lao and Mitsubishi, who donated over 80 million kip to the Ministry of Information and Culture for the construction of billboards in Vientiane and the provinces. The messages on these billboards were, for example: "To build and expand the system of people's independence under the leadership of the party is the way to achieve prosperity." Where in 1985 one found the word "socialism" (*sankomniyom*), in 1995 it was now replaced by "prosperity" (*wattanataworn*).

Television that night also ran two short documentaries; one on Lao culture, focusing on temples and Buddhist relics and emphasizing the need for aid to preserve this heritage

---

7. Most Lao watch Thai television, which clearly has had a very important impact on young people, but the complex nature of this influence remains to be investigated. I recall a conversation with a young Lao woman in 1993 who said that although she mainly watched Thai television she was aware that it is biased in its presentation of Lao history and she looked forward to the day when she could also view more "truthful" programs on Laos. In the run-up to the opening of the Friendship Bridge in April 1994 the Thai telecommunications giant, Shinawatra, was given permission to begin broadcasting from a new channel in Vientiane. Channel 3, broadcasting in Lao, was operated by the International Broadcasting Cooperation (Laos). Its target audience was to be Vientiane and Nong Khai, and it was to provide a counter to Thai TV. The experiment lasted a year when in April 1995 the Lao government moved to take control of the station, renaming IBC-3 as Lao Television 3, and the Thai staff left. No official reason was given for the move, but clearly it involved the Party's reluctance to give up its monopoly on information and propaganda.

21

"that few people know about." The second, was a propaganda documentary narrated by a medical doctor who told
viewers about the poor health conditions in Laos before 1975,
and about how people had indulged in "superstitious"
practices, consulting *moh dtoo* and *moh phi* (fortune-tellers and
shamans) when family members were sick, and about how
health care had improved under the new regime.

National days are ritual occasions for generating solidarity
and "pride in the nation," and for propagating myths of
foundation. As one political anthropologist writes: "No
matter how culturally artificial or historically serendipitous
the new national entity, it must be endowed with sacred
unity and made to seem a natural social unit. . . . Without
rites and symbols, there are no nations" (Kertzer 1988:179).
For obvious reasons most national days tend to be state-
centered, but in communist regimes this logic is taken to
extremes whereby the state dominates all activities and
occasions, leaving nothing to the masses and nothing to
spontaneity. In many places sports games are held as a kind
of substitute popular participation. Thus, it is perhaps no
accident that in Laos sports have come to play an increasingly
important role in social and political life. In 1995, for example,
athletic games were held in the main stadium in Vientiane to
celebrate National Day, overseen by the deputy prime
minister who handed out the prizes at the end of the event
(*Vientiane Mai* 4/12/95). Several days later Lao athletes
competed for the first time in the Southeast Asian Games in
Chiang Mai, Thailand, and it was reported in the Thai press
as a sign that "Brave Laos is making an emphatic march
towards progress in every field" (*Sunday Post* 10/12/95).
National sports games were first held in Laos in 1989.
Opening the 1991 games, Kaysone said they were "aimed at
promoting and building dynamic physical and mental health
and strength in our youth. This can then be utilised in
carrying out production and national defence work, in
instilling in them worthy qualifications, discipline and a good
lifestyle, and in forging relations of friendship and unity
among athletes from all zones and provinces throughout the

country" (*SWB* 24/12/91). The importance of national sports in the rituals of modern power, in particular, communist state power, have been analyzed for China. Brownell (1993:60) argues that there "National Games are one aspect of a whole system of technologies of the body by which Chinese people's habits are slowly but surely altered." And, unlike elite state-centered rituals they are "witnessed by hundreds of thousands of Chinese people through the media" (Ibid:61; see also Brownell 1995). Therefore the linking of games to the nation and to its political leadership is of utmost importance to those in power. Laos has only begun to move along this road.

Since 1991 another key event has been added to the state ritual calendar: Constitution Day, which is celebrated on 15 August. It was a major event in 1996 because it was the fifth year of its proclamation, and so the state organized official celebrations around the country and a grand meeting in Vientiane presided over by President Nouhak who claimed:

> Five years ago, it was the first time in the history of the nation that the Lao people of various ethnic groups exercised their freedom and democratic rights to create the most fundamental legal document of the nation. (*VT* August 16-22/96)

While this occasion certainly registers the attempt by the regime to move towards some form of rule of law, it unwittingly draws attention to the fact that for fifteen years it ruled without a constitution and was effectively "lawless." Nouhak and state propaganda speak as if Laos had never ever had a constitution before, but of course the RLG had one for the whole of its existence, and had celebrated its Constitution Day on 11 May. But this was not something that Nouhak and his party wanted the Lao people to remember.

# THE "CULT" OF KAYSONE

*Kaysone*
*leader of Lao comm party*
*& LPDR*

**K**AYSONE Phomvihane died at the age of seventy-two on 21 November 1992 after leading the Lao communist party since its foundation in 1955, and the LPDR since 1975. A seven-day period of nationwide "deep mourning" was declared. What followed was a state-sponsored sequence of nationalist and religious rites. On 22 November, Kaysone's body was placed in the National Assembly building to lie in state. Here religious rites began with alms being offered at lunchtime to twenty-two monks from various monasteries in Vientiane who chanted blessings for the soul, and who later at 5:30 P.M. chanted a mantika prayer before Kaysone's remains. The state drew up a schedule for paying homage to the late leader: on the first day party and state organizations, the next two days for provinces and mass organizations. Companies or individuals who wished to pay homage had to inform sub-committees established for the occasion. The final days were for foreign embassies and international organizations. On 28 November his coffin was carried to a bier constructed in front of the National Assembly and in the early afternoon eighty monks led the funeral ritual. The actual cremation took place at 8 P.M. that night. Three days later, in accordance with Buddhist practice, merit-making and alms offerings to Buddhist monks took place at the National Assembly building.

24

As we know, death temporarily opens a gap in the social structure, and ritual sets out to fill it. For a brief time people and structures are disoriented and in some situations it is through this gap that chaos, say in the form of political protest, may surge. This has been the case in China where the deaths of Chou En-lai and then Hu Yao-bang were both occasions for the demonstration of political dissatisfaction. Thus the Lao government was quick to issue instructions calling for "vigilance" and to "smash schemes to create disturbances and all acts of sabotage and subversion," as well as banning "banquets, soirées or entertainment programs" *to avoid disorder* (*SWB* 23/11/92). The state quickly appointed a new president, Nouhak Phoumsavan, on 25 November, and both his statements and all others stressed continuity with the past, calling on the people to "turn the grief and sorrow . . . into patriotic deeds, love of the new regime and unity . . ." *rhetoric* (*SWB* 28/11/92). At the state memorial service he urged those present to "remember the comrade's teaching," but ended with the apparently extraordinary exhortation for a long-time Marxist-Leninist: "Comrade President Kaysone Phomvihan's cause remains with us forever. Comrade, we wish your soul may reach paradise and the state of bliss" (*SWB* 30/11/92). Two weeks later the party leaders gathered to commemorate the seventy-second birthday anniversary of Kaysone, along with six hundred Buddhist monks, and all stood in one-minute silence "to express condolences to the soul of the late beloved leader . . ." (*SWB* 16/12/92).

Kaysone was the key figure in the LPDR regime and it is not surprising that full state control was maintained over his funeral. By way of contrast, Chou En-lai and Hu Yao-bang were both popularly considered to be opponents of the hard-line Maoists in China and therefore could become vehicles for protest. Kaysone's funeral also successfully integrated into its ritual the central pillar of Lao culture, Buddhism, and demonstrated strikingly the increasing reliance of the state on Buddhist and nationalist themes.

Not long after Kaysone's death the former head of the recently disbanded Committee for Social Sciences, Sisana

Sisane, was put in charge of the creation of a museum to commemorate the former party leader.[1] Since then the state has sponsored a Kaysone cult, but it is a pale shadow of the political cults we have seen in East Asia, something which registers an important cultural shift between East Asia and mainland Southeast Asia.[2]

The creation of political cults within Stalinist political systems arose out of a need for some kind of transcendent legitimacy. The leader becomes like a God, all-knowing, all-seeing and all-powerful—the embodiment of a totalitarian system.[3] Begun by Stalin after Lenin's death, the former drew on the cultural well-springs of Russian orthodox belief and rhetoric, creating the illusion of life beyond death through the embalming of Lenin's body. This was anathema to rationalist Marxists like the historian Isaac Deutscher who denounced it: "The Mausoleum was the monument which primitive magic erected to itself in the very heart of the Russian revolution, the very totem pole and the shrine of Stalinism. . . . Under Stalin the story of Bolshevism came to be re-written in terms of sorcery and magic, with Lenin and Stalin as the chief

1. Long-time comrade of Kaysone's, Sisana Sisane, was minister of information and culture from 1975 to 1983 when he was relieved of his position for making anti-Soviet remarks at a party. In late 1985 he was given the position of director of the Committee for Social Sciences, about which see fn. 8 on p. 170.

2. In this section I focus on the cultural roots of the cults, but for an examination of the political coordinates of the cult in China see Martin (1982), especially chapter 10, "Canonical Writings and Forms of Personality Cult at China's Periphery," which examines Vietnam and North Korea.

3. One thing that is noticeably absent from communist countries is political cartoons and caricatures of incumbent political leaders. No doubt this is because jokes about "deities" are a form of blasphemy. I was reminded of this in early 1996 when I showed a Lao friend the newly published collection of Martin Stuart-Fox's essays, *Buddhist Kingdom, Marxist State* (Bangkok 1996), whose pages contain several caricatures of Lao leaders. Flicking through it my friend first happened upon the caricature of Khamtay and whooped with laughter, then of Kaysone, and he shrieked. "If you published these in Laos . . ." and he made a gesture with a finger across his throat. The caricatures are not grotesque, and I had looked at them without any reaction at all, habituated as I am to such lampooning and more. But to a Lao they were sacrilegiously funny.

totems" (1969:50-1). Reflecting his Eurocentrism, Deutscher saw this as a capitulation to "semi-Asiatic" mysticism as against Western rationalism.[4] Without wishing to repeat Deutscher's error we can, nevertheless, observe that the cult of personality thereafter seemed to strike deep roots among East Asian communist states—in China with the cult of Mao Zedong, in North Korea with Kim Il Sung, and in Vietnam with the much milder and more "avuncular" cult of Ho Chi Minh— "Uncle Ho." These "charismatic" cults were begun while these leaders were still alive, but the important role played by the state in their promotion somewhat obscures the deeper cultural meanings obviously expressed by these charismatic figures.[5]

As is well known, ancestor cults are a fundamental to East Asian cultures, and indeed with the rise of Confucian doctrine they were enforced by the state. In dynastic China spontaneously generated religious cults were appropriated by the state while others were actively promoted by the state (Watson 1990). Recent studies have argued that the power of the Mao cult was derived from its syncretism, its ability to overlay itself on pre-existing symbolic structures. Thus Landsberger (1996:208) argues: "The presence of his official portrait in every home, often occupying the central place on the family altar and replacing the ancestor tablets as the principal object of worship, added to the already god-like stature of Mao." Indeed, his portrait replaced the Kitchen God who kept an eye on the household for the Jade Emperor, which was an accommodating template for the totalitarian state. Aijmer (1996) shows how the cult related to a deep cultural code of image making. Since the collapse of the politically sponsored cult of Mao in China, Mao has been incorporated into folk religion (Xin 1995; Lee 1996), and in Vietnam the state had to crack down on "a religious cult that worshipped the late president Ho Chi Minh as the 18th king in

---

4. Tumarkin (1981), however, provides an interesting account of the cultural background of the Lenin cult in the Soviet Union.

5. For a discussion of the meaning of charisma, see Anderson (1990:74-77).

a dynasty of rulers said to have founded Vietnam" (*South China Morning Post* 15/12/95). The crackdown confirmed the state's control of this cult.

By contrast, even in Cambodia under the Khmer Rouge there was no cult of Pol Pot, and indeed he remained a shadowy figure throughout the regime's rule, although paintings found after the fall of the regime indicate that there was to be an attempt to project Pol Pot as a national leader.[6] In Laos, the LPRP has projected a collective profile. This is most evident in the portraits of the leadership hung in offices since 1975 which always featured groups. Initially it was common to see the photos of all seven leading members of the politburo (Kaysone, Nouhak, Souphanouvong, Phoumi, Khamtay, Phoun, Sisomphone), or Kaysone (prime minister), Souphanouvong (president), and Faydang (vice president, but signaling ethnic representation because he was Hmong). Death has depleted this line-up, and there has been no attempt to project new leaders through portraits, and so it has been increasingly common to see individual portraits of Kaysone. But compared with either Vietnam or China there has been no comparable tendency to produce billboard-size portraits of any of the leaders. Only Kaysone has ever made it onto a billboard, and only then as a small placard held by revolutionary youth (see cover illustration).

Furthermore, the idea of a mausoleum for an embalmed body in these cultures is anathema given the religious commitment to the immateriality of this world expressed through the ubiquitous practice of cremation. The cultural roots of these differences clearly lie in the ideology and practice of Theravada Buddhism. As Keyes (1987:185) has suggested: "Belief in rebirth aborts a tendency on the part of the Northern Thai [and Lao] to think of the dead as ancestors having persistent interest in the world of the living. The *anisong* texts connected with death point to an ultimate transcendence of the cycle of death and rebirth . . ." The common practice of merit-transference could, he says, be seen

---

6. A photograph of one of these paintings can be seen on the cover of Evans and Rowley (1990).

28

as a type of ancestor worship (ibid:198), and in Laos this is most apparent during the festival of the dead, *boun khao salak*, where offerings with the name of a dead person are given to monks. But the overall emphasis on transience means that even the remains of Buddhist monks which are venerated "are not those of a person who can still act in the world but are, rather, the material residues of merit that continue to have potency for the living" (ibid). Popular preoccupation, therefore, focuses on how to tap into these "residues of merit," these sources of metaphysical power, and direct them towards one's own ends. Yet these attempts to tap sources of transcendent power, especially by people who in everyday life are powerless, drift easily in the direction of heterodox cults of, for example, *phu viset* or *phu mi boun*, that is, magically powerful monks, who from the point of view of sangha- and state-promoted orthodoxy are seen as potentially disruptive.

The enormously popular cult which has grown up around the former Thai King Chulalongkorn (1853-1910) in recent years, however, should make us wary of easy cultural generalizations and contrasts between East and Southeast Asia. As we shall discuss further below, the Thai state over the past thirty years has built up a cult of the king, and this has been extended to other kings, with the current king presiding over an annual cycle of rituals of homage to former monarchs. But the current cult around King Rama V (Chulalongkorn), argues Thai historian Nidhi Aeusrivongse, is different because it has evolved independently from the state. Here he is referring to gatherings, which began in 1992, of Thai at the equestrian monument of Rama V in Bangkok every Tuesday because it is believed that the spirit of the king descends then. The unstructured individualistic nature of this ritual gathering, he suggests, is indicative of the cult's democratic and popular nature. Chulalongkorn "is the symbol of a compassionate, accessible state, a visionary monarch . . . [who] stands for modernity, progress, and prosperity. In short, he is the symbol of an ideal state that people want, but does not exist in reality. A state that is efficient, accessible, accountable, and compassionate" (cited by Sanitsuda 1993). He is the object of worship by the new Thai middle class seeking a point of stability in times of rapid change.[7] This cult has also spread to Vientiane, and perhaps for roughly the same reasons. The amulets and images that have sprung around the king (Panyacheewin 1992) have deep roots in Thai Buddhism (Tambiah 1984), and the king is believed to be *saksit* (metaphysically powerful). Popular or not, this cult is easily assimilated by the Thai state's cult of the king, and posters, calendars, books and other memorabilia are produced by, for example, the National Museum in Bangkok. But the important difference between the cult surrounding someone like Chulalongkorn and Ho Chi Minh, for example, is that the latter was a secular politician, while the former was a figure filled with religious merit, and semi-divine.

State-promoted "cults of personality" are clearly attempts to establish transcendent points of reference within secular authoritarian regimes. Secular liberal democracies like the United States have transcendent "sacred" documents like the Constitution which, through various sleights of hand, is a "God-given" charter (Kertzer 1988:65); in France the ideals of the bourgeois revolution "liberté, egalité, fraternité" are transcendent; while constitutional monarchs elsewhere—England, Thailand, Japan, for example, are transcendent sources of national unity and continuity, even if the incumbents have renounced their divinity. The other main sources of abstract, transcendent power in modern societies are, of course, "the people" and "the nation," and all regimes claim to rule on their behalf. Indeed, Bruce Kapferer (1988) has suggested that nationalism is religious in inspiration.

7. Anthropologists are now acutely aware that individual motivations surrounding religious cults like this are likely to vary. Thus one individual explained his devotion in conventional Buddhist terms: "The reason for having King Rama V amulets is to remind wearers to be ashamed to commit sin. It's not for self-promotion or devil protection" (Panyacheewin 1992). Others, however, directly connect their worship of Rama V with their business success. These different tendencies may in fact reflect differences between the Sino-Thai population in Bangkok and the Thai-Lao populations there. Such polyvalence, of course, is the mark of a potent symbol.

The central problem of legitimacy is how to make convincing claims to rule. In Stalinist regimes there has always been a fundamental tension between claims that the people rule and the stark reality of an authoritarian exercise of state power in all realms of life. While this tension can be contained by crude coercion, there is still an attempt by the state to legitimize its coercion by appeal to a higher source, in this case the transcendent person. Thus "traitors," "counter-revolutionaries," or whatever, are seen not only to be against the nation but also against the person of the "great leader." While neither Mao nor Kim Il Sung, let alone Ho Chi Minh, ever went so far as to claim divine status, much of the visual and written representations of them only just stopped short of suggesting they were the new "Sons of Heaven." This kind of development could occur in East Asia because of the continued cultural salience of ancestor worship. In Cambodia and Laos, however, because of the historically close relationship in these countries between kingship and Theravada Buddhism, any cult of personality drifts dangerously in the direction formerly occupied by the overthrown monarch. The continued cultural salience of Theravada Buddhism thus aborts tendencies towards the full blown personality cults seen in East Asia, because its logic demands a king and this demand cannot be fulfilled without undermining the whole rationale of the revolution.

The cult of Kaysone in Laos today is part of the state's ongoing attempt to invent national legitimating myths.[8] The cult is being promoted through three main mediums: the establishment of memorial museums; the erection of memorial busts and statues; and in journalism and speeches.

8. A book in honor of Kaysone was published by the Comittee for Social Sciences in 1991, *Kaysone Phomvihane: Man of the People* (in Lao). "*Luuk kong pasason,*" which literally means "child of the people" is, I think best rendered in English as "man of the people." The book contained mostly hagiographic articles by Lao and "fraternal" comrades from the USSR, Vietnam and China. Two foreign academics contributed, Martin Stuart-Fox and myself. I do not know about Stuart-Fox's contribution, but mine had all critical comments (mild as they were) cut out. In 1995 a pure hagiography was published, *President Kaysone Phomvihane Hero of the Lao Nation,* Vientiane (in Lao).

The Kaysone Memorial Museum was opened on 13 December 1994, Kaysone's seventy-fourth birthday anniversary, its purpose being to, as one party magazine stated: "train members of the younger generation to succeed in and perpetuate the cause of the party. It will honor the nation to which Kaysone Phomvihane devoted his entire life for the sake of building the beloved fatherland and to make it a wealthy and strong nation serving the well-being of the Lao people of all ethnic groups" (*Laos* 1/1995). It is located at "Kilometer 6," Kaysone's headquarters in Vientiane after the communists came to power in late 1975. Situated well away from the center of the city, down a dusty road, it hardly occupies a place comparable to Mao's or Ho's mausoleums. The compound, until then, was off-limits to most people and therefore often shrouded in mystery. As one long-time resident of Vientiane quipped: "the party came down out of the caves of Vieng Xai [Houa Phan province] and went into another set of caves just out of town." While one normally goes there officially, it is now open to the general public on working days. "Many people come here. Important visitors, and guided groups of school children and tourists," said the guard at the gate.

On my visit to the museum in early December 1995 only one section of the planned complex was yet open: Kaysone's office and residence. This section of the museum presents his "homely" side, Kaysone as a simple man, a "man of the people." Just inside the first building hang two naive oil paintings of Kaysone sitting in his garden reading, and one of the first things the guide points to is an old-fashioned telephone which he refused to have replaced despite the entreaties of his entourage. And certainly, among the mini-palaces of the new rich in Vientiane today, one is struck by the simplicity of Kaysone's surroundings.[9] Later in the tour, one is shown a newer house built for him by his "comrades," and a wooden Russian-style house, a gift from the Soviet Union before its

9. Interestingly, Lao and foreigners who visit the palace in Luang Prabang also remark on the simple living conditions of the king. Fantasies of opulence no doubt always surround powerful men.

demise, but we are told he rarely used them. The message is that he was a man not distracted by the trappings of the material world, but had a higher calling. The guide narrates the ritual orderliness of his day—he "always" sat here, his advisers "always" sat there, he sat in this rocking chair to read, etc., imparting to his life a certain timelessness. The guide stresses Kaysone's passion for reading, and for a Lao his personal library is well-stocked (though an academic outsider like myself is struck by how few books he has); yet, there is a discordant note for a nationalist narrative—most of the books are in Vietnamese, and even his notes on one of the tables are in Vietnamese.

Care of the people for their leader is also narrated: his lounge room has a cabinet full of old, and what appear to be valuable, Buddha images—"given to him by the people." One cabinet full of traditional medicines in Johnny Walker whiskey bottles stands to one side—also "gifts from the people" who cared about his health. And in the corners of the room two elephant tusks. "Are they real?" "Yes, the people gave them to him." But the room also contains gifts to Kaysone the statesman given by President Suharto of Indonesia, the king of Thailand, and the presidents of Vietnam and China.

A walkway between his office and residence was built by *Rhetoric* his "comrades" so that he wouldn't get wet in the rainy season, and here the guide pauses to point to a traditional herbal garden out the back whose herbs, she informs us, are especially good for newly pregnant mothers as these herbs help to produce a lot of milk. Thus, does Kaysone become both father and mother to his people![10]

On 13 December 1995 President Nouhak Phoumsavan opened another section which is organized more like a standard museum exhibit, giving a cradle-to-grave account of Kaysone's life:

---

10. On another occasion, however, a guide told a reporter that he "gave medicinal herbs only to his very close friends" (*VT* 8-14/12/95) thereby shifting the emphasis to his care for his friends.

*Notes*

On a background of a panoramic view of the rich plain of Savannakhet bordering on the Mekong river are displayed a wood and bamboo bed on which, like any other mother in the country, Kaysone's mother spent some time after his birth sweating over hot ashes and drinking decoctions of medicinal roots boiled on a nearby fire.

Also on display is a *kadong* [winnowing tray] on which a newborn baby is placed during the first three days of his life.

Another section is devoted to his youth and school years. Kaysone's father, Pho Leuan, was a severe and intransigent man while his mother, Mae Dok, was sweet and caring and loved to tell him stories such as *Sinsay*, the famous epic poem he often referred to during his life. (*VT* 15-21/12/95)

While the authenticity of the bed and *kadong* are not vouched for, his school desk has been brought from Savannakhet and installed in the museum. The rest of the exhibition is a more conventional political history of Kaysone as revolutionary, at the early party conferences, visiting the people after 1975, and photos of his international contacts. It ends with photos of his funeral. The last section is devoted to the current leadership and the tasks of national defense and economic growth.[11]

The second main activity associated with the cult has been the erection of memorial busts of Kaysone throughout the country. All 150 of these statues were, not surprisingly, produced by North Korea. Some were officially donated by the North Korean ambassador on behalf of Kim Jong Il, the new "great leader," on the day of Kaysone's anniversary

11. I visited the revolutionary museum in Savannakhet in May 1996. It contains the usual run of photos of Kaysone and the revolution. It was, however, interesting to learn that the museum, now housed in a large French-style villa beside the Mekong, would soon have to move because the villa had been rented to a Thai tourist company. A new location had yet to be found for the museum. Kaysone, architect of the "new economic mechanism," would understand, I am sure.

(*Vientiane Mai* 15/12/95). The completion and the cost of these memorials was regularly recounted in the press. For example in late November 1995 Xieng Khouang province installed its bust of the "beloved leader" at a cost of 28 million kip (*Khao San Pathet Lao (KPL)* 30/11/95), while in the first days of December they were completed in Oudomsay for 28.6 million, in Luang Nam Tha for 29 million, in Phongsaly for 35 million, in Sayaboury for 28 million, and reportedly completed or nearly completed in the other provinces. The memorials have also been an occasion on which new entrepreneurs could demonstrate their patriotic spirit too. For example, in October the director of the Mekong River Saw Mill presented 500,000 kip to the vice chief of Khong district, Champassak province for the memorial's construction (*KPL* 11/10/95), while the Lienching Agricultural Development Firm of Taiwan donated 13 million kip for the construction of a memorial in Thakhek, Khamouane province. But at the popular level there has been little enthusiasm, with people complaining about the waste of money and about how it would have been better spent on schools or clinics.[12]

The spatial location of these busts, however, demonstrates that they are part of a state cult rather than being open to popular pilgrims. The main bust in Vientiane municipality, inscribed with the words "Kaysone Phomvihane is in our thoughts whenever we carry out our duty,"for example, is set deep within the main municipal office grounds, past a guard at the gate. Indeed, only high party officials were at its inauguration on 20 November 1995. They sat in the open air, while in the distance the rest of Vientiane rode past the front gate oblivious to the ceremony. Furthermore, the spatial location of these statues across the country is revealing. Larger busts of Kaysone (1.2 m) are installed at the provincial level, while the smaller (0.75m) busts are installed at the district level. In August 1996 the regime received three full-

---

12. These complaints have not been without good humor, however. I asked one woman in Luang Prabang if she thought the bust of Kaysone was handsome: "Yes!" she replied. "Much more handsome than Kaysone in real life!"

size statues of Kaysone (made in the PRC) which were placed in Vieng Xai, at the museum in Vientiane and at the museum in Savannakhet. One can see in this layout shades of the older *muang* structure, with smaller units being subordinate to and incorporated by larger and more central units, culminating at last in the main statues in Vientiane—in the National Assembly and in the museum. They are undisguised attempts to symbolize national unity by the new regime. Furthermore, the design of the memorials draws on Buddhist architectural motifs, using the nine-tiered parasol on the pinnacle, usually reserved for royalty. Is this an unconscious cultural trope, or perhaps a pale imitation of the Mao cult's ability to insinuate itself into traditional symbolic structures?

The political rhetoric that surrounds the Kaysone cult is predictable inasmuch as he is credited with great foresight, greater than the rest of the leadership. One can, however, discern a little tension in the rhetoric here as the Lao Party to date has insisted on the collective nature of its leadership, and to single out Kaysone goes against the grain of this. Indeed, when the idea of a museum was first mooted there was grumbling among some members of the party and outside along the lines of "Did Kaysone make the revolution all on his own?" and "If there is going to be a museum why not include Souphanouvong and the other leaders as well?" This would suggest the possibility of factions in the party wanting to use the Kaysone cult to advance their own interests. Yet there is not much evidence of serious division. State rhetoric all emphasizes Kaysone's responsibility for introducing the "new economic mechanism," and there is no evidence of any opposition to the privatization of the Lao economy like one may discern in China or Vietnam where some interests are still tied to a threatened state sector. While some journalists in the party-controlled press may engage in hyperbole about Kaysone's wisdom and about him being a "national hero," the tone of Prime Minister Khamtay Siphandone's speech on Kaysone's seventy-fifth birthday anniversary was relatively mild. He preferred instead to mobilize the memory of Kaysone to emphasize current policies. Kaysone, he said, "deserves the title of a great revolutionary and a nationalist. . . . President Kaysone Phomvihane was the center of unity and unanimity within the party and integrity of the entire people. He initiated the policy of renovation in our country. . . . It was President Kaysone who laid the foundation for a theory of developing the socialism-oriented people's democratic regime. He was an outstanding theoretician and man of action" (*VT* 15-21/12/95). Such instrumental references to Kaysone's economic policies are now commonplace and justify the establishment of a capitalist economy in Laos. The references to "socialist-oriented," and so on, which became more frequent during 1995, partly reflect the influence of Chinese views in Laos. But more fundamentally, and as I suggested earlier, socialism really means no liberal-democratic reform, and indeed the final part of Khamtay's speech spoke of strengthening the hold of the party and opposing "the multi-party concept." Kaysone's memory, then, is useful in an instrumental way for politicians in Laos.

But there is another aspect of the cult which is emphasized in the press, and that is the more avuncular side of Kaysone. Perhaps in this respect the influence of Ho Chi Minh and Vietnamese communism shows itself. In the run up to his anniversary *Pasason* ran a series of articles on "Kaysone the Family Man" written by his eldest son, Saysomporn Phomvihane, minister of finance. While these series of recollections will no doubt be useful for any future biographer of Kaysone, their interest from our point of view lies in the way they provide identifiable everyday details of a man who, while he was alive, was in fact very remote from most Lao people. They are an attempt to place Kaysone within the mainstream of Lao culture.

In these articles we are given access to his habits, and in particular the advice he gave to his children. So, we are told he used to rise at four in the morning because he felt his mind was sharpest then. And although he was a very busy and serious man (*kaeng kat*), he was always very concerned about his children's schooling, and from when they were little would always try to be available to help them. "He said, you must look first, observe, and then you must study hard, seek to understand and be prepared to ask questions" (*Pasason* 12/12/95). Although he was the only son, and therefore a favorite, his father was strict with him, and this he continued with his own children. When they were separated he wrote often and would always enquire after three things: "first, my health, second my studies, and third about my relationships with schoolfriends" (13/12/95). When Saysomporn returned from his university studies in the Soviet Union his father counseled him that although he had a very high university degree and knowledge he would not know how to put that knowledge into action unless he went down among the people, and so he was sent off to work in Savannakhet. "He always told me: 'The best university is the university of the people'" (15/12/95). Kaysone also instructed him that he may have to sleep and eat among the ethnic minorities as his father had during the revolutionary years. But lest the reader think Kaysone reminisced often about his days in the mountains we are assured that he did not dwell on them, and only spoke about them a little, sometimes while relaxing with his son and family when visiting Savannakhet. Kaysone was neither a fussy eater, nor a big eater, and his favorite food was country food (*kong gin peun muang*) about which he was particular, insisting that a certain dish, for example, had too little *pa daek* (a typical Lao fish paste condiment). We are also told that he was especially fond of Lao traditional literature and arts: "I have seen him when visiting Savannakhet enjoy going to listen to *Lam Savan, Lam Phu Tai, Lam Dang Vay,* . . . and he doesn't just go to listen either; he will call the *moh lam* over and tell him whether he is singing the song correctly or not, after which the singer corrects himself . . . and sometimes he complained that the *lam korn savan* should be sung slowly and not so fast as some singers do today" (16/12/95).[13] This

---

[13] The *lam* is a traditional style of singing in Laos, usually accompanied by playing of the *khene* (a type of pan pipe) in which a tale is told. *Moh lam,* the specialists of this style, have been an important source of information historically in Laos and in Thailand. There are regional and ethnic

emphasis on the non-political, homely side of Kaysone appeals to the everyday cultural practices of Lao society and attempts to show that he was a common person with common interests who cared for his family, just as he cared for the Lao people and the Lao nation.

*R helpful*

With the decline of full-blown socialist rhetoric following the shift to a post-socialist regime the Lao government has increasingly emphasized Lao nationalism, and nationalism needs its heroic figures and myths. The actions and achievements of individuals rather than groups are much better stuff for mythmaking, and as a central architect of the new regime Kaysone can fulfill this role as well as anyone. But this only underlines the fact that the new regime is remarkably short of charismatic figures. The other colorful characters of modern Lao history, such as Prince Phetsarath, Prince Boun Oum, or Katay Don Sasorith, or the prime minister in the old regime, Prince Souvanna Phouma, were all on the "wrong side" from the perspective of the current regime, and perhaps only the demise of the LPRP can allow them to play a role in a more rich tapestry of Lao nationalist historiography. For the moment, excepting Kaysone, Lao nationalist mythologizing usually has to reach back into the early nineteenth century to the uprising of Chao Anou against the Siamese in 1828, before it can continue its heroic narrative. The following account "of unyielding struggle against feudalists and foreign domination" produced for the fortieth anniversary of the party, however, includes references to leaders of minority revolts (although they are not marked as such) against colonialism in the north and the south, but more specifically it is a history of Lao kings and princes:

*only Kaysone "wrong side"*

> They were Chao Fa Ngoum who united the Kingdom of Lane Xang in 1353, Chao Phothisarath who defeated the hegemonists' scheme of the Siamese feudalists in 1536, Chao Saya Sethathirath who salvaged the nation from the

---

variations of style, such as a Savannakhet style, e.g. *Lam Savan*, or an ethnic style, *e.g. Lam Phu Tai.*

Burmese feudalists' invasion in 1563-1569, Chao Anou, who in 1827-1828 bravely fought against Siamese domination, Phokadouat, Ong Keo and Ong Khommadam, who fought against French colonialists in central and southern Laos between 1901 and 1937, and Chao Fa Patchay, who also fought the French between 1918-1922 in northern Laos. (*VT* 17-23/3/95)

The demands of nationalism to produce a fuller historical narrative will, no doubt, be one of the pressures which will finally undo the current hegemony of the LPRP's version of history. Furthermore, Laos's engagement with intellectuals from other parts of the world, and Thailand in particular, will make its historians aware of their fragmentary understanding of Lao history and the crudeness of their methodology. This could already be seen at a seminar for historians and geographers held at Dong Dok College in Vientiane on 27 April 1996. After a presentation by Sisana Sisane, in which he said historical analysis and politics had to go hand in hand, several Lao speakers from the floor challenged him, saying how could they write "true history" (some also used the phrase "patriotic history") if history was always subject to the whim of politics. "In 1979 when we were having problems with China, what could we say? We simply had to avoid it. And with Vietnam, because of the close relations with Vietnam, we've been unable to examine Vietnam's historical role in Laos clearly." Sisane (one of the more liberal-minded figures of the regime) had no clear or convincing answer. The important point is, such challenges would not have been heard even a few years ago. And they are likely to continue.

# THAT LUANG: "SYMBOL OF THE LAO NATION"

I N August 1991, with the proclamation of the first constitution of the LPDR, the That Luang, or Grand Stupa, of Vientiane replaced the hammer and sickle as the centerpiece of the national symbol which adorns each ministry and all official Lao documents, and became the emblem on the 1000-kip note released that year. It signaled a clear shift away from socialist iconography and the promotion of re-cognizeably nationalist iconography, following the collapse of communism elsewhere and the regime's desire to re-legitimize itself.

This stupa has become the central symbol through which the nation remembers itself. Introducing a book on the stupa published in 1995 the vice minister of information and culture proclaimed: "That Luang recalls for us the grandeur of Laos, it was built at the height of Lane Xang, the Kingdom of a Million Elephants, by King Setthatirath whose statue stands proudly close by the monument. Destroyed and pillaged several times in the past centuries, each time it has been rebuilt to its initial splendour with love and patience by the Lao people. It symbolizes the perseverance and the gen-erosity of the Lao people. It is also a symbol of the unity of the country, demonstrated each year as people gather enthusiastically at the time of the great festival of the That" (Editions *VT*:1995). Here, not for the first time, we encounter the theme of the vicariousness of the Lao nation, and its

*main stupa*

dogged persistence. In a turning world That Luang is the nation's still-point.

Held in November each year between the thirteenth and fifteenth day of the twelfth month in the Buddhist calendar, the That Luang festival is one of the most popular Buddhist festivals in Laos, although it is an urban festival focused in Vientiane.[1] Coming just before the National Day celebrations on 2 December, the spontaneous fervor it generates among the population contrasts almost embarrassingly with the bureaucratic organization of the state-controlled celebration. On these days thousands of people stream towards the That Luang to pay homage, while the white stupa to the unknown soldier stands forlornly at the other end of the grounds, visited only by officials of the state before National Day. Over the years the state-sponsored celebration has slowly given ground to this popular celebration, and finally retreated indoors.[2] Meanwhile the state has attempted to appropriate the That Luang festival.

*like past*

It was under the RLG that the That Luang festival was promoted as a national festival and it became a time for swearing an oath of fealty to the king at Vat Ong Tue.[3] "The ritual prayers having been recited by the monks, the Master

1. Around this time festivals associated with regional stupas are also held, and these festivals are consciously linked to the main festival in Vientiane.

2. Explaining the modesty of the National Day celebrations in 1995 an official of the Lao Front for National Construction (NLSS) said the reason was that the state did not have enough money and wanted to concentrate on economic development. However, a little earlier in the interview, in response to a question about the large celebration at That Luang, he said, "Now that Laos is prosperous the state can afford to spend much more on the That Luang festival." It is significant that he did not notice the contradiction between the two statements.

3. At one time this ceremony had been held at Vat Sisaket, initiated by the Vientiane ruler Chao Anou (reigning 1804-28) who built the temple. After his overthrow by the Siamese it was at Vat Sisaket that Lao notables in Vientiane had to swear an oath of fealty to them. Then, after the French took over in 1893, an oath of loyalty was sworn to them in this *vat* as well (Raquez 1902:103-4). The ceremony of swearing fealty to the king was revived in Vientiane after the establishment of the constitutional monarchy. It was moved to Vat Ong Tue because this *vat* is associated with its builder,

of Ceremony then dips the extremities of swords and rifles into alms bowls filled with lustral water, and three times repeats the following Oath written on latania leaves: 'We, Chao Muongs . . . take the solemn oath of loyalty to His Majesty, our August sovereign.'" (Nginn 1959:290) Afterwards the royal cortege would proceed to the That Luang to join the thousands of people gathered there for the religious festival. The atmosphere is caught by Nhouy Abhay:

> Nearly everywhere, "bean banks" can be seen, where games of chance will produce some unknown formulas to the inexperienced gamblers, all this amid shouts of pleasure and mumbles of disappointment. Smiling or long faced gamblers, *phusaos* slipping, full of curiosity and merriment, among so many both expressive and strange faces there is an intense bustle around the *That*, shining in the moonlight. The crowds are so dense and so many high pitched voices around that a general hubbub can be heard everywhere. Men and women, young and old, Vietnamese, Chinese, Mountain People and Laotians, are inextricably mingled, pressed and squeezed together. All of them speak, laugh, shout and swear in hundreds of tongues which fuse and echo from all parts. (1959:291-2)

A fair preceded the religious festival, and this too was presided over by the king. Indeed, one of the last major public acts of King Sisavang Vatthana was to give a banquet for all the local headmen and village chiefs who had taken part in the fair and festival, on 19 November 1975.

Already under the RLG the organization of the festival had been bureaucratized and come under the aegis of the Ministry of Religious Affairs. After 1975 Buddhism was no longer designated as the state religion, and the organization of Buddhism and popular festivals fell to the *Neo Lao Hak Sat* (Lao Patriotic Front), later the *Neo Lao Sang Sat* (Lao Front for National Construction (NLSS)), who continues to organize

---

King Setthatirath, who "unified the Lao nation," and it took place at the time of the That Luang festival.

the festival. In the years immediately following the revolution "extravagant" religious rituals were discouraged by the state, under the rhetoric of "practicing thrift" to mobilize economic surpluses and effort for the process of construction and development. As Kaysone put it during an address in June 1976: "All religious gatherings and rites under the new system have been reorganised with the emphasis on national values, jubilation and entertainment by spending less money, effort and time in organising them" (*SWB* 21/6/76). Earlier, instructions on the celebration of festivals were issued, which among other things said: "The That Luang Pagoda Festival will be held as usual because it provides a place for our people and friendly countries to display their economic and cultural achievements. However, the organization of this festival must be improved to ensure public security. All kinds of gambling at the festival are prohibited" (*SWB* 12/4/76). The concern with security and control also led to a ban on the sale of alcohol during the festival.[4] In the absence of the king, the leading state figure presiding over the festival each year has been the minister of education, religious affairs and sport, who for most of the period since 1975 was Phoumi Vongvichit, and he was occasionally accompanied by other senior figures like Nouhak Phoumsavan.

---

4. It is of interest that the pre-1975 display of anomalous animals (i.e. those with various deformities) has been banned from the fair. In popular belief such anomalies are associated with metaphysical power—the Buddha for example, is believed to have had thirty-three teeth, and folklore has it that the founding king of Lane Xang, Fa Ngum, had the same number of teeth. One is also reminded of symbols of many-headed elephants or many-armed *thevadas*. A book published by Princess Maha Chakri Sirindhorn (1994:58-9) about her travels in Laos shows her visiting a "sacred" pig at Vat Siamphon, Vientiane. The pig has five toes. The banning of the anomalous from popular festivals by the regime comes as no surprise to anthropologists because anomalies defy categorization and therefore can symbolize disruptive and un-controllable forces—they are anathema to an imagination which craves total control and predictability. Yet, to my surprise, I noticed a small pavilion at the Luang Prabang boat racing festival in September 1997 inviting people to view "the strange" phenomenon of "Siamese twins." Perhaps it is one more small sign of the decay of totalitarian control.

A discussion with Lao Front for National Construction officials of the Vientiane prefecture in late 1995 concerning the history of That Luang revealed memory processes which mix legend and fact freely, and signaled a re-traditionalizing of official narratives which no longer conformed to Marxist-Leninist historicism. The officials' story begins with the fanciful travels of the Buddha or his disciples through Laos some two thousand years ago when the site was allegedly originally marked for a stupa,[5] and the narrative takes a more conventional historical form with the coming of King Setthathirat (1548-71) who built the current stupa, and this is followed by a heroic description of how subsequent Lao kings protected Buddhism and the stupa. "But what about after the monarchy was overthrown in 1975?" I asked. The historical reverie of the NLSS official was temporarily suspended in mid-air, and he stared blankly at me for a full moment, a lapse which underlined the discontinuity. "The people continued the celebration, and the leaders of our state, such as Kaysone, attended," he replied. In fact neither Kaysone nor Souphanouvong ever attended the That Luang festival after 1975, but this substitution of Kaysone is revealing in ways we shall need to consider further on.

The festival has always included a traditional game of hockey, *tiki*, which as Charles Archaimbault (1973) has recorded, is found in various parts of Laos, and in which the two teams represent variously the sacred and the profane, the aboriginal inhabitants versus the invaders, the ordinary people versus the state, with the latter being the dominant meaning played out at That Luang. Before 1975 during this "rite of reversal," the king's side (*gasat*), or the state's side, would be dressed in red, while the people (*ladsadon*) would be dressed however they liked, and it was always vital that the people's side won as this would be a sign of future calm and prosperity. After 1975, however, the new state has tried to reformulate this ritual and suppress the element of "reversal" by simply recruiting two teams, one of which will

5. This particular narrative can be found in a publication released by the Committee for the Restoration of That Luang in 1985.

be, say, the blue-shirt team, the other the white-shirt. Under the new "democratic," "people's" regime there is, of course, no need for reversals because there are, allegedly, no hierarchies to reverse and ritually reconfirm. Yet, while official language attempts to neutralize the meaning of the teams, some onlookers still refer to one side as *gasat*, the other as *ladsadon*, thereby not only recalling older meanings but also drawing attention to the continuing reality of political hierarchy.[6]

As the state has withdrawn from its totalitarian project of trying to organize all aspects of daily life, so the festival has spontaneously grown. Furthermore, following the state's adoption of That Luang as its national symbol in 1992, it has stepped up its identification with the ritual and since then the president of the country has been the main officiant at the ceremony, just as the mayor of Vientiane, replacing the older *chao muang*, presides over the game of *tiki*. In recent years, following the changes in economic policy in Laos, the That Luang fair has become a major trade fair, and 1995 saw the biggest yet organized "to mark the 20th anniversary of the People's Democratic Republic and the 75th birthday of the late President Kaysone Phomvihane" according to the *Vientiane Times* (10-16/11/95). The six hundred pavilions by foreign and local companies and ministries promoted economic growth and advertised future development plans, such as a future national railway network.

The importance of That Luang as a national symbol, however, predates the LPDR. As Marcel Zago wrote:

> The That Luang of Vientiane contains the spirit, the *Ming Khouan* of the Lao nation, and is the barometer of the nation's fortune, and simultaneously the cause of its prosperity. Every monarchy has its *That*, just as it has its protective palladium and statue. When in the sixteenth

6.  Another process is at work too, and that is the transformation of traditional games into "sport," something increasingly promoted by the Lao state. One can also see this, for example, with the boat races held throughout the country.

century the capital was moved to Vientiane, the *That* and the *Lak Muang* at Vat Si Muang were constructed. Since independence, the That in Vientiane has once again become the center of the new kingdom, including Luang Prabang, Xieng Khouang and Bassac; it is therefore following the line of tradition. This is why the King of Luang Prabang comes down to Vientiane for the festival. . . . The *That* is considered the receptacle of power, while the divinities who reside in the *Lak Muang* are considered as the center of the city. (1972:328-9)

It symbolizes the structure of the world; it is the center of power, a source of merit, and a symbol of Buddhism. The new regime was never able to generate an equivalent center of symbolic power, and so as time has passed the rituals of the state have become more attenuated, while more traditional rituals, some of which like That Luang can perhaps be called rituals of the nation, have grown in strength. In anthropologist Victor Turner's terms, National Day in Laos could only celebrate structure, whereas That Luang also celebrates communitas.[7]

It should be pointed out that the above passage from Marcel Zago is reproduced in the book *Le That Luang: Symbole de la Nation Lao,* produced by the Vientiane Times 1995, but it omits all references to the king and to independence. In fact this book is an extraordinary work of scissors-and-paste designed to avoid all references to the former king and the

---

7. The classic formulation of this concept is by anthropologist Victor Turner: "All human societies implicitly or explicitly refer to two contrasting social models. One . . . is a society as a structure of jural, political, and economic positions, offices, statuses, and roles, in which the individual is only ambiguously grasped behind the social persona. The other is of a society as a communitas of concrete idiosyncratic individuals, who, though differing in physical and mental endowment, are nevertheless regarded as equal in terms of shared humanity. The first model is of a differentiated, culturally structured, segmented and often hierarchical system of in-stitutionalized positions. The second presents society as an undifferentiated, homogenous whole, in which individuals confront one another integrally, and not as 'segmentalized' into statuses and roles" (Turner 1977:177).

RLG. This would not be so bad, except there is no indication in the texts, by using, for example the standard use of three full stops (. . .), that a part of the text is missing. It is sewn together seamlessly so that one may think that the text is as Marcel Zago wrote it. Thus, in this Orwellian book, we are not even given the opportunity to be reminded that something has been "forgotten."[8]

8. In September 1996 an English version of this booklet was produced which also fails to acknowledge the censoring of the texts. It was translated into English by the Australian ambassador to Laos, Roland Rich.

# "BUDDHISM IS INSEPARABLE FROM THE LAO NATION"

T HERAVADA Buddhism is the main religion in Laos. But unlike its neighbors in Thailand and Cambodia where the majority of the population are either ethnic Thai or ethnic Khmer and therefore Buddhists, perhaps only between fifty to sixty percent of the people of Laos are ethnic Lao and Buddhist, the rest of the population being made up of *all things in nature have souls* diverse minorities practicing animism. In this respect it is more like its other neighbor, Burma, but unlike the latter, Christianity has made no significant headway among its ethnic minorities.

Prior to French colonial control of the country in the late nineteenth century the polity was a "galactic" one (Tambiah *Fr ruled end 19th c* 1976) in which Buddhism played a central role in the ruler's legitimation and in everyday life of the Lao. A pale version of a galactic polity centered on Luang Prabang in the north continued under a French colonial umbrella, while in the south the French ruled directly, although the traditional aristocracy in Champassak retained their status. Throughout Laos, therefore, the aristocracy maintained their customary ritual relationship with Buddhism.

A full study of the impact of French colonialism on Buddhism in Laos has yet to be done. The still current received wisdom is expressed by Zago (1972:38): "The French authorities favored Buddhism in Indochina because it assisted their domination there." While this is no doubt partly true it fails to grasp both the complex motivations for the French support of Buddhism in Laos, or its long-term effects. The French began the restoration of many Buddhist monuments, such as the That Luang, destroyed during the previous century in wars with Siamese or Ho armies, thus providing recognizable national symbols. In this one could argue they were simply transposing the practices of French nationalism into the Lao context (e.g. the preservation of "heritage," to be discussed in a later chapter). The colonial state, of course, also transposed elements of the modern state into this context, which included an increasingly elaborate set of bureaucratic rules and regulations. Thus in 1927 a detailed code for the conduct of the Buddhist sangha (order of monks) was enacted (*BEFEO* 1929:522-30). Perhaps more importantly, attempts were made to improve the theoretical sophistication of the clergy in both Cambodia and Laos by the establishment of a Buddhist institute in Phnom Penh in 1930 and in Vientiane in 1931, both under the "protection of the sovereigns of Cambodia and Luang Prabang." The political motivation for the establishment of the institute was clearly to counter Thai influence on Cambodian and Lao Buddhism. This was made explicit in the establishment of a Pali school at Bassac in the south of Laos, which could also serve Cambodia: "Here they inevitably come under the influence of Bangkok and, each year, Lao monks go to the capital of Siam for their religious studies. The creation of a Pali school in Bassac would be able to remedy this undesirable situation and retain with us youth who wish to undertake studies in the sacred language" (*BEFEO* 1932:335). The institutes were to become an arena for the interaction of Lao religious intellectuals and French intellectuals, an interaction which no doubt influenced in some way the direction of Lao Buddhist studies. The influence of a Western discourse can be seen, for example, in the speech given by the Venerable Nath from Cambodia (ibid:340) at the opening of the institute in Vientiane in 1931 where he talks of them as being places for the "instruction of monks in religious *science* and morality" (my emphasis).[1] Thus a Buddhist revival in Laos began under the French.

1. An interesting attempt to consider the impact of Orientalist

In 1947 a constitutional monarchy, not unlike the one already installed in Thailand, was formed.[2] The preamble to the constitution said: "Buddhism is the state religion. The King is its high protector. . . . He shall be a devout Buddhist." This trilogy of nation, king and Buddhism, like in Thailand, was the foundation of national ideology, and all key state rituals drew on religion. The king appointed the head of the Buddhist sangha, while a Ministry of Religion and Cults was formed to oversee religious affairs. Religious instruction was carried on in the schools and state radio broadcast special programs dealing with Buddhism. The ritual calendar of the state was organized around religious festivals, or state-royal-religious festivals. The main exceptions being the national holidays for Constitution Day on 11 May, Independence Day on 19 July, and the international (Gregorian) New Year.

The formation of the RLG thus saw attempts to bolster Buddhism, building in part on French-created institutions such as the Buddhist Institute. Nhouy Abhay, a prominent figure in the RLG, was a leader of this revival. In a key text on Lao Buddhism, first given as a speech in 1949, he wrote:

> How much ignorance among the monks! The Pali tongue which is less and less understood has become a screen behind which they hide their ignorance. . . . This lack of reasoning goes with a daily slackening in the performance of religious rites. Monks relax their discipline, and it can be noticed in temples as well as in the streets, in cemeteries and in homes. In its essence, Buddhism is deeply tolerant; but ours in fact has lost too much of its authority. . . . In the field of manners, as in religion, our monks are far from being the elite they are supposed to be. (Nhouy 1959:253)

---

Buddhologists on Buddhist studies East and West is the various essays in Lopez (1995).

2. Though, as Ishii (1986:37) observes, the Thai constitution simply refers to *sasana* (religion) without specifying Buddhism, it says that the king who is the protector of religion should be a Buddhist.

*Budd*

The revival saw an increase in the number of Pali schools throughout the country, programs for further education of monks abroad and the introduction of approved texts for studying Buddhism. In the 1960s meditation schools were established in some temples and a publishing program of Buddhist texts by Lao monks was begun. Writing in the early 1970s Marcel Zago could say: "Today, some twenty years after Nhui Abhay advocated [his] reforms, many of them have been realized, thanks in large part to the actions of the responsible ministries" (1976:123). Indeed Zago, who is rightly considered one of the foremost experts on Lao Buddhism in this period, spoke of a "renaissance of Lao Buddhism" (ibid:124) which he saw in the growth of lay Buddhist associations, meditation schools, and in missionary activity.

The increasing role played by the modern bureaucratic state in the affairs of Buddhism in Laos was, compared with Thailand, a belated reform of state/sangha relations. Such reform had begun in the second half of the nineteenth century in Thailand, and paralleled the modernization of the state there (Keyes 1971; Ishii 1986). After the establishment of the RLG we see similar attempts at modernization in Laos. Thus, for example, in 1959 a royal ordinance was passed in order to establish closer state supervision of the sangha's activities.

*past roots*

Some writers, observing the close control established over the Lao sangha by the communist regime after 1975 see the roots of this policy in the RLG. In some respects they are correct. Modern states, communist or non-communist, create extensive bureaucracies and exercise more regulation of their societies than their predecessors. However, I would like to briefly take issue with Martin Stuart-Fox and Rod Bucknell in their influential article "Politicization of the Buddhist Sangha in Laos" (1982) whose most questionable assumption is that somehow Buddhism was traditionally above politics, when in fact Buddhism had always been linked to state legitimacy. The main difference after independence was that with the attempt to create a modern liberal state different political parties of the right and left were trying to yoke Buddhism to their political cause, a demonstration in and of itself of the

*bind budd to political cause*

importance of Buddhism within Lao culture and society. The first main sign of this was the appointment of a communist, Phoumi Vongvichit, as minister of cults during the first coalition government in 1957. In this position he is claimed to have "skillfully indoctrinated a number of bonzes in the justness of the Communist view of world affairs" (Dommen 1971:76). It was this which no doubt led to the tightening of *gov't* central government control over the sangha two years later by the right-wing Sannanikone government, both over appointments and over internal communication within the sangha.[3] This caused some resentment, which was perhaps Pathet-Lao–inspired, but it was nothing compared to the opposition one has seen to reforms in Thailand this century, such as violent millenarian outbreaks in the northeast (Keyes 1977; Ishii 1986). Stuart-Fox and Bucknell cite one demonstration against the transfer of a monk, but besides this there does not seem to be a lot of evidence for the claim that the 1959 ordinance seriously undermined the legitimacy of the sangha. In fact, another source, going to the other extreme argues that: "The close relationship between the religious hierarchy and the state has not led to the direct involvement of the sangha or individual bonzes in politics" (Whitaker et al. 1972:112). Compared with neighboring Burma, for example, the sangha in Laos was very quiescent despite the continual political jockeying which went on around it, such as the Pathet Lao formation of the United Buddhist Association in 1960, or the Vientiane side's Young Buddhist Association in 1963.

Having alleged that attempts to "politicize" the sangha were weakening its influence and assisting secularization, Stuart-Fox and Bucknell then, in a contradictory vein, berate *Table* the state and its French-educated elite whom they allege were "predisposed . . . to a view of the state which entailed a sharp division between secular government and ecclesiastical affairs" because they supposedly excluded the sangha from

---

3. The right-wing Sarit Thanarat government in Bangkok passed similar legislation in 1962. (See Jackson 1989: chapter 4.) For the rules under the RLG until this time, see Kruong (1959).

political influence causing the monks to "withdraw into lives of seclusion"](1982:64). They further claim that the RLG gave Buddhism "no sense of social responsibility in the building of a Lao nationalist identity" (ibid:63-4). In the face of the centrality of Buddhist ritual to RLG legitimacy and its attempts to promote Buddhism it is hard to see how any of these claims can be sustained.

A third factor they point to is the division of Lao Buddhism into two sects—Mahanikai and Thammayut—which they claim weakened it. In fact the first sect was much larger than the second which still had little influence on Lao Buddhism. Furthermore, the centralizing of the sangha which these authors deplore, was one attempt at avoiding serious damage from such schisms. The Thammayut was strong in Thailand because of its close connections with the palace historically, and this also tended to be true in Cambodia. But no such connection existed in Laos, and the Thammayut was strongest in the south of the country where it had existed since at least the beginning of the century, while a couple of temples in Vientiane adhered to the Thammayut order.[4] There were none in the royal capital, Luang Prabang. Strangely,

---

4. Information on the relationship between these two sects in Laos is scarce. We are given some insights by one Lao Thammayut monk, Maha Canla, who defected to Thailand in 1976: ". . . in Laos the division was very wide. It was as if neither sect recognized the other as made up of Lao people. They were completely distinct from each other, and were always trying to get the better of each other . . . The entire Lao population was divided on the same basis, so that a young man who was an adherent of the Mahanikai could on no account marry a young woman who was an adherent of Thammayut, because their parents would not allow it. The trouble was the political left was aware of this weak point and they managed, by inciting the two sides and spreading evil rumors, to make the gap wider and wider." (1977:71) The depth of sectarianism cannot be doubted, but in Laos it had much less import than in Thailand where the Thammayut, although having a minority of monks, held the key positions in the sangha because of royal patronage, and this was deeply resented by the Mahanikai majority. In Laos the latter were predominant in numbers and in power, and thus the stakes were less high, and the sectarianism had less impact on Buddhism as a whole. There is no doubt, however, that the Pathet Lao would have tried to capitalize on what factionalism there was.

what these authors do overlook is the role of politically conservative Thai Thammayut monks in Laos before 1975.

Finally, they argue that "the sangha saw itself as the principal guardian of Lao culture" (ibid:65) and this made a significant number of monks sympathetic to the Pathet Lao cause. This I think is broadly true, but it is not a factor which counts for the weakening of Lao Buddhism before 1975. As Tambiah (1976) documented for Thailand, a majority of the monks in the main temples of Bangkok are from rural backgrounds and the sangha is an important avenue of social mobility for poor country boys in Thailand. This was also true in Laos prior to 1975 (Zago 1972:43), and it is not surprising that these poor country boys should resent the conspicuous big-spending of the Lao elite in that period made possible by a large influx of US aid dollars. This they contrasted in distinctly Buddhist terms with the lifestyles of the Pathet Lao. Speaking of the "Red Prince" Souphanouvong, one young monk told Joel Halpern in the early 1960s: "He visits the monks at the wat and tells them of his troubles and the hardships suffered by his army when they were fighting in the forest. The soldiers were not paid any salary, and they had to beg rice in the villages. I like Souphanouvong and the Pathet Lao because they are honest people" (Halpern 1965:160). Once he passed his exams and became a Maha, this young monk hoped to become an official in the foreign ministry. The French educated elite tended to dominate the upper echelons of government, but not to the total exclusion of upwardly mobile country boys, as Stuart-Fox and Bucknell try to suggest (1982:63). It is also of interest that a significant number of monks who sympathized with the Pathet Lao were from the Thai northeast, no doubt after fleeing from tight state controls there. And following right-wing coups in Vientiane (sympathetic to Bangkok) they fled to the mountains with the Pathet Lao. Others, such as the recently deceased (24/12/96) Phra Ajaan Maha Bouakham Voraphet became radicals during their studies in Cambodia in the early 1940s where the sangha was radicalized by French attempts to reform the calendar and other aspects of Cambodian culture.

Later than their confrères in Thailand (see Tambiah 1976:chapter 18), Lao monks also began to be involved in rural development (Boutsavath and Chapelier 1973), and indeed Thailand was the model for their involvement. Zago (1976:124) speaks of one prime mover being Maha Pal Anantho who both sought a "return to the fundamental essence of Buddhism and to live in accordance with it while at the same time giving heed to the demands of contemporary society." But this move towards a more socially engaged Buddhism was also sponsored by the RLG and USAID in an attempt to bolster support for the RLG among the peasantry. There is no evidence, however, that this weakened Buddhism's appeal any more than it did in Thailand.

Of course, secular forces were at work in Lao society prior to 1975. The fact that a constitutional monarchy had been established meant a certain desacralizing of the political realm. Furthermore, partly because of the political divisions in the country, there was no concerted attempt to create a modern cult of the king as occurred under the right-wing dictatorships in neighboring Thailand. While all political factions—including the Pathet Lao—swore their allegiance to the monarchy and to Buddhism, much political debate took place without reference to religion. Moreover, the attempts to create a modern state in Laos, with modern education and health systems for example, saw the *vat* (temple), which had previously functioned as a school or as a center for traditional medicine, slowly pushed to one side by professional teachers and nurses—at least in the main towns.

Urbanization also meant that the *vats* stood in a different relationship to the community, compared with rural villages. Martin Barber commented: "Social relations in the towns are now determined not so much by residence or kinship patterns as in rural areas, but rather by class and occupation. In Vientiane many people say 'we don't have time to go to the *vat*. We're too busy making a living.' Others note that young people only go to the wat these days in order to meet each other at a *boun*." (1974:49)

The communist takeover in December 1975 saw the victory of a radically secular political movement. The king was forced to step down and with him went the centrality of Buddhism. Modern nationalism's triumvirate of monarchy-religion-nation were swallowed up by the singular communist party state.

Given that the Buddhist sangha in Laos was one of the main vertical organizations to reach down into the villages, it was inevitable that the communist government after 1975 would wish to gain control over it. Thus it reorganized the sangha into the United Buddhist Association, which in turn was subordinate to the Communist Party's national front organization, and the Ministry of Religious Affairs was integrated into the Ministry of Education, Sports and Religious Affairs. Buddhism lost its status as a state religion, and the government announced that "every Lao citizen is allowed to practice any religion he wishes. He also has the right not to practice any religion" (*SWB* 13/1/76). Inevitably this also meant a reorientation of state ritual away from religion towards purely state-based secular rituals. Thus the official ritual calendar involving public holidays reads as follows: New Year's Day, Pathet Lao Day (6 January), Army Day (20 January), Women's Day (8 March), LPRP Day (22 March), Lao New Year (13-15 April), May Day, Children's Day (1 June), Lao Issara Day (13 August), Liberation Day (23 August), Freedom from the French Day (12 October), National Day (2 December). These were festivals which primarily affected state organizations, the bureaucracy and schools. For festivals like the New Year, celebrated by other ethnic groups such as Hmong, Yao, Goh (Akha), etc. in December, the state gave allowance for its officials from these ethnic groups to have days off for the celebrations. In general, however, in the rural areas the traditional calendar, centered as it was on the *vats* and associated with the agricultural cycle, remained in operation beyond the reach of the state. Had the government's plans that the agricultural cooperatives function as political as well as economic organizations (Evans 1990a:chapter 8) been successful, then this state-based ritual calendar could have extended its reach. In fact, it never did, except for some isolated cases, and then only for a short period of time.

Nevertheless, the government attempted to extend its influence into this ritual domain, and in April 1976 issued detailed regulations on Buddhist festivals. A central feature of the state's political rhetoric at the time related to the importance of thrift for economic development (Evans 1993). Thrift applied to both time and money, and extravagant festivals were seen to be wasteful of both by drawing resources away from development. Thus the rhetoric of control tended to be phrased in economic rather than political terms. For example, the That Luang festival was to continue as usual "because it provides a place for our people and friendly countries to display their economic, cultural and arts achievements." But, "all kinds of gambling at the festival are prohibited." Similarly, the Boat Race Festival was to continue, but "all gifts given to the winners should be in the form of production tools so that they will be utilized in work." It was suggested that festivals be "rationalized" and adjacent temples were encouraged to hold joint festivals under the guidance of the local administration. Depending on the zealousness of local cadres (and zeal was abundant in the early years of the revolution) this sometimes led to the discontinuation of some temple festivals or their extreme attenuation, leading some refugees to speak of the total suppression of Buddhism. These restrictions caused a great deal of popular resentment. For example, concerning the *Boun Bang Fai* (Rocket Festival) held around May, the regulations said the "festival must be restricted to each locality. The people in a province must not congregate in the provincial capital to celebrate the occasion as was done in the past. If the worshiping of a town center shrine has to be performed on the same day as the Rocket Shooting Festival, the administration of the district where the shrine is located must be responsible for preparing the rite." In 1977, in some localities, attempts to control this festival led to its virtual suppression by, for example, not allowing holidays for preparations (Sicard 1981:49), or led to such disruption of customary practice that it was seen to have severely compromised the effectiveness of the rite. For example, the participation of *nang tiam* (female spirit mediums) in this rite was strongly discouraged. The Rocket Festival is a fertility rite which invites the monsoon rains. The subsequent poor rains in Laos in 1977 were blamed on restrictions on this festival, causing a great deal of resentment among the peasantry. Subsequent rice shortages gave rise to other restrictions: "The use of rice or corn for liquor distillation must be strictly minimized, and we must avoid unnecessary parties or religious rice donations" (*SWB* 15/7/77). Thus even the free flow of liquor and good times that normally go with a Lao festival were under threat. For ordinary people the new regime had definitely become *boh mouan* (unpleasant). Indeed, government attempts to restrain alcoholic revelry is echoed in subsequent years through various instructions released before festivals.

Other attempts were made to try to reorganize the everyday merit-making ritual of giving alms to monks during their morning rounds in the villages and towns. People were encouraged to take their alms to the *vats*, and in some cases the local administration tried, unsuccessfully in the end, to designate specific *khum* (a village sub-unit) with responsibility for giving alms on specific days. Some attempts were also made in the interests of "thrift" and the importance of everyone devoting their time to production and development, to encourage monks to establish gardens and work for their food. In some cases the monks were openly accused of being "parasitic" like the old "feudal classes." Besides doctrinal objections, such as the need of the monks to be aloof from the mundane world, people objected to these changes because they deprived ordinary Lao of the opportunity to make merit through alms-giving whenever they wished or needed to. In the long-run none of these changes survived.

As in their misguided attempts at collectivizing peasant society where the communists misunderstood the relations of reciprocity among peasant families (Evans 1990a), they also did not understand the relations of reciprocity between the sangha and the people, which as Strenski (1983:470) argues, constitutes "Buddhist *society*. . . . It is undeniable, I take it, that ritual giving sits squarely in the center of the relation between the *sangha* and lay society." Monks are "fields of merit" and gifts to them enter a system of generalized exchange which is essential to the social solidarity of these societies.

In Theravada Buddhist societies monks embody Buddhist principles, the dhamma. Their withdrawal from the mundane world into the *vat* where they dress differently, follow a different daily regime from the rest of the society, are subject to elaborate codes of conduct, including codes of avoidance, especially of women who tempt them back into the mundane world—all of these rules demarcate the sacred space within which they move. As Tambiah remarks:

> Curiously, the question of "orthodoxy" in the behavior of monks related in Buddhist countries not so much to the propagation of heretical doctrines as to the breaking of rules of conduct and etiquette as laid down in the *vinya* code. In the history of Buddhism there have been, of course, major sectarian splits on doctrinal matters, but, more characteristically, schisms within the sangha have arisen on questions of "discipline" relating to details of ritual, etiquette and conduct, such as methods of ordination, of wearing the robe, or the laxness of behavior regarding the handling of money or sexual behavior. (1976:520-1)

Transgressions either point back to the rules or call them into question.[5] After the revolution the new regime attempted

5. Maha Canla says that the Pathet Lao was able to weaken the sangha before 1975 by sowing doubts about the discipline of monks: 'The . . . thing monks who joined the movement did was to produce leaflets and anonymous circular letters and distribute them among the young monks and novices in the monasteries. These leaflets said that this or that elder or high-ranking monk was behaving badly, that he was breaking the monk's code of discipline, and so was, strictly speaking, no longer a monk. Ought

to redefine these rules, as well as doctrine, and often met with resistance. However, one might argue that the importance of rules over doctrine, compared with the communist fixation on doctrine, partly helped to insulate the sangha from the powerful revolutionary winds which blew after 1975.

The new rulers of Laos set out to politicize the sangha. In early January 1976, the leading radical Buddhist Maha Khamtan Thepbouali, author of the seminal tract *Buddhism and the Lao Revolution* (1975), said: "We hold that the country and Buddhism cannot be separated. . . . Therefore, since Lao society is changing favourably, it is certain that Buddhist monks and novices will undergo changes. . . . We will try our utmost to stamp out the vestiges of the old society and build a new, pure and bright one. In the religious sphere it is necessary to correct many mistakes such as Buddhist textbooks which do not conform with the principles of Buddhism—textbooks compiled by capitalism and feudalism to hoodwink the people . . ." (*SWB* 21/1/75). The Lao People's Democratic Republic banned the two main sects in Laos, the Mahanikai and the Thammayut, and formed the Lao United Buddhist Association, which proclaimed at its nationwide conference held in Vientiane in mid-1976: "In the social field, the Association will defend all fine customs and habits of the people and the good morality of religions, while eliminating superstitious practices and all other social evils left behind by the old regime. . . . The spread of Buddhist morality must accord with the line and policies of the Lao People's Revolutionary Party . . ." (*SWB* 30/6/76). Later in the year Phoumi Vongvichit gave the new regime's keynote speech on Buddhism, where he said that in contradistinction to the "old regime which prohibited Buddhist monks from engaging in politics" the new regime encourages it. The Buddha's original path of learning, he claimed, led him to the

---

one to go on bowing and paying respects to such a person? When the young monks and novices read this, they talked about it and discussed it so much that the news soon spread widely. This caused people to lose faith in the order, and to look with suspicion on the elders and high-ranking monks." (1977:33)

same conclusion as communists: "the Lord Buddha gave up all his worldly possessions and became an ordinary person with only an alms bowl to beg food from other people. That meant that he tried to abolish the classes in his country and to create only one class—a class of morally conscious people who were respected by other people. It was in this way that the Lord Buddha became involved with politics . . ." (*SWB* 1/11/76). He requested that monks go out and preach in support of the state's developmental programs.

Significantly, Phoumi situated himself and his government in the same position as the Theravada kings of old who, in their role as defenders of the faith, occasionally acted as purifiers of the sangha. By retraining monks, the new regime, he said, "will help purify and make Buddhism in this country more scientific than in other countries." Interestingly, the LPDR's "scientific" hostility to "superstitious" practices gained endorsement for a while from modernist Buddhists in Thailand, the followers of Buddhadasa, who, according to Lafont (1982:159) saw Lao Buddhism as "reverting to the Buddha's original teaching."[6] In a brief message to Lao Christians in 1982, Khamtan Thepbouali, told them: "Under this regime, everybody has a right to his own religion. But be careful. Don't believe just anything. Choose a belief which has some foundation and logic. Christianity is a good example. It has a set of scriptures which you can study and understand" (cited by Peachey 1983:19).

For many monks and for many laymen this political reorientation of the Lao sangha was unacceptable. As a result some left the order and returned to ordinary life, some fled to Thailand, and among the flood of Lao refugees to Thailand from 1975 until the early 1980s, many cited dissatisfaction

6. This view appears to have been temporary, and subsequent publications of Buddhadasa, for example, *Dhammic Socialism* (1986), make it clear that the two movements have little or nothing in common. Interestingly, Zago (1972:45) notes in his study that the Buddhist texts produced for moral education in elementary schools in Laos in the 1950s and 1960s by the Ministry of Education (using US aid) placed the accent on the moral aspect of Buddhism and not the ritual component, and made no mention of spirits.

with the changes to Lao Buddhism among their reasons for leaving. Paradoxically, the inroads which the state education system had been making on the educational role of the *vats* stalled after 1975 because so many teachers fled the country as refugees and the new regime had to fall back on the monks. According to the Peacheys (1983:19), a network of Buddhist schools serving both the religious community and the society had nearly eight thousand pupils. But this made control of Buddhist ideology and the training of monks in Marxism-Leninism even more imperative.

During these austere years people were reluctant to display their wealth by giving to the temples, obstacles were placed in the way of men entering the monkhood, and many people were wary of showing too much religious fervor. Typically, these measures were most effective in the main towns. In the early 1980s, however, close government control of Buddhism began to relax, and even party members could enter the monkhood for a short time to earn merit for parents who were sick or who had died. By the mid-1980s an efflorescence of Lao Buddhism had begun. Growing prosperity in the towns as a result of economic reforms begun in 1979 and accelerated after 1986, saw money flow towards the *vats* for their repair and for the building of Buddhist monuments, all highly visible forms of merit-making.

The revival of Buddhism has been attributed largely to these macro-economic reforms. But I would also like to suggest that an accumulating existential crisis within the Lao leadership contributed to it as well, for as Gellner remarks: "Marxism has nothing to say to personal tragedy and bereavement" (1994:40). Thus one of the areas in which we can trace the gradual reemergence of non-secular Buddhist rituals at the level of the state is in funeral rituals. Perhaps fortunately for the new state the first of its old leaders to die was Sithon Kommadan, a member of the non-Buddhist Loven minority from the south of Laos, in May 1977. A simple state funeral was held for him at the That Luang square in Vientiane. In late September and October 1978, a number of leading figures died, and pressures was clearly building up for the reinstitution of full Buddhist funeral rites. At these ceremonies there was some attempt to keep the party orations and the religious ceremony separate. Nevertheless, by 1980 we begin to see the regime relaxing its controls across a range of traditional religious rituals. By the time Prince Souvanna Phouma, the former RLG prime minister and now adviser to the president, died in January 1984, time was ripe for a Buddhist funeral in high style.

And as we have seen, when Kaysone Phomvihane died full Buddhist rites were also accorded to him. Further evidence of this existential crisis among the leadership is revealed by the fact that as Kaysone's health began to fail him he turned increasingly to traditional remedies, which included visiting famous and mystically powerful monks in search of traditional medicines and also religious protection through prayers and amulets. One such religious figure now lives in a retreat he has created close to Vat Dong Savang in a forested area on the outskirts of Vientiane. Ajaan Phimpo had been arrested in 1987 because he spoke of spirits, *thevadas* and gods, and because people were making claims that he could "fly" *(phuba haydua/visa duabao)*, i.e. someone who was observed to be in one place and soon after to be in another place far away. Ajaan Phimpo was expelled from the monkhood and his library confiscated. By 1989, however, the authorities admitted that they had made a mistake and invited him to rejoin the sangha, but he refused and today simply wears a white robe. He told me that from his retreat he can say and do what he likes without being subject to the sangha's control, something that would have been impossible until the late 1980s. "If people are holy inside then each person is like a *vat*, and therefore don't need *vats* or the sangha." Kaysone visited him several times, beginning in 1989, in search of medicines and spiritual protection.

A formal shift in the government's attitude was registered in a March 1989 national meeting of the sangha in Vientiane. The fact that it was held just prior to the collapse of the "communist world" can be seen in the continual references to "socialism" and the support of Buddhism for the "socialist

64

system." Subsequently there has been a tendency to refer to the "development system"(*labop ganpattana*). The rules for the organizational structure for the sangha (the first made public since the RLG ordinance of 1959) adopted at this meeting made it clear that it would "take the religion forward along the road of socialism under the leadership of the party" (ULBA 1989:90). But it established the right of young men to enter the *vats* "so long as they get permission from the local persons concerned; and before leaving the Sangha they must have a good reason and carry it out according to the customs of Buddhism; the Lao United Buddhist Association does not restrict the beliefs of the people . . . but it reserves the right to decide on all problems relating to the work of the Sangha" (ibid 1989:91). It reiterated that the organization was opposed to "superstitious" beliefs in spirits and *thevadas*, and opposed all forms of intoxication and gambling (ibid 1989:92). No mention is made of the sangha having to provide for itself, but monks were encouraged to grow trees or bushes around the *vat* to improve their way of life, and to spread their knowledge about useful plants to villagers (ibid 1989:96-7). As for overseas contacts, these were to follow party policy, and the text refers explicitly to Vietnam, Cambodia, Mongolia and so on, but also to "international cooperation" in general. Since 1990 the emphasis has fallen on the latter, and monks in Laos have been allowed to go and study in Thailand,[7] and arrangements for Thai aid with Buddhist texts for teaching are made on a temple-to-temple basis, which is a radical departure from the recent past when contacts with Thai Buddhists were strongly discouraged.

In the constitution enacted in August 1991, the profile of Buddhism was also upgraded from one religion among others, to being the one specific religion named in the document: "The State respects and protects all lawful activities of Buddhists and followers of other religions, mobilizes and encourages the Buddhist monks, novices and priests of other faiths to participate in those activities which are beneficial to the country

---

7. In 1995 officially there were nine monks on a six-month study course in Thailand. My guess is that there may have been more unofficially.

and its people." No statements here, like Phoumi's of 1976, about upholding people's right to not believe in anything.

A major meeting on Buddhism and Lao culture held in July 1995 saw Khamtan Thepbouali continuing to proclaim that "Buddhism is inseparable from the Lao nation; Buddhist monks are inseparable from the Lao people." But a defensive note had crept into his rhetoric, and references to socialism were replaced by the cover-all of "revolution":

> [I wish] to clarify to all whether Buddhism and revolution are in contradiction to one another? There are some people who have always said that it is not right for the Sangha to engage in revolutionary activities because the Sangha does not engage in politics. These people have not read their history of Buddhism! And also they do not understand what the Sangha is, or for that matter, revolution. The truth is that the Sangha and revolution are not in contradiction, even though they do have separate basic assumptions. . . . Now I will speak about the problems of revolution. Revolution does not only mean the use of weapons. Struggle over ways of thinking is also revolution, struggle inside oneself over the right way of thinking and the wrong way is also revolution. It is the Sangha that really has the need to struggle day and night. To struggle to solve what is right and what is wrong, and not just once but again and again. Speaking generally, revolutionary struggle is a social struggle in which we search for what is right and what is wrong in order to weaken the latter and strengthen the former. (Khamtan 1995)

Khamtan's rhetoric skillfully interweaves Buddhist ideas about seeking for the truth with the more ominous communist idea that there is a single truth which the party knows. The emphasis, however, has shifted onto a more abstract moral plane and obvious socialist political rhetoric has been de-emphasized.

This meeting signaled a new phase in Buddhism's relationship with the LPDR. Throughout the whole period since 1975, because the sangha was one of the organizations making up the National Front, monks were present at most major state occasions and festivals, such as the beginning of National People's Assembly sessions, or at May Day or National Day, so a profile for Buddhism was maintained even though it was no longer the state religion. During the liberalization of the 1980s Buddhism, although flourishing, was still subordinate to the party's long-term aim of building socialism in Laos. The collapse of communism in Europe changed all that and the regime has turned increasingly to Buddhism in its search of new ideologies of legitimation, and of a reformulated Lao nationalism. This is especially apparent in the importance the media places on photographing or filming for TV the party leaders making merit during major Buddhist festivals.

Buddhism historically has been ready-made for this task, and I believe we can see a re-Buddhification of the Lao state. This is occurring in the context of Laos opening up to the outside world and growing concerns in Vientiane about the "decaying of traditional values" (Evans 1994). Thus, at the June 1995 conference, Buddhism and the monkhood were being championed as the "leaders of cultural pride," and the conference was told that monks are traditionally the keepers of knowledge and culture. Jan Nong Inthavong (1995), president of the NLSS, said: "Right now the Buddhists are extremely important for their moderation and their care for the national culture, because Buddhists are part of the spirit of the national Culture." The president of the Lao United Buddhist Association, Venerable Phra Ajaan Vichit Singalat, urged Lao monks "lead the way in a cultural renaissance which will ensure the longevity of the Lao way of life" (*VT* 23-29/6/95). The history of Lao Buddhism he gave to the conference was a litany of the exploits of Buddhist kings in defense of the faith, and made pointed reference to King Phothisarath's campaign against spirit cults.

This heroic history of Lao Buddhism is the history of Laos which circulates in the temples and increasingly is the one given out by cadres of the state, rather than a more orthodox Marxist-Leninist history as can be found in Kaysone's own book *La révolution lao* (1980), serialized once again in the Lao press in 1995 in the run-up to the anniversary of his death. Just how far this re-Buddhification can go without alienating its non-Buddhist ethnic minority constituency is one problem faced by the LPDR, and memories of the old king are not so dead that any moves to reinstate Buddhism as a state religion might undermine in a fundamental way the current state's legitimacy. Clearly, older hopes of the ethnic minorities moving from animism to atheism—"bypassing" the high religious stage in the same way that the regime hoped to "bypass" the capitalist stage in history—have had to be scrapped. But will this commit the regime to Buddhist missionary activity and the conversion of minority people into ethnic Lao?

The LPRP and spokesmen for the sangha maintain their public opposition to "superstitious" beliefs, but today this must be counted as one of the least successful of the regime's campaigns. Immediately after the revolution all forms of astrology and fortune telling by monks were repressed or heavily restricted. With the relaxation of restrictions in the 1980s all of these practices and beliefs have gradually returned. Significantly, in 1993, the long-time supporter of the LPRP and president of the Lao Buddhist Association, Maha Bouakham Voraphet, produced a traditional Lao calendar in which he said: "Lao astrology in the past and now is still a very important tool of the nation and of all Lao people, it is still a useful tool for officials and all Buddhists. . . . Astrological calculations like these are not only popular among Lao but they are also popular in many countries who continue to use them" (1993:2). He also claimed that this knowledge could also help in curing, and so on.[8]

---

8. An added feature of this calendar is that it carries a great deal of other miscellaneous information, such as Lao vital statistics, and statistics which "map" the Lao nation, such as highest mountains, longest rivers, etc.

A detailed study of the long-term impact of the communist-directed reforms of Buddhism in Laos remains to be done. Religious instruction is still excluded from the school curriculum (although some Buddhist references have made a comeback in school textbooks, as we shall see later on), and Buddhism is not promoted in the mass media as much as it was under the RLG, although newspapers and magazines carry much more information about Buddhism, or at least Buddhist festivals, today than they did in the recent past. One can now hear debates about the conduct of the monkhood, similar to those voiced by Thao Nhouy Abhay many years ago, among lay people who complain about the lack of discipline among monks. They talk of their careless attitudes, such as smoking cigarettes, walking along roads looking around just like ordinary people, rather than concentrating on a direct path, and some speculate about monks accumulating money in overseas bank accounts, and so on. Some people attribute this to the collapse of Buddhist values under communism.

There is little doubt that the communist state has hindered the theological development of Buddhism in Laos and led to a fall in the number of knowledgeable monks in the country. It is much harder to evaluate the theological developments it has encouraged, such as the the strong rationalist emphasis in the interpretation of doctrine, such as Khamtan's demand that belief have "some foundation and logic." Or the earlier insistence on the historical relativizing of Buddhist doctrine, and the insistence on the worldly direction of religious action in support of government policies. It is my opinion that these interpretations are primarily upheld today by those monks who have long been associated with the communists and have gained power through that association. Outside of that, in my conversations with senior Lao monks I have been struck by how orthodox and traditional their Buddhism remains.

It also contains a history of modern Laos in the form of significant dates, and these all conform to the orthodox LPRP story. Consequently, the calendar must also be seen as potentially communicating a range of other political and historical information.

Moreover, the new interpretations of Buddhism called for by Khamtan in 1976 have not materialized, and the last few years has seen the republication of texts used during the RLG, as well as the importation of texts from Thailand.[9]

In the new atmosphere in Laos in which the state is relying increasingly on Buddhism for legitimation one might expect greater attention to be given to modernist developments in Thai Buddhism, especially the teaching of someone like Buddhadasa whose critique of beliefs in spirits and *thevadas* would appear to be in accord with NLSS and sangha rhetoric. In this regard one could perhaps argue that one consequence of the communist moment in Lao history is that it may have created the conditions for a more rapid absorption of these modernist developments than would have occurred otherwise. We will have to wait and see. For the moment, however, I can only observe that I have come across few Lao monks who are familiar with Buddhadasa's teachings, and one of them was the dissenting former monk, Ajaan Phimpo. While Thai Buddhism's organizational changes initiated by King Mongkut in the mid-nineteenth century have filtered through into Laos and constitute one element of modernization, one gets little sense among monks and certainly not among lay people of a fundamental shift in cosmography that began among the Thai elite in the nineteenth century (Reynolds 1976) and subsequently fanned out into the population at large through the medium of mass education. As suggested earlier, with the collapse of socialist ideology an older Buddhist discourse on Lao history has reemerged to fill its place—a discourse which is centered on righteous kings and was suddenly interrupted by the historical hiatus of 1975.

9. In this context it is of interest to note that in 1994 Douangsai Luangpasi, one of the regime's most prolific propagandists, produced a small booklet on *The Various Religions Around the World (Sasana Dang Dang Nai Lok)* in the interest of "religious understanding."

# MEDIUMS AND RITUAL MEMORY

THE communist regime's relentless criticism of "superstition" in its early years reflected not only its claim to be the bearer of "scientific socialism" (indeed most modernizing states claim to represent scientific reasoning against "backward" or "ancient" superstitions), but also the demands of their project to create a "socialist man." In conformity with the latter project the state could attempt to purge Buddhism of its "superstitious" accretions, and through the sangha, both control and link Buddhism and monks to the state's various policies. This was not possible with spirit mediums and shamans who operated independently of established institutions.

Female *nang tiam*, and male *moh cham*, through their possession by spirits—sometimes from the historical past—represented uncontrollable forces within a political structure aiming at total social control. Mediums, of course, act as conduits for the social and cultural concerns of the people around them and therefore, through the words of the spirits, can express dissatisfaction and discontent. There were obviously fears that the spirits of dead kings or recently dead RLG politicians could come to life in these ceremonies to, for example, predict the coming demise of the regime.

This fear of mediums is found elsewhere. Of course, the pattern for communist regimes was first set in the Soviet Union where militant campaigns were carried out against shamans (Balzer 1990), and followed with equal ferocity in China after 1949 (Anagnost 1987). But it can also be found in authoritarian developmental regimes which are staking their control over the whole country. Thus in the early 1960s the Ne Win socialist government moved against *nat* worship in Burma (Smith 1965:296). Gehan Wijeyewardene (1986:90) reports from Chiang Mai that police in the past, presumably during the military dictatorships of the 1950s and 1960s, attempted to suppress spirit mediumship. No doubt aware of these past attempts and of their marginal status, modern urban mediums in Chiang Mai are often possessed by heroic nationalist warrior spirits.[1] "The images of *caw* [princes] as loyal protectors of the polity are well-tuned to current State-promoted preoccupations with protection of the Nation. Their heroic biographies indicate unselfish self-sacrifice in the name of communal survival and identify the *caw* and their mediums with the interests of the State, at a time when the phantom of communist aggression structures political perception and gives renewed impetus to traditional practices" (Irvine1984:319). These mediums in Thailand often make ostentatious displays of their allegiance to Buddhism by, for example, refusing to hold sessions on Buddhist holy days or by donating "money trees" to the monks. State hostility to "superstitious" mediums in post-1975 Laos had the effect of weakening or even severing these ties with Buddhism and making mediums the reluctant scribes of the culture's "hidden transcripts."

Campaigns against "superstition" in the temples meant that monks were less available to provide fortune telling, interpret dreams, and generally help ordinary people interpret the vicissitudes of their lives. Despite proclamations of a "new dawn"[2] after the revolution, problems of life and death and love did not disappear. Ironically, therefore, with the path to the temples closed off, or at least felt to be closed

1. This is also the case in Laos where I know of mediums for Chao Anou, his son Ratsavong and another for Prince Phetsarath, all of whom are national heroes.

2. "New Dawn" (*Aloun Mai*) is the name of the LPRP theoretical journal.

off, one consequence of the new government's policies was to direct people to the more private, less easily monitored, world of the spirit mediums. Austerity after the revolution also had this effect, as medicines became more scarce and expensive throughout the country. Monks were encouraged to practice traditional forms of medicine, but many people also turned to spirit mediums to help with illness.[3]

The cultural milieu in which the communists were operating, however, could not abide such sharp and uncompromising distinctions between "science" and "superstition." Many cadres, especially at lower levels, had not imbibed the rationalist spirit of Marx and they and their families faced the same vicissitudes of life as most Lao. Thus localized compromises were reached with both mediums and their spirits all over Laos, and some cadres even took the revolution to the world of spirits. During 1977 in Luang Prabang, for example, one such cadre claimed that all spirits attached to temples in the old royal capital were *sakdina* (feudal) and therefore he conducted a ceremony at the shrine of the spirit in his temple to call all of these spirits to court, whereupon he told them that the king had been deposed and sent to seminar and that the spirits too had to change. They could, he said, choose to become monks attached to the temples, they could choose to follow the king to Vieng Xai, or they could choose to leave the country. He then sent the spirits away telling them to think it over and to decide. That night "all the villagers" dreamt that they could hear pandemonium among the spirits. Subsequently, full *boun kong bouat* ceremonies were held to induct some of these spirits into the sangha. A ceremony was also held for sending others to Vieng Xai to be with the king, and "you could hear the sounds of elephants" as they began their journey. No ritual was required for the other spirits who became "refugees" and

3. I recall a conversation with a French-trained vice minister of health in the early 1980s who at that time was implacably hostile to the idea of somehow drawing traditional healers into the orbit of the health system, and thereby being able to dispense with any harmful practices, while keeping the genuinely therapeutic ones. Their practices were uniformly condemned as "superstition."

fled away stealthily. Telling the story in 1996, this former cadre remarked that the fame he acquired from this operation meant that some people still approach him to help conduct purification ceremonies, but he says he is no longer young and bold and no longer has the power to do this. Of course, what he narrated was the story of the revolution transposed onto the plane of ritual, just as his contemporary loss of the power to expel spirits suggests the decline in revolutionary militance and power *vis-à-vis* the realm of the spirits.

In the mid-1980s increasing tolerance was accorded to spirit mediums, and *nang tiam* covens started to be held in Vientiane. Yet, still in 1987, when I attempted to attend one of these gatherings, after being there for about an hour and a half I was chased off by a policeman from the Ministry of Interior, who made no move to stop proceedings, only wishing to remove me from them. He claimed I would make "propaganda against the Lao government on the BBC" by, presumably, exposing "superstitious" practices in socialist Laos.

From the early 1990s onwards, however, I have attended similar functions without any problems. *Nang tiam* ceremonies have flourished in Vientiane and other urban centers in ways similar to Thailand. In Savannakhet in 1994, for example, the *chao muang* threw his weight behind a money raising campaign to build a new *ho* (hall/altar) for the *lak muang* beside the Mekong River, and it is at this altar, twice a year, that local spirit mediums gather (in this case *moh tiam*, the term used there rather than *moh cham*) to carry out their rituals, inviting spirits from various *ho* in Savannakhet to gather at this central altar. One of these spirits is Chao Anou's son, Ratsavong, along with the spirits of various previous *chao muang*, including the great grandfather of the notorious right-wing RLG general, Phoumi Nosovan. Thus we now see active government participation in not only Buddhist ceremonies but also its sponsorship of local spirits cults.

There remains, however, a certain schizophrenia in state attitudes. While various forms of "superstition" now flourish in civil society, discussion of it is systematically excluded from the state-controlled mass media. This is especially true, for example, of ethnic minority practices of spirit worship. Discussion of similar practices encompassed by Buddhism sometimes sneak through because an ethnocentric Lao cultural state apparatus does not recognize its own practices as "superstitious."

The destabilizing of Lao culture and society by attempts at revolutionary transformation in the recent past, and the rapid commercial changes which have been occurring in the past decade, especially in the cities, has seen people flock to all varieties of religious consultants in an attempt to find some orientation and meaning in all of these changes. This search has been as intense among the well-educated and the small new middle class seeking success, as it has among the poor. This is especially evident in what I call "lottery mania" and the attempt to get rich quickly. For a time it seemed that everytime I sat down with Lao in Vientiane the conversation would drift towards lottery numbers and how to divine them: through dream interpretation, consultations with monks or nuns who would be asked for numbers, or other spirit mediums. With the collapse of socialist ideology no other explanations are offered for the confusions thrown up by economic, social and cultural change, and religious belief in all its variety has rapidly filled the gap.

No doubt it is against this background that we can also view the participation of some villages on the outskirts of Vientiane in the "widow ghost" scare that spread throughout Isaan (northeast Thailand) in April and May of 1990.[4] This scare occurred in response to the sudden deaths in their sleep of Thai migrant workers in Singapore, and elsewhere. These deaths were interpreted to be the result of a sexually voracious widow ghost in search of husbands. The villagers erected large, carved wooden penises outside their homes, and paraded them through the villages, in the cases I know of accompanied by *nang tiam* and monks. Mary Beth Mills

4. I only have information for Vientiane, but it is quite likely that other villages along the Mekong, especially in the southern half of Laos, also participated.

(1995), in analyzing this scare in Isaan argues that the villagers responded in this way because this ritual was a medium for expressing anxieties about the destabilization of gender relations between men and women as the latter roamed further from home in search of work (e.g. in Bangkok's infamous bars), and of the impact of "international capitalism" on village life as men travel overseas in search of work. No one in the village she studied had died, however, and the people there had simply responded to reports on Thai radio. This was also true for the Lao. But the causes of the latter's anxieties were somewhat different. Relatives and friends had been scattered around the world as a result of revolution. But like migrant workers these people sent back money, and like them they brought new ideas and new ways of acting back into the villages when they began returning to visit Laos in large numbers in the late 1980s. To some extent the women returnees represented the new worldly-wise woman, and they had been preceeded by letters, videos and stories about the changing and sometimes culturally disturbed lives of young Lao overseas. Furthermore the new capitalist economic reforms were just beginning to bite in Laos and cause economic differentiation, at least in areas adjacent to cities, thus straining previous bonds of solidarity. Thus some viewed the opening to the world with trepidation and they asked, would it bring with it the violence and sexual mayhem that they had seen on Thai television? In response, therefore, they carved their large wooden penises and, led by their traditional officiants, *nang tiam* and monks, attempted to ritually control these changes.

Writing about *nang tiam*, Mayoury Ngaosyvathn (1995:153) argues that "by controlling rites and practices linked to the past, women provide the Lao with a sense of calculated assurance about the continuity of interpersonal and communal relations in the future." She also argues that when possessed by their spirits these woman embody a sense of control over one's fate compared with the more fatalistic stance of Buddhism, and of course, it is this activism, this unpredictability, that earned them the hostility of the state in

the early days of the LPDR. Mediums also represent historical
continuity because of the fact that they are possessed by
princes and lords from past kingdoms whose power is drawn
on to overcome trials and tribulations of the present. In other
words they remain potent forces, and in the future it will be
interesting to see what figures from the past emerge to find
their mediums. One thing we can be reasonably sure of
however, is that Kaysone is unlikely to be one of them. But as
with shamans and spirit mediums elsewhere, *nang tiam* and
*moh cham* also attempt to articulate the present with the past.
To give a simple example: one day when I was traveling to a
coven with a *nang tiam* she insisted that I stop and buy some
Benson and Hedges cigarettes. She explained that her lord-
spirit from the south of the country would, when he
possessed her, only smoke these! Executives of Benson and
Hedges would surely be delighted by the depth of their
market penetration!

One of the most pervasive of Lao "animistic" rituals is the
*sou khouan*, or *baci* ([klua), which according to Thao Nhouy
Abhay (1959:129) is a "pompous kingly term" reserved for
more formal occasions.[5] Today, however, throughout Laos
*baci* is the term most commonly used. *Sou khouan* can be
roughly translated as the calling or entreating of the spirits of
a person or persons, and is performed as a transitional rite,
such as for births, marriages, entering the monkhood, going
away, returning, New Year and so on. It has been referred to
by many authors, somewhat hyperbolically, as the quin-
tessentially Lao ritual (Abhay 1959; Zago 1972; Ngaosyvathn
1990, among others), although it is also found in adjacent
groups of Tai, and among non-Tai groups, thereby providing
a point of ritual linkage across ethnic groups in Laos. It is,
therefore, not surprising that this has been elevated into a

5.   "Animism" is the belief that elements of the material world possess
souls or spirits and that the souls of the dead persist as ghosts. Spirit beings
can assume many different forms: they can be found in trees or streams or
amulets, or they can be guardians of a household or a village, or embodied
in hunted animals. In practice, the *sou khouan* and Buddhism interpenetrate
in many spheres, and ordinary Lao experience no sense of contradiction as
they move from one sphere to another.

"national" custom. The pervasiveness and frequency of the ritual certainly distinguishes it from the *tham khwan* ritual of central Thailand (Heinz 1982). At one pole the *sou khouan* rituals are virtually indistinguishable from Buddhism, starting as they do with the recitation of Buddhist prayers, while at the other pole no references to Buddhism are made at all. Among the ethnic Lao the *moh phone* (the officiant) himself is invariably an ex-Buddhist monk of some standing; when I have been present on such occasions in the Black Tai villages or Austroasiatic Sing Moon villages, the officiant was the local *moh cham*.

The fundamental mediating role of this ritual between several realms of belief and across ethnic boundaries is striking. Around New Year, for example, one can attend in the space of a few days a *baci* held at a company or a research institute where it will, in part, mediate the relationship between Lao and foreigners, then attend a *baci* held in a household. This ceremony begins with several Buddhist monks first chanting prayers to expel evil spirits from the house, whereupon the ritual is taken over by a *moh phone* who conducts the *sou khouan*. Monks sit seemingly aloof from this, but during the fastening of the souls to the body by tying strings of cotton around the participants' wrists (*mat kaen*) young children in particular will be presented to the monks who will participate in this soul-fastening part of the ceremony. Then one of the monks will bless the participants by sprinkling water over them and throughout the house. On the first day of the New Year one may attend (as I have) a *baci* held by a *nang tiam* and *moh tiam* together who, not unlike the monks, sat apart facing the spirit shrine, smoking and delivering advice to people who prostrated themselves at their side. The *baci* itself is conducted by a *moh phone* and the *nang tiam* and *moh tiam* turn away from the shrine and join in with the rest of the people around the *pha khouan*. They also participate in the soul-fastening ceremony, and as with the monks, young children in particular are presented to them for the spirit-tying. It is the *moh tiam* who, like the monks, carries out the ritual blessing with water. Indeed, throughout the latter ceremony one is acutely aware of the similarities of bodily gestures with those associated with Buddhist ritual, and through these gestures congruities with larger cultural patterns are enacted (see the following chapter).

The importance of this ritual for Lao social life meant that the state could only have suppressed it against a great deal of resistance, but it has been suggested by some authors that attempts were made to both control these rituals and suppress their appeal. In the early years of the revolution, permission to hold the ritual had to be sought from the head of the locality or village, and waste of time and expenditure on them was frowned upon (Sicard 1981:43-4). Among LPRP members and officialdom, at least in some areas, the ritual was strongly discouraged. So, for example, the Sicard's report on their attendance at the marriage of two communist officials in 1977. Lao marriage is traditionally a *sou khouan* ritual; by contrast:

> We entered into a bare room; on a kind of altar covered in a white sheet was the flag of the new popular democratic republic; no *phakuan* for the baci, or flowers; and above were the portraits of the President of the Republic and of the Prime Minister. The chief of the locality lectured those present on the requirements of a good citizen under the new regime, and encouraged the young couple to put all their effort into helping the people. We all applauded, shook their hands, as in the West, and left. Everything had been said, without embellishments, and with no wasted gestures. (Sicard 1981:48)

The marriage rituals that I attended in the early 1980s in villages and in the suburbs of Vientiane were in fact traditional *sou khouan* rituals, presided over by former monks. The main noticeable political influences on these ceremonies was some toning down in the blessings which formerly called for the couple to get rich or powerful, and at the end the officiant called on the couple to be good socialist citizens and to work hard for the development of the country. By this time most communist officials had started to participate in these rituals.

We know relatively little about the use of this ritual among the communist elite in the immediate aftermath of the revolution. It is perhaps significant that we get our first glimpse into their secret world in 1980, after the late 1979 relaxation of hardline policies. *KPL* reported that for the Lao New Year in 1980 the administrative committee of Vientiane province held a *baci,* and that those attending were Kaysone Phomvihane, Souphanouvong, Nouhak Phoumsavan, and other key figures in the regime, including the government adviser, Souvanna Phouma. This snippet of publicity sent a signal to people at large that the *baci/sou khouan* was a legitimate practice and it has subsequently flourished.

It has been interesting to observe the role of the *baci* in the LPDR. It has played a fundamental role in mediating relationships between Lao and foreigners of all persuasions, and ironically, in this capacity, it has been at its most animistic (i.e. "superstitious") pole of meaning. The motives of the rite, as Zago observes, are quite complex: "This rite is not only held as an honor to visitors, but also as a way of accepting them into the community; they are accepted as members. It is also a protection of the community against the strangers, who are unknown and therefore dangerous, just as it is equally a protection for the person receiving the rite" (1972:154). In a sense this has been its "secular" role, as observed by Zago (1972:131), and this secular role has continued to expand since 1980.[6] The main context in which foreigners encounter this ceremony is in "threshold" ceremonies, to use Tambiah's (1970:225) term, that is for the beginning of an enterprise, or marking the arrival or departure of someone or some group. Thus aid workers, consultants, researchers (such as anthropologists), upon leaving a house-

---

6. "Secular" in this context means independence from Buddhism. The *baci* would usually be perceived by foreigners, and Westerners in particular, as being distinct from their cultural idea of "religion," and if anything part of their cultural idea of "superstition."

hold or a community, or beginning a project, will be invited to participate in a *baci*. The *baci* in Laos therefore plays an overtly political role as a vehicle for underlining a certain achieved "solidarity" in a particular enterprise. Today it has also regained an important place in state ceremonies in Laos. For example, during the visit of King Sihanouk of Cambodia to Laos in December 1995 *Pasason* (11/12/95) carried pictures of Sihanouk, his wife and President Nouhak all sitting in their gilded chairs, holding their strings of cotton connecting them to the *pha khouan*.[7] During the 1980s in particular the *baci* for many Lao was also a way of stating something about their "Lao-ness" to foreigners, as distinct from the regime's political stance. It drew foreigners close in a non-political way, and in a way that Buddhism could not, and it had the desired affect of causing many foreigners to swoon about Lao culture, and drew their attention away from the regime's policies. In the 1990s it continues this role. But today *baci* have also become commercialized and in the tourist industry they are now included in package tours.

Commercialization is not restricted to tourist *bacis*, and one can see in Vientiane that money offerings (sometimes substantial) at *bacis* have become crucial, whereas in other centers, such as in Luang Prabang or Champassak, for example, this is not so. There are, of course, regional variations in the required offerings at *bacis*. But in Vientiane one can also see in the ritual a growing individualism. That is, if a *baci* is thrown by or for someone then the focus is on them, and the *mat kaen* part of the ceremony is directed towards them, whereas outside Vientiane it remains much more a ritual of communal solidarity and attempts are made to spread its blessings evenly among the participants.

An interesting feature of both spirit medium rituals and the *baci/sou khouan* is their imitation of "royal style." According to van Esterik (1980:102-3) it is "*royal style* which brings local ritual into a specifiable relation with royal or court ritual.

7. It is perhaps worth noting that in the series of articles in *Pasason* on "President Kaysone Phomvihane, the Family Man" referred to earlier, the issue of 12/12/95 ran a photograph of Kaysone at a *baci*.

Royal style in village ritual provides a symbolic pattern for visualizing and manipulating the relation between royalty and commoner." Here she is referring to Thailand and its intact monarchy, whereas in Laos today the structure of the rituals can only allude to this relationship while drawing participants into a mythical time associated with an ideal Buddhist community. Royal style is most apparent in *nang tiam* ceremonies where the women dress as princes or lords, because while they are possessed they *are* princes and lords, and are treated as such in this idealized ritual time frame. In marriage ceremonies the bride and groom dress as a princess and a prince. This is much more apparent in recent times, especially for grooms, who are forsaking the austere style encouraged after 1975 and returning to formal, courtly style. Abhay (1959:140) records elements of the traditional banter on the arrival of the groom's party at the bride's house. Representatives of the latter ask: "Where does the master come from? What mountains did he come across, and what is his wish?" To which his side replies: "We are coming from a Palace built of stones, where innumerable quantities of gold and silver are piling up. Every new day brings us treasures of gold, and each new night, silver." Of course, it is precisely such rhetoric that the new regime objected to after 1975, but the very structure of the ritual is making its return in recent times irresistible. Young men about to be ordained are treated as young princes who are about to enact the passage of renunciation of Prince Gautama. And in the ritual sequences of all of these occasions there is a *baci*, the centerpiece of which, the *pha khouan*, images Mount Meru and invokes a broader Buddhist cosmology. For the duration of the ritual the *pha khouan* becomes the center of the world. Before 1975 a *baci* would begin: "This is a very propitious day, a very appropriate one, the day when the victorious King re-enters his Palace!" (Abhay 1959:130). Such explicit royal references were dropped after 1975, but the overall royal style could not be erased. In fact, the very structure of ritual language was shot through with royal style and has left an indelible imprint on this most widespread of Lao rituals.

# BODIES AND LANGUAGE

I N thinking about the apparent ease with which "the old
regime could come back" it is worth considering Paul
Connerton's argument concerning "inertia in social
structures" (1989:102). He argues:

> Both commemorative ceremonies and bodily practices
> therefore contain a measure of insurance against the
> process of cumulative questioning entailed in all
> discursive practices. This is the source of their im-
> portance and persistence as mnemonic systems. Every
> group, then, will entrust to bodily automatisms the values
> and categories which they are most anxious to conserve.
> They will know how well the past can be kept in mind by
> habitual memory sedimented in the body (ibid).

Much of what is "sedimented in the body" among the Lao
comes from religious practice. Zago writes of young boys
"who may go to the pagoda school and there learn to read and
recite sacred texts. Even in home life, and in conversations,
ritual practices furnish multiple occasions in which they come
to understand, feel and model themselves within a Buddhist
vision of existence. Later, a short period passed in the
monastery deepens this experience" (1972:44). The respect and
deference paid to monks and buddhas (and kings) through the
*wai*, the clasping of the palms of one's hands together in a

prayerful motion, is the model of respectful behavior and deference. This action is repeated in front of elders and other superiors, and as a general greeting (also called *nop*), with added subtleties of height of the hands, length of time held, degree of bowing of the head, etc. For some years after the revolution this gesture was discouraged in political/state public spaces, except in the countryside, to be replaced by the more egalitarian handshake, or hugging and kissing if receiving "comrades"—something acquired from Soviet practice. These latter practices were problematic, in that they not only blurred status, but they also entailed physical contact with strangers, which was especially disturbing in cross-sex encounters, and caused considerable psycho-physical unease—often coped with by a typically Lao burst of shy laughter. These practices were happily abandoned with the disintegration of socialism, but well before that the *nop*, with women in the lead, began to reappear in public life.[1] Today this gesture is widespread, although not as common (nor as compulsory) as in Thailand where its practice is buttressed within the state by the fact that public servants are servants of the king.[2] For a long time this form of salutation of teachers in

1. One, perhaps, should also make reference to how these hierarchical modes of thought and practice are also "sedimented" in the organization of social space. Thus Bernard Formoso's study of social space in northeast Thailand (1990) demonstrates how this encodes a conceptual pattern of *hua* (head)/*diin* (feet), the former representing higher, the latter, lower.

2. One aspect of what Foucault would have called "technologies of the body" are the gymnastic displays introduced into Lao, Khmer and Vietnamese societies from the Soviet Union. At state theatrical functions, or now at the That Luang festival, one will see young girls in tights (normally an almost obscene form of dress in Laos) going through motions learnt from an instructor from some European communist country. I have always found this somewhat out of place. I also recall being shocked and bewildered when a display of traditional dancing in Cambodia in 1992 was followed by a young girl in tights giving a completely incongruous gymnastic demonstration. The Lao and Khmer around me, however, do not seem to register the same sense of incongruity. (Perhaps for them, being subject to apparently uncontrollable forces of cultural change, the whole world is a little surreal!) Or perhaps it is in fact culturally congruent with the forms of bodily control demanded of women in traditional dancing. But

Lao schools was also suppressed, but it has returned in the 1990s.

In 1976 the new regime had moved quickly to enforce certain dress codes, condemning boys with long hair, girls in high-heeled shoes, and couples walking with arms around each others' waists. "We regard this as an indirect, or direct challenge to the Vientiane city administration's order prohibiting fancy clothes, long hair, etc. You may argue that the whole civilized world dresses like this, but we ask you not to base your arguments on foreign ideas. You should be ashamed to appear like this before the Lao people" (*SWB* 3/ 3/76). This enforcing of dress codes in the early days of revolutions can be found from the French revolution onwards. That dress is connected to a cluster of meanings is recognized consciously or unconsciously by revolutionaries. Certain forms of dress and fashion were explicitly associated with the "capitalistic West" or the "feudal" past and for that reason suppressed. The new code stipulated that women were to wear their hair long, not use makeup (or not too much of it), and were instructed to wear the full-length Lao skirt, the *sinh*. However, *sinhs* with colorful and elaborate designs, and expensive silk *sinhs,* were frowned upon, and so these were stored away in draws and wardrobes to await sunnier days. Jeans were out, as were even the more loose-fitting dresses one could observe in Thailand, and of course short skirts. Dress for men was simple, and at least among

---

I also think that, in part, this type of body control is an aspect of modernization in the same way that sport is.

In this regard I also recall being amazed in the early 1990s on seeing body-building posters in Hanoi displaying not only muscly men, but muscly women as well. Similar posters can be seen in China (though, significantly, I have never seen them in Laos, Thailand or Cambodia). This is strange at first sight because masculinity and femininity are so strongly marked in these cultures. It has been suggested by some writers on culture change in China that the attractions of muscle building there are related to the emergence of a sense of self—of a private self and a private body. For a very interesting book on how bodies are molded by a political regime, see Brownell's (1995) discussion of China, especially "The Bikini Debate" (270ff).

party cadres it was along the lines one has seen in other Asian communist countries (though not to the extremes one saw in China) of "worker-peasant uniform." These egalitarian forms of dress were to complement the other egalitarian reforms introduced by the new regime, and to differentiate themselves from the elaborate regalia of functionaries in the RLG, and the economic differentiation displayed in dress by the old elite.

Slowly, however, this reform too broke down. In the early 1980s one might observe a bold young girl riding along on her bicycle in jeans! Others would quickly join in. But soon it would be stopped, only to reemerge again some months later. This guerrilla war of fashion went on until the reforms began in earnest in the mid-1980s, and by the mid-1990s dress among the young imitated youth in Thailand. The only enforced dress codes now are for female public servants who continue to wear the *sinh*, though outside of work they can wear what they like.[3] The wearing of expensive jewelry has also made a dramatic comeback. The Lao leadership has, along with post-socialist leaders elsewhere in Asia, abandoned their more egalitarian uniforms for smart business suits and ties—a dress statement that they are committed to capitalist reforms! Yet, the elaborate forms of dress associated with the old regime, with their braids and sashes, like one can see in Thailand, cannot be resuscitated, the one exception being the traditional courtly style dress for men, the *sampot* with an accompanying white, tightly-fitted jacket.[4] It has been the customary wedding dress for Lao grooms, which is one source of its wide, popular appeal, and this form of dress can now be seen publicly at New Year during the procession in Luang Prabang, and during the That Luang festival. The sartorial status differentials associated

3. Now that Luang Prabang is a World Heritage site (see "Customizing Tradition"), a rule that women leaving Luang Prabang by plane must wear *sinh* is occasionally enforced.

4. It would seem that this style of dress was adopted by the Lao aristocracy in the nineteenth century under the influence of the Thai, and subsequently adopted by other social classes in Lao society as "custom."

with the monarchy have gone, and have been replaced by the status differentials of consumerism associated with modern capitalism (to which can be added, besides dress, cars, houses, etc.). Hierarchy in dress has returned, but it is not a pure return to the past, because, once again something has been left behind—a system of dress rules which encoded a particular hierarchy, and which pointed to religion and history through its reference to the monarch. Modern forms of dress point only to money and power, and because it is simply fashion it contains no history or memory. In a country like Laos new forms of dress point to a future imagined modernity, not to the past. To some extent this is qualified by the boom in traditional weaving brought on by tourism, and its incorporation into Lao fashion (and indeed into New York fashion due the entrepreneurial skills of some). But it is, for all its "traditionalness," a modern marker of Lao ethnicity as encouraged and articulated within the modern Lao state and its tourism agencies.

The ease with which Lao people reverted to an older deferential language in everyday life, and then increasingly in official speech, but still less so in print, is also remarkable. As I observed in *Lao Peasants Under Socialism,* many peasants ignored the language reforms anyway, and because they constitute the linguistic majority, as well as being the ones most likely to need deferential political language, they therefore constituted an enormous source of linguistic inertia. Alongside the everyday reality of deferential linguistic habits within the family and village, the realities of political hierarchy, and the renewed reality of socio-economic inequality following the implementation of the new economic policies, drew the older forms of language out of hiding and they have today swept most of the revolutionary terminology *past* aside. For example, the more neutral appellation of *pathan,* president or vice president, was introduced at all levels of organization, such as for the head of the Buddhist association who became *pathan song,* rather than *phra sangkarat,* and *chao khoueng* became *pathan khoueng,* and this reform went on right down to the village level. But today one rarely hears the term

87

*pathan*, except when people refer to the president of the country. Similarly, at the opening of all meetings in the past one would refer to the people gathered as *banda sahay* (all comrades), whereas today it is the more respectful *banda tan* (all sirs). In the early days one would hear the more populist village style *hao ni*, (we/I), but now it is the older form *khapachao* (I, literally, "slave of the Buddha"), which first began to appear in speeches by Kaysone in the early 1980s. The polite response *doy*, sometimes coupled with *kanoy* (lit. "small slave"), has swept back into linguistic fashion since 1996, especially in Vientiane. Nevertheless, in the absence of the monarchy, royal language has not made a full comeback in Laos although, as we have seen, it is encoded in rituals. Yet, through various forms of mass media Lao are exposed to Thai *rachasap* (royal language) and the higher status forms that this entails. In the main cities of Laos today one can observe widespread imitation of Thai forms of speech. Many years ago, Charles Keyes (1967:60) observed that the ethnic Lao in the Thai northeast admired Thai elite culture because it held out the attractions of upward social mobility. Something similar has been occurring in Laos in the past decade, especially among youth.[5]

Yet while the sense of relief experienced by the throwing off of bureaucratically imposed regulation and a return to customary forms of bodily and linguistic practices was palpable in Laos, its opening to the wider world saw the beginnings of a challenge to them from a new direction: consumerism, ideas of individualism, pop music culture, and those other elements we now gloss as "global culture."

5. For a Lao view on this, see Houmphanh Rattanavong's essay (1995). Adding to the earlier footnote on the organization of social space, one can see the rapid transformation of architecture in Vientiane and elsewhere into an extension of Thai *nouveux riches* styles from just across the border, in which case it may be possible to talk of a middle-class Thai-ization of Lao social space.

# RECALLING ROYALTY

A fact rarely noticed about King Sisavang Vong (1885-1959) of Laos is that at the time of his death on 29 October 1959 he was the longest reigning monarch in Asia, having ascended to the throne of Luang Prabang in April 1904. To be sure he only became the king of the whole of Laos in August 1946 following a *modus vivendi* between the French and an increasingly assertive Lao nationalism. Nevertheless, compared to monarchs in surrounding countries this lifespan is, superficially at least, impressive. Given the often asserted central importance of the monarchy to Theravada Buddhist societies, the low profile of the Lao monarchy in writings about Southeast Asia is striking. The following, therefore, is a brief attempt to place the Lao monarchy in its modern context.

It has often been said that Laos and Cambodia and their respective monarchies only saw the modern world because of the protection given them by French colonialism. With an eye on the steady encroachments of both Vietnam and Siam on his territories the Cambodian King Norodom sought French protection in the mid-nineteenth century. Luang Prabang, still a vassal of Siam in the late nineteenth century, also sought French protection as a result of the depredations of marauding warlords from the borders of China. An 1893 treaty with Siam established French control over the land east of the Mekong. A protectorate was established over the kingdom of Luang Prabang (which included at that time the present provinces of

Luang Prabang, Oudomsay, much of Houaphan and later Sayaboury) where the king remained enthroned encompassed by a colonial system of indirect rule.[1] The annihilation of the aristocracy around Vientiane following Chao Anou's uprising against the Siamese in 1827-28, and the destruction of the Phuan kingdom in Xieng Khouang by Chinese warlords in the late nineteenth century, meant that the only other royal center in Laos was Champassak in the south, but this also had been enfeebled by Siamese conquest in 1828, and so here the French ruled directly, simply allowing the royal family to maintain its aristocratic status.

The king of Luang Prabang presided over his simple, traditional administrative structure, paralleled by a tiny number of French officials. He also continued to carry out the calendrical and ritual duties of a Buddhist monarch, as indeed did the prince of Bassac (Champassak). It may be asked, then, how does one legitimately claim to be a king or a prince of a ruling house under foreign colonial rule? The problem was particularly acute in the south where the prince of Champassak exercised no real power. Studies of ritual in the south by Archaimbault (1971) and a commentary on the latter by Keyes helps explain this. Rituals of purification of the realm previously carried out by mediums were taken over by the princes around 1900. "For the populace, the merit acquired by the princes by virtue of their position continued to generate power; however, the power could be employed not in the secular realm but in the realm of the spirits of the locality. For the populace, the prince had become a priest, a substitute for the mediums of old" (Keyes 1972:613). One could say that in Luang Prabang throughout the French era and culminating in the formation of a constitutional monarchy, we see the progressive attenuation of royal power in the secular realm and its increasingly important ritual role in relation to the metaphysical realm.

Direct questioning of French colonial power did not arise until the protective cloak of the French was swept aside by the

1. For a brief description of the initial French administrative structure in the north, see Raquez (1905:1786-1791).

Japanese during World War II. French administrative centralization had caused revolts in peripheral areas, as Geoffrey Gunn (1990) has documented, but these revolts were not specifically anti-colonial as Gunn and the current Lao government historiography would have it; rather, they were forms of resistance analogous to the revolts against modernizing state centralization in neighboring Thailand around the same time (Chatthip 1984; Evans 1990b). Meanwhile, the king did not have to concern himself with defense of the realm, and this left him time to expend on ritual duties and on his role as defender of the faith. Indeed, the French assisted him financially in his duties and in fact the royal palace standing in Luang Prabang today was built for the king by the French at the beginning of this century to replace the one destroyed in 1887 by the Black Flag Chinese warlords and White Tai during the sack of Luang Prabang.

Even though the Japanese occupation shattered the aura of French colonialism and gave rise to a Lao independence movement, the Lao Issara, in which three members of Luang Prabang royalty figured prominently, the king remained loyal to the French. The reason for this appears to have been the king's fears that Laos could not protect itself from Chinese and Vietnamese encroachments. Hence he was briefly deposed by the Lao Issara after they had stepped into the power vacuum left by the Japanese in late 1945.[2] As the fortunes of the Lao Issara government faded as a result of fiscal problems and lack of international recognition, and in the face of French and pro-French forces, they offered to restore the king (Deuve 1992). Soon, however, the French reestablished control and a little

2. Within current nationalist discourse promoted in Laos these strategic concerns of the king are not taken into account and he is simply pilloried for wanting to invite the French back. That the king had his own game plan with the French is rarely acknowledged; for example, his demand (combined with a threat of abdication if the demand was not met) for an extension of the Luang Prabang monarchy's authority after the loss of Sayaboury Province to the Thai in 1941. Initially he sought suzerainty over the whole of Laos, but he settled for control over Vientiane and the whole of the north of Laos.

later, in 1947, Sisavang Vong became the first constitutional monarch of the Royal Lao Government.

But the conduct of the Lao monarchy in the 1950s and 1960s contrasted with Thailand where military dictatorships promoted a cult of the king, and with the political activism of Cambodia's Norodom Sihanouk, who as king shrewdly led a " crusade for independence" and then stepped down as king in favor of his father in 1955 to engage in politics (Osborne 1994). Christine Gray (1991) has documented how the initial ritual competition between Field Marshal Phibunsongkhram and King Bhumibol Adulyadej gave way to cooperation under Phibun's successor Field Marshal Sarit Thanarat who "adopted the strategy of 'latching on' to or 'borrowing' the royal virtue. In 1959 he publicly observed that the king was upholding the ten virtues of the Dhammaraja, that he was far-sighted and had a personality worthy of worship. For the first time since 1932, a Thai king was conveyed up the Chao Phraya River in a splendid royal barge procession to offer *kathin* robes at royal temples" (Gray 1991:51). As distinct from the dramatic overthrow of the Thai absolute monarchy by the military in 1932, the Luang Prabang monarch under the French had already lost absolute authority and then become increasingly a symbolic figurehead, something which was formalized by the formation of a Lao national government in 1947. The king's ritual calendar had encompassed Vientiane after 1941 when the Luang Prabang sovereign's rule was extended south following the temporary loss of Sayaboury to the Thai. Yet much of his ritual activity remained focused on Luang Prabang, and even as Lao king his ritual duties were largely confined to the northern parts of the country.[3] All political

3. Royal ritual in Champassak in the south remained centered on a descendant of the southern principality, Prince Boun Oum. In an annex to the agreement drawn up between the French and the Lao in August 1946 which recognized the unity of Laos under the Luang Prabang monarchy, Prince Boun Oum renounced all claims to sovereignty in the former southern kingdom, but retained his royal title. The Luang Prabang monarchy appears to have respected the ritual autonomy of the south, although the king or the crown prince regularly attended the Vat Phu and boat racing festivals in the south.

parties proclaimed loyalty to the king, but the petty jealousies of a geographically and politically divided aristocracy, and the absence of political dictatorship, meant that there was no concerted state promotion of the monarch as there was in Thailand. Furthermore, during the 1950s the aged king was enfeebled by arthritis and other illnesses, and his son, Sisavang Vatthana, carried out most of his duties. The king's illness in turn, enfeebled the monarchy. By the time Sisavang Vatthana ascended the throne in November 1959 the nation was already deeply divided politically.

The weak nationwide education system contributed to disunity as well, for education systems are major instruments of modern nationalism. For example, the development of a modern, national education system in neighboring Thailand has played a vital role in cultivating the cult of the king there. Charles Keyes (1991:116) writes: "More important than simply respect for the King is the idealization or even sacralization of kingship. . . . King and Buddha are placed on equal planes for 'worship' . . . by the students and teachers. The educational program firmly establishes the monarchy as an important element in the villagers' world view. The recognition of the particular Thai king and the idealization of the Thai kingship are the main elements which underlie the villager's sense of citizenship." In Laos much was made of a survey done in the late 1950s which showed that "only" 60 percent of Lao villagers could name their king (Le Bar & Suddard 1960:231; Fall 1969:128),[4] yet among lowland Lao the king was much

4. One gets the impression that these sources did not consult the original survey, but simply repeated press reporting at the time. The survey asked: "'Can you tell me the names of the two most important leaders in Laos?' Among those responding at all, 'Don't knows' were given by more than half in Vientiane and in the capitals. Over three-fourths of the villages [villagers?] also answered 'Don't know.' The king of Laos, Sisavang Vong, the most frequently named, was mentioned by about a third of the respondents in Vientiane and in the capitals, and by a fifth of the villagers" (BSSR 1959:30). The prime minister at the time, Phoui Sananikone, was known by less than a third in the urban areas, but by only 6 percent in the villages. After him the crown prince, Sisavang Vathana, was better known than all other politicians, including Prince Souvanna Phouma (BSSR 1959:35). The interpretation of this survey is problematic for a number of

better known than any other political figure, especially in the villages. Lowland Lao knew of the palladium of the kingdom, the Prabang statue, and most could cite fragments of the legends of Lane Xang. Fall remarks, in the remote mountains among the "hilltribes" who make up a significant proportion of the population, one would not expect to find a strong awareness of the king. "The fact remains that the old King was," writes Fall (ibid), ". . . a 'King's King'—courteous, wise, kind, and to the last endowed with a glimmer of humor and worldliness in his eyes that earned him the esteem of Laotians and foreigners alike." In August 1959 Crown Prince Sisavang Vatthana became regent, and in the political turbulence of the time "many Laotians associated the decline in health of their sovereign with the gradual disintegration of the kingdom" (Fall 1969:128-9). Sisavang Vong died two months later, and one commentator who attended his grand funeral in April 1961 commented:

> The ashes of the old King were carried to their last resting place in a royal pagoda. The dignified little procession made its way through the narrow main street to the accompaniment of the thin sweet, Lao music, played on the traditional flutes, xylophones and drums. There was a gentle, sad finality about this last rite. It contrasted painfully with the military and political chaos in which the *ancien regime* of Laos seemed to be foundering. The King's funeral seemed to symbolize the probable demise of the old Buddhist monarchy itself. (Field 1965:130)

Arthur Dommen (1971:329) writes of King Sisavang Vatthana expressing deep pessimism about the future of Laos at this time as well, and is alleged to have said to Prince

---

reasons. First, commentators assumed that somehow ordinary Lao held a modern view of politics. Second, they tended to assume that people in modern industrial societies are well-informed politically. This is questionable. Opinion poll surveyers have often been shocked by the ignorance of the public about political affairs.

Sihanouk of Cambodia who was attending the funeral: "Alas, I am doomed to be the last King of Laos."

Sisavang Vong is not forgotten. His large figure, located in a park outside Vat Si Muang which houses Vientiane's *lak muang*, stares down at passersby, and on several occasions I have noticed women kneeling before his statue, burning incense and praying to the old monarch.[5] At the main temple in Luang Nam Tha in mid-1995 I photographed a banner made of old 100-kip notes (which escaped the ceremonial burnings of the old kip notes in mid-1976), with proud profiles of the old king, hanging down from the ceiling of the temple to make merit for its donor. During research in the early 1980s on the attempted collectivization of the Lao peasantry, I sometimes came across faded photos of King Sisavang Vatthana hanging in battered frames in village houses. By this time photos of the old king were frowned upon and were being pushed aside by the ubiquitous photos of the main members of the politburo, in particular Kaysone, Soupha-nouvong and Faydang Lobliayao. I recall going into one house in 1983 where, above the window, hung portraits of the farmer and his wife when they were young; Souvanna Phouma, the former RLG prime minister, then still adviser to the new regime; and a photo of the Lao crown prince, Vong Savang. I asked what he was doing with photos of Souvanna Phouma and the former king's son still up in a prominent place. He smiled wryly and replied: "I keep them there to tell my children how bad the old regime was!"

As has been remarked upon many times, the cities which housed monarchs in Southeast Asia represented sacred centers—centers of mystical and material power. The growing centralization of power focused on Bangkok over the late

5. This statue was donated by the Soviet Union in the early 1970s. A similar statue stands in the grounds of the old palace in Luang Prabang, described by two Swedish consultants as "a unique and quite impressive piece of 'socialist realism' [they seem to say this simply because it was made in the USSR] . . . one could be tempted to propose its removal, even if for no other good reason than for its sheer size and pompous monumentality" (Lind & Hagmuller 1991:51). The statue in fact is typical of its genre, and similar ones can be seen all over the world, including Sweden.

nineteenth and throughout the twentieth century, has further served to bolster the power of the Thai monarchy in all respects. By contrast, in Laos, the French established their administrative capital in Vientiane. There they built their offices, and also rebuilt traditional Lao monuments such as the That Luang and established conditions for the restoration and revival of Buddhist temples in the capital which had been left in ruins since 1828. Vientiane has remained the political capital of Laos to this day, but after 1947 the king did not move to Vientiane, although he was encouraged to by Lao Issara members (Deuve 1992:194 ). Luang Prabang simply became the royal capital of Laos. Thus royalty in Laos remained geographically aloof, or off-center, from the mundane world of real politics, and histories dealing with the period of the Royal Lao Government are punctuated by the decamping of the prime minister and his entourage to Luang Prabang to attend this or that festival and royal ritual, or of feuding politicians or ambassadors going to Luang Prabang for an audience with the king.

Commentators on the bitter factional struggles that took place in Vientiane during the days of the RLG remark on the attempts by the king to play a neutral role. For example, Stevenson writes, "since 1959, Savang Vatthana, has played a careful balancing role, always acting to preserve the royal position in the struggles between the various contending factions" (1973:13). Marek Thee confirms the impression that the king "did not wish to mix in the political game," and said "most of my Laotian contacts wanted the King to act independently, to play a balancing role" (Thee 1973:161). Recently released American archival material, writes Arthur Dommen, shows King Sisavang Vatthana "as a far more complex character than he has generally been portrayed" (1995:159), and strongly anti-communist. Nevertheless, he remained a conciliator and in fact delayed his coronation ceremony so that it could be a symbolic crowning point of national reconciliation.[6] Subsequently, LPRP propaganda has

---

6.   François Gallieni reports in *La Revue Française* (Octobre 1967:23) that the coronation was planned for the end of 1968.

tried to insinuate that he was not really king because this rite had not taken place, when in fact it was delayed as a peacemaking gesture towards them, and it was the LPRP which in 1975 dissolved the coalition government formed in 1974 and made the coronation impossible.

In contemporary (private) discussions among some Lao about their recent history, when the role of the king comes up he is sometimes compared unfavorably with the Thai monarch. For example, Maha Canla Tanbuali, the senior Thammayut monk who defected to Thailand in 1976, said that while "the Lao people did in fact love their King too, . . . they lacked the feeling of closeness to him, and the feeling of solidarity with him that the Thais have for their King" (1977:19).

> The Lao monarchy had existed for more than six hundred years. But the Lao King differed from the Thai King in his general attitude and behavior. The Lao King never made much contact with the people; he did not go out to see the people in times of distress. Mostly he stayed in his court. So the Lao King was not close to the hearts of the people in the way that the Thai King is. I am Lao, but I never once saw the King of Laos. On the other hand, in the ten years that I spent in Thailand I met the King of Thailand several times. I would also like to point out that the King of Thailand is endowed with three important qualities: he is concerned for the people, he is accessible, and he is brave. (1977:15)

But, when considering these remarks, one must be aware that Maha Canla was at one of the main royal temples in Bangkok, Wat Bowornives, and therefore was more likely to come in contact with the king. His *retrospective* remarks should also be compared to the observations of outsiders on the nature of Lao royalty. For example, Australian academic C.D. Rowley, then working for UNESCO, comments on traveling with the king's son and *chao khoueng* of Luang Prabang in the mid-1950s: "I was interested to see how easily M. Tay, a career official, took his place with the son of the King; and how the prince-governor consulted easily with his boatmen. One felt that in Laos the distance between the humble and the great is not really great" (Rowley 1960:169).

Some Lao will opine that the Lao kings, unfortunately, were not as clever as the Thai king when it came to politics. Had they been, it is claimed, Laos would not have become communist. And drawing on their observations of the Thai king as presented on Thai television today which shows him touring his kingdom and surveying various royally sponsored development projects, some people are likely to echo Maha Canla's sentiments and say the Lao king never did this and was not "seen." Of course, this is not true, and there is a great deal of evidence to show that the Lao king and his son the crown prince, also attempted to tour the kingdom, sponsoring religious celebrations and surveying development projects. But this was only recorded on newsreels which could be seen in cinemas, and not on the more powerful medium of television. In this way the much more visible Thai king of today is compared favorably to the less visible (pre-TV) Lao king of yesteryear.[7] But I recall a conversation with a taxi driver in Vientiane in 1995 who, wishing to offer me tourist commentary, informed me without prompting that " we Lao once had a king like in Thailand, you know. And we respected him like the people in Thailand." These unfulfilled desires for a righteous monarch continue as part of the Lao social memory.

King Sisavang Vatthana was forced to abdicate on 1 December 1975, a day before the declaration of the LPDR, and he and former RLG prime minister, Prince Souvanna Phouma, were appointed advisers to the new President Souphanou-vong. "The abdication," writes Dommen, "deprived the

---

7.  In Evans (1990a:113), however, I cite a rather idiosyncratic counter-memory of the king by a Lao cooperative head: "The television had shown the Thai king, who he remarked was a good leader, and his family out inspecting cooperatives [in Thailand]. To which he added the observation that the old Lao king had been a good gardener, implying that he too would have approved of cooperatives."

majority of Laos's inhabitants of their country's soul, both spiritual and temporal" (1985:113). The abdication came as a shock to many Lao because the Pathet Lao had promised to retain the monarchy. Thus, Phoumi Vongvichit, was compelled in late December to respond to "rumours spread by the enemy that we had dismissed the King. . . . Realising that the monarchy had blocked the progress of the country, the King abdicated and turned over power to the people. He abdicated intentionally. . . . The King is still in his palace, and is now Supreme Adviser to the President of the country. He is still enjoying his daily life as before, and his monthly salary will be sent to him as usual. The only difference is that he is no longer called King" (*SWB* 31/12/75).

After 1975 Lao royalty continued its off-center trajectory. Indeed in April 1976, the now ex-king Sisavang Vatthana was enjoined to vacate his palace in Luang Prabang. In a ceremony presided over by none other than Phoumi Vongvichit, the palace along with its relics, including the Prabang, were "donated" to the state as a museum and Sisavang Vatthana moved into Hong Xieng Thong, his private residence beside the royal Vat Xieng Thong. In March 1977, following *pattikan* activities in the north, with whom they were alleged to have had some association, the ex-king and his wife and two sons (Vong Savang, the crown prince, and Prince Sisavang) were arrested and sent to Houaphan where they apparently died of illness. Mystery still surrounds their arrest[8] and deaths, and the regime itself has never offered an official explanation, while the whereabouts of their remains is a closely guarded

8. The day after the arrest the governor of the province called a meeting of government functionaries to explain that the ex-king had been sent to Vieng Xai in Houaphan province. Three days later, Phoumi Vongvichit arrived to explain to these same officials that the ex-king would stay in Houaphan until he had been "reeducated." A *tuk tuk* driver in Vientiane who said he was in the Lao Revolutionary Youth movement in Luang Prabang at the time of the king's arrest claimed the following story was circulated by the party in Luang Prabang: On the day before the king was taken away a shaman suddenly appeared in the quarter near the palace. When police tried to capture him he would simply slip out of their hands. When they tried to stab him with a knife it would not cut him and

secret.[9] As late as December 1996 I have overheard guides in the palace museum telling tourists that the king is still away "at seminar." When challenged about the truth of this they say the king's whereabouts is a "state secret."

Prince Souvanna Phouma, on the other hand, continued to act as an adviser to the president until his death in January 1984, whereupon he was given a state funeral. Led by chanting Buddhist monks and his half brother, President Souphanouvong, his cremation took place at the That Luang pagoda, but his remains were taken to Luang Prabang where they were interred in a family stupa at Vat That which also contains the remains of the legendary Prince Phetsarath, his older brother.

Phetsarath was the son of the uncle and viceroy, *ouparat*,[10] to King Sisavang Vong, and grew up with the king. He studied in France and briefly at Oxford, returning to Laos where he earned a reputation as an effective administrator. He was elevated to the position of *ouparat* in 1941. He played an important role in the Lao Issara (Free Laos) government which seized power in Vientiane in October 1945 after the Japanese surrender. Against the will of the king, they proclaimed their independence from France, leading them to depose the king briefly which left Phetsarath as head of state. This government was soon dispatched by returning French forces, and its members fled to Thailand, forming a "government in exile."

---

when they tried to shoot him, bullets would not penetrate him. According to the story circulated, this man was a danger to the king and therefore the police persuaded the king to fly away with them in a helicopter. Perhaps some version of this story was in fact circulated in Luang Prabang. It expresses a certain paranoiac logic inasmuch as the new regime felt it was dealing with uncontrollable opposition forces, while the king was also under threat from forces beyond his control. The two ideas come together in the story.

9. During a visit to France in December 1989 Kaysone finally confirmed that the king had died of malaria in 1984, but no other details were provided. Only in the proofreading stage of this book did I read Christopher Kremmer's (1997) excellent account of his attempt to trace the final movements of the king.

10. The *ouparat*, often translated as the "second king," played a key administrative role in the traditional political structure.

Over the next few years, due to substantial changes in the relations between Laos and France which satisfied the aspirations of most of the Lao Issara members, the Lao Issara was dissolved in 1949 and its members returned to Vientiane, except for Phetsarath and Souphanouvong.[11] The latter went to work with the Viet Minh and participate in the formation of the Lao communist party, while Phetsarath remained in exile until 1957, when he returned and was reinstalled as *ouparat*. He died in late 1959.

Because of his role in the Lao Issara, of which the LPRP claims to be the heir, Phetsarath remains a legitimate royal figure under the LPDR. In recent years a cult not unlike that surrounding Chulalongkorn has begun to form around him and so one will often come across his photo in houses, shops or temples. For example, I asked the monks as Vat That Luang Dai in Vientiane why they had a picture of Phetsarath up on the wall in the *sala* instead of the old king. "Because he was on the revolutionary side. You can't use the old king." Significantly, permission was given by the government for the publication of Maha Sila Viravong's biography of Phetsarath (originally penned in 1958), and it appeared in print in August 1996. But Phetsarath is a popular figure not primarily because of his political role, although important legends have grown up around this, but because he is considered to have magical powers; he is *saksit*.[12] This reputation partly arose from his deep interest in astrology, about which he published a book in Thai in the 1950s. Anthropologist Joel Halpern recounts how during an expedition with Phetsarath in Luang Prabang in 1958, villagers would approach Phetsarath to carry out purification rites. He also tells stories he heard about the prince:

11. A proper analytic history of the Lao Issara, and Phetsarath's political career remains to be written. No doubt it will reveal a much more complex, and perhaps less heroic, view of the prince. Phetsarath's own account of his role is contained in an "autobiography" that he published anonymously as "3349" in Thailand in the mid-1950s, and it was later translated into English. (See Phetsarath 1978.)

12. *Saksit* is usually translated as "holy," "sacred," or "powerful" in dictionaries, and it most often combines all of these meanings.

One asserted that Prince Phetsarath had the power to change himself into a fish and could swim under water for long distances. It was said that bullets could not harm him. He was also reputed to have the ability to change his form, so that at a conference with the French at the time of the Free Lao Movement, he became angry with them, changed himself into a fly, and flew out the window. . . . People from many parts of the Kingdom often write to him requesting his picture, and some of them place it in their rice fields to keep away malevolent spirits. (Prince Boun Oum is felt by some to have similar powers.) (Halpern 1964:124)

On the other hand, Maha Sila's account (1996) of Phetsarath's life, interestingly, emphasizes how the prince was able to overcome local superstitions and fears of, for example, dangerous spirits inhabiting forests or lakes, through rational rather than ritual action.

But ideas about the prince's magical powers are still widespread. His pictures are used for protection against malevolent *phi* (spirits), a protective amulet of him is now on sale, and in the current lottery mania in Vientiane it is said that if you have a genuine picture of Phetsarath you can divine the lottery numbers. A tract I acquired from a holy man outside Vientiane contained a picture of Phetsarath, alongside those of a buddha and other sacred images, with protective holy words written in *tham* script surrounding his head like a halo. This same monk suggested that Sisavang Vong also had special powers, but not Sisavang Vatthana.[13] When I asked a

13. This, of course, conforms to the traditional cosmology of kings. Kings who reign successfully to the end of their lives, by definition are *phu mi boun*, men of exceptional merit. King Sisavang Vatthana was overthrown, and therefore by definition did not have sufficient merit. Other tales underline this, such as one which claims King Sisavang Vong forbade his son from attending his funeral; and a related story which claims that during the dressing of King Sisavang Vong for his funeral, a role reserved for the son, Sisavang Vatthana could not lift his father in order to carry out the task, thus showing he was not a true child of the king. Only Sihanouk (the latter in fact flew to Luang Prabang for the funeral) could lift him, which shows that he was in fact a true child of the king. The same storyteller

shopkeeper in Luang Prabang who kept a picture of Phetsarath on the wall whether he was more respected than the old
king he replied: "Yes. Phetsarath was *saksit*. He could go for
days without sleeping, walk in the rain without getting wet,
and could fly up and sleep in the crown at the top of the
forest." And there are other elaborations and variations. It is
this religious or "priestly" role which keeps Phetsarath alive in
the memory of Lao today. He was not a communist like his
younger brother Souphanouvong; neither did he line up with
anyone else under the RLG. He simply maintained his stature
as a leader of the Lao Issara. This makes memory of him
politically acceptable.

The other commanding royal figure of post-independence
Laos was Prince Boun Oum na Champassak who, as the quote
from Halpern indicates, was also thought to be *saksit*, and was
"high priest" of the major festivals held in the south, such as at
Vat Phu. But his close alignment with the right wing makes
him politically unacceptable, and therefore no cults that I
know of have sprung up around him. Indeed, Pathet Lao ire
seems to have led to the almost complete elimination of the
remnants of the southern aristocracy associated with the
principality of Champassak.

This is most apparent in the realm of ritual. The New Year
ceremony at Bassac (Basak) described so carefully by
Archaimbault (1971) has been completely suppressed. Prior
to 1975, the New Year ceremony was centered on the figure of
Boun Oum who would in the first days of the New Year
celebrations go in procession to the cardinal points marked
by the *vat*s in Champassak to expel *(bok)* evil influences from

---

continued by saying that Sisavang Vatthana's father was in fact an
Englishman, which you could tell from the size of his nose. A final further
"fact" from this storyteller was that Sisavang Vatthana had never placed a
roof over the statue of his father outside Vat Simuang, and this also showed
that he was not a true child of the old king. This rather bizarre tale of
legitimacy and racial purity is spun out of a cultural fabric which attempts
to rationalize the rise and fall of kings. Many other stories are told which
"explain" his fall and de-legitimize him, such as that he could not speak
Lao properly, for example, and could only speak French. This false claim is
happily bolstered by Pathet Lao propaganda

the *muang* (principality). It would culminate on the final day with a calling of the spirits of past rulers of Champassak by a *moh tiam* and in a *baci* ceremony at the main house of Boun Oum, where on this day the palladium of the principality, the *pha gaew pheuk*, would be brought out, and the local populace would file past the prince himself sprinkling him with water as a blessing.

There are parallels in this ritual with the one conducted in Luang Prabang, which I describe in the chapter "Customizing Tradition," but unlike the ritual in Luang Prabang, it has not been revived in recent years. Today, the *bok* ceremony is no longer practiced, and all rituals which express the structure of the old *muang* have disappeared. New Year in Champassak has been atomized, and celebrations, if any, occur only at the level of the respective *baan* and most commonly in individual households. The *moh tiam* ritual has been revived, and the spirits from across the city of Champassak are called, as are the spirits of past princes. But for the people at the ceremony I attended, these princes were non-specific, and people were content to simply say that many princes come (*lay ong ma*), though they were quite explicit that Boun Oum's spirit did not attend.

The *moh tiam* does not go in parade to the main house of Boun Oum as in the past because this is not allowed. Older people in Champassak are quick to remember these grand parades, but younger people have no memory of them at all. Since 1996 at Boun Oum's former residence the palladium has been placed on the veranda on the first day of the New Year ceremony (*sangkhan bai*, the day of the passing of the old year) for the ritual splashing by the populace, while a traditional orchestra plays.[14] This slight allusion to past practice is all that remains of the traditional ceremony.

Three days later on the first day of the New Year (*sangkhan keun*) a *baci* is held in the main house in front of the ancestral

14. Several members of this orchestra had been sent off to "reeducation" camps after 1975. After ten years away, several of the instruments had fallen into disrepair and had to be remade. They began playing again in 1988 as the revival of "tradition" began.

shrine, overseen by two large photos of Chao Khamsouk and Chao Rasadani (Boun Oum's grandfather and father, respectively). This ceremony takes the guise of a household ceremony, and the government seems determined to keep it there. Yet any visitor to the south, in particular to Pakse, cannot avoid the presence of Boun Oum because his huge, unfinished palace, towers over the whole city. In the early 1990s this was taken over by a Thai company and converted into the sixty-room Champassak Palace Hotel.[15] "Whose palace was it?" is, of course, the logical touristic question. Thus is the memory of Boun Oum, who died in exile in Paris in 1980, kept alive. The advertising brochure produced by the hotel contains a brief reference to the fact that it was Boun Oum's palace (and this must be the first neutral reference to him inside Laos in the past twenty years), but curiously this is only in Thai and not in English. Is it thought that only the Thai are likely to be attracted by a brush with royalty?[16]

It has been the numinous figures of Prince Phetsarath and Prince Souphanouvong who have maintained a high profile for Laos's royal past. Souphanouvong became a powerful symbolic figure "precisely because, like all dominant or focal symbols, he represented a coincidence of opposites, a semantic structure in tension between opposite poles of meaning" (Turner 1974:88-9). Almost always referred to in official pronouncements as either "comrade" or "president," in everyday speech he was commonly called "Prince Soupha-nouvong." Interestingly, this lapse was also registered in the

15. Folkloric speculation about why Boun Oum needed so many rooms claims that it was so that the palace could accommodate his many concubines and girlfriends. Thus the building continues to symbolize the sexual potency of traditional rulers.

16. Indeed, I'm not sure what to make of this difference in texts. After all, hotels in Luang Prabang directly pander to French and other foreigners' fascination with old royalty. For example, at one hotel, the Souvanna-phoum, the former Luang Prabang residence of Prince Souvanna Phouma, one can stay in what used to be the prince's bedroom for a higher price compared with other rooms in a newly-built wing. Currently, on the outskirts of Luang Prabang a Thai company is constructing a huge hotel around the former residence of Prince Phetsarath.

title of a collection of essays about him published in 1990, where in both Lao and English he was referred to as "prince." The title in Lao is "Prince Souphanouvong: Revolutionary Leader."[17] Unexpectedly, *Pasason* (30/11/95) also referred to him as "prince" instead of "president." Foreign journalists and politicians regularly called him the "Red Prince."

In the run-up to the communist takeover Souphanouvong was seen to represent in his person continuity with the kingdom's past, and the Pathet Lao's claim to want national reconciliation, which was further embodied in Souphanouvong because the neutralist prime minister, Souvanna Phouma was his half brother. When he returned to Vientiane on 3 April 1974 to join the short-lived coalition government, journalists spoke of the "almost hypnotic spell of Souphanouvong," and of a "new era" in Lao history:

> Possessing a degree of vitality that was unusual in a Lao politician, he drew enthusiastic and demonstrative crowds wherever he went. He seemed at ease in any company, a veritable "people's prince" whose rapport with the populace was reminiscent of Prince Sihanouk of Cambodia, though Souphanouvong was more reserved and he had a sense of mission. He had come to restore Laos' faith in itself. He was the hero of the Lao student movement. He had presence, if not charisma, and this rubbed off on the men who came down from Sam Neua with him. (*FEER* 1975:208)

He was a powerful symbolic figure, whatever his personal beliefs. Indeed, there is little evidence that Souphanouvong personally was anything other than a committed communist political activist.[18] Because of his numinosity, however,

17. The English title is *Autobiography of Prince Souphanouvong*, published by the Committee for Social Sciences, Vientiane, 1990. However, the book is not autobiographical.

18. He was a long-time associate of the Vietnamese communist leaders. Nevertheless, foreigners and some Lao like to insinuate that Souphanouvong's communist commitment can be attributed to the

many people wished to believe that somehow he was not deeply committed to the LPRP which he fronted for so successfully. Even after "the abolition of the outdated monarchy" (Kaysone's words), the aura of royalty clung to Souphanouvong and made him a symbolic enigma to the end.

For this reason, on his death on 9 January 1995, one may have expected an overflow of nostalgia for the past.[19] The state, however, maintained strict control over the funeral. Five days national mourning was declared for "one of its best loved leaders," and his body lay in state at the National Assembly until the final high Buddhist funeral ceremony on 15 January. The tears rolling down the cheeks of some monks, those who should have been most detached, perhaps bore silent witness to this final physical break with the royal past in the public sphere of Lao politics. As with Souvanna Phouma there had been some speculation about whether the funeral would be held in Luang Prabang, or whether his ashes would be returned there. But, one hundred days after the cremation, led by fifteen monks, Souphanouvong's family made merit for him along with President Nouhak and other party leaders, and his ashes were placed in a stupa at That Luang.

To bury him in Luang Prabang would have reconfirmed that city's claim as a royal and ritual center.[20] Souphanou-

---

influence of his Vietnamese wife. The suggestion rests on an inference of "scheming Vietnamese," a sexist inference of "scheming wives," and also the inference that a "real Lao," and especially one who was raised as a prince, could not have chosen of his own free will to become a communist. There is no good evidence for these inferences which are supported primarily by popular prejudices. I have suggested elsewhere (Evans 1995:XIX) that the traditional system which allowed major and minor wives produced jealousy and disaffection and a search for alternative routes for advancement by those in a minor line, and that this may apply to Souphanouvong.

19. In fact, after 1975 it is not at all clear how popular Souphanouvong was. Many people associated with the RLG saw him as having betrayed their trust and his own royal heritage. Indeed, these days, one rarely sees photos of Souphanouvong displayed in offices, shops or houses. If anything, he is completely overshadowed by Phetsarath.

20. Souvanna Phouma's ashes were taken to Luang Prabang and placed in a stupa at Vat That. This stupa also contains the remains of his older

vong, however, now rests at what is today firmly established as the national shrine, That Luang. While this may seem to be the final eclipsing of the Buddhist monarchy by secular politics based in Vientiane, the shrine where he rests is a Buddhist shrine built by a Lao king.

Nothing, perhaps, registers the continued symbolic ambiguity of Souphanouvong's royal heritage better than the fact that no member of the Thai royal family attended his funeral, whereas HRH Prince Maha Vajiralongkorn, as representative of King Bhumibol Adulyadej, and HRH Princess Maha Chakri Sirindhorn, attended the funeral for Kaysone. While the attendance of royalty at Souphanouvong's funeral is more "logical" than at Kaysone's, it would have focused too much attention on his royal, rather than revolutionary, lineage.

Yet, almost as substitutes for Laos's "disappeared" royalty, Thai royalty since 1990 has been playing an increasingly important, if subtle, role in Laos. They act as patrons of development projects, just as they do in Thailand, and as patrons of Buddhism, as they do in Thailand too. Ordinary Lao seem to obliquely recognize the parallel. Indeed, on walls in shops and businesses and in private homes throughout Laos, one will find calendars with pictures of Thai royalty occupying the same place that Lao royalty would have occupied in the past. In the showrooms of some retailers in Vientiane one can see proudly displayed the photo of an elite Lao family during their audience with the Thai king. Others who have met Princess Sirindhorn also proudly display photos of their encounter. Calendar pictures of the Thai king by himself or with his wife, and calendars with pictures of

---

brother, Prince Phetsarath, and some assumed that Souphanouvong's ashes may have been destined for this stupa too. Vat That in Luang Prabang was historically connected with the "Vang Na," the front of the palace, compared with Vat That Luang in Luang Prabang, historically connected with the "Vang Louang," the central palace, and the remains of King Sisavang Vong rest there in a large stupa. Souvanna Phouma, despite his titular status under the LPDR, was part of the old regime, and not as symbolically important as his half brother, and therefore there was less political need to control the disposal of his remains.

Princess Sirindhorn, or the crown prince of Thailand can all be found. While these are distributed much less widely than in Thailand, their mere presence is significant because of the symbolic space they occupy, and because similar pictures of the former Lao king have been taboo. This taboo appears to apply especially to Sisavang Vatthana, and less strictly to Sisavang Vong. It was only after 1990 that people started to bring out of hiding old photos of the former kings, but much of this memorabilia had been destroyed after 1975, and is not reproduced yearly on calendars, for example, as with Thai royalty.[21] Thus there is a diminishing supply of such reminders of the Lao royal past. On the outskirts of Luang Prabang in a Lue village which has historical connections to the palace, however, one can find an unusual concentration of such memorabilia, combined now with the cult figure of Chulalongkorn.

In his essay on the first visit to Laos by Princess Maha Chakri Sirindhorn (commonly known as Prathep), in March 1990, Charles Keyes (1993) investigates the way her visit registered, symbolically, Thai recognition of the independence of Laos, and of the revolution. This she did by visiting several key places and monuments in both Vientiane and in Luang Prabang. While in Luang Prabang the princess also met twice with the widow of the Lao crown prince, Princess Maneelai. Keyes learned that "when Princess Sirindhorn approached Princess Maneelai she saluted her by putting her hands together and bowing so that her head was lower than that of Princess Maneelai's. This indicated that Princess Sirindhorn acknowledged that Princess Maneelai was of high status." He continues: "I was told by a number of Lao . . . that the respect she showed Princess Maneelai helped to bring the Lao royal family back to popular attention in a positive way." Keyes was encouraged by the fact that when he visited Luang Prabang in 1993 he found a small hotel had been opened by Princess Maneelai and was called Villa de la

---

21. In 1988 Lao refugees in America produced a calendar with a picture of Sisavang Vong on it, but naturally only a few copies found their way into Laos.

Princesse. There is no doubt that the existence of this hotel brought the old royal family back into public view in a way not seen since the revolution. But it is interesting to also note the subtleties of this maneuver. The owners were careful not to use the Lao name for princess (*chao ying, lasabudii*), thereby invoking the officially abolished *rachasap* (royal language) but simply transliterated the French name into Lao (ແປຣງຄສສ). Nevertheless, during 1994, pressure was brought to bear on the hotel by local authorities to change its name to *Santi*, for they were clearly disturbed by this resurfacing of Lao royalty.[22] In 1996 the new name was displayed outside, but the old plaque still hung on the wall behind the reception desk, and the stationery still carried the old name. Indeed, taxi drivers and locals all continue to call it the *Hong Haem Princet*, and so the quiet tug-of-war between popular and official views continues.[23] Perhaps it was the visit by Princess Sirindhorn which supplied the impetus for this move back into the public eye by Lao royalty, and the Lao authorities have acted to nip it in the bud. There has been no repeat meeting between the Thai princess and Princess Maneelai since 1990.

Prathep appears to act as the special envoy of Thai royalty to Laos. She has visited Laos every year since 1990, traveling to different parts of the country to familiarize herself with it and to hand out largesse at schools and hospitals, and of course to be received enthusiastically by the various *chao khoueng* and their wives. She has given large donations to two of the oldest royal temples in Vientiane, Vat Inpheng and Vat Ong Teu, and to temples in Luang Prabang and elsewhere in Laos. She has, in a sense, become Laos's princess.[24]

22. In Vientiane around the same time a guest house called *Wang Sadet*, "Princess's Palace," also had to change its name. The Champassak Palace Hotel transliterates "palace" into Lao (ໂຣງແຮມຈຳປາສັກພາເລດ). But this use of "palet" may simply be the Thai use of English, as the Grand Palace in Bangkok is commonly called the "Gran Palet."

23. It is perhaps worth noting that in advertising outside of Laos the hotel combines "Villa de la Princesse" and "Villa Santi" and invites tourists to come and stay in the old royal quarter of Luang Prabang, whereas inside Laos only the latter name is now used in advertising.

The most important occasion, however, was the visit of the Thai king and queen to Laos on 8-9 April 1994 for the opening of the Lao-Thai Friendship Bridge. It was the first visit abroad by the Thai king in twenty-seven years, a significant fact in itself. But it was also significant because the Thai king had never visited Laos when it was a kingdom. Only when the Lao king was no longer present did he visit. Indeed, it is said that for as long as there was a king the Thai king could not enter the Lao kingdom. This parallels the story of the relationship between the Prabang and the Emerald Buddha, the palladiums respectively of the kingdoms of Laos and Thailand, in which it is said that they cannot coexist within the same space. Thus the Prabang which was taken to Thailand in the nineteenth century following the sacking of Vientiane was returned by King Mongkut in 1867 because it was considered a "rival" of the Emerald Buddha (Reynolds 1978). King Bhumibol and King Sisavang Vatthana did meet once, however, on a floating pavilion moored in the middle of the Mekong River off Nong Khai on the occasion of the inauguration of the Ngam Ngum Dam on 16 December 1968.[25] Photos at the time show the much younger Thai king and the Lao king, both dressed in ceremonial military uniforms, shaking hands.

In April 1994 the Thai king once again stood in the middle of the Mekong, this time in a pavilion erected on the new bridge, and this time with the aged communist president, Nouhak Phoumsavan. That night after a reception at the Presidential Palace in Vientiane a Lao orchestra played songs composed by the Thai king. The next morning the king paid an official visit to the national shrine, That Luang, accompanied by President Nouhak, Prime Minister Khamtay,

24. Rumors which have circulated, particularly in Luang Prabang, have idly speculated about the possibility of a "dynastic marriage" between a Lao prince now living in exile in Paris, and Prathep. In fact, this is nothing more than rumor. But what is of theoretical interest to us here is the *wishful* and nostalgic element contained in the rumor.

25. Ngaosyvathn (1994:124) incorrectly states that this meeting occurred in 1972.

and a large entourage. The king and queen and the princess offered flowers, incense and candles as tribute to the Lord Buddha while monks chanted their blessing. They then made offerings to the monks and presented a contribution to the president of the Buddhist Association, Venerable Vichit Singalat for the maintenance of the stupa. It was pointed out in the Lao press that "the King showed keen interest in the rehabilitation of Buddhist temples in the country, educational institutions for Buddhist monks and the civic and religious role activities of Buddhist monks in the country" (*VT* 8-14/4/ 94). After That Luang they visited an orphanage placed under the patronage of the princess during her visit in 1990, and again in 1992, and for which she had raised the equivalent of 342,000 baht and donated a further 285,000. While there, the king officially opened a building named after the princess, donated teaching aids and made a personal financial contribution. Later they visited an agricultural development and service center north of Vientiane established jointly by the king and the Lao government, which according to a speech by Lao foreign minister Somsavath Lengsavad, was established to commemorate the late President Kaysone Phomvihane and as a symbol of friendship between the two countries. In an audience with the king that afternoon Thai businessmen in Laos donated a further 2.5 million baht in support of this royally sponsored project, a conventional way for Thai business people to earn merit through association with the king.

Finally, a *baci*, sponsored by the president and the prime minister and their wives was held for the royal couple and the princess at the Presidential Palace. In attendance were all the ministers, vice ministers, selected high officials and their wives. The seating arrangements only partially conformed to Thai protocol. The Lao president and prime minister and their wives sat on chairs at the same level as the Thai royal visitors underlining their equality, while before them seated on the floor around the *pha khouan*, were the Lao high officials and their wives, acknowledging their own ritual inferiority (*VT* 11/4/94). What is striking about this occasion is the ease with which the Lao officials and their wives conformed to royal protocol, and the obvious delight they took in moving within the charmed circle of the Thai king.

One of the most important occasions in the ritual calendar of the Thai king is the *kathin* ceremony held at the end of the Buddhist lent. In October 1995 the Thai king extended his yearly sponsorship of the sangha to Laos. General Siri Thivaphanh from the Ministry of Foreign Affairs in Thailand, on behalf of the king, offered one set of monk requisites and donations of 510,000 baht to Vat That Luang Neua in Vientiane for the renovation the temple and the promotion of Buddhism. What was most interesting about this occasion was that joining in the merit-making were President Nouhak, Prime Minister Khamtay, and Foreign Minister Somsavath. The offerings were made again in 1996 and it was as if the Thai king had become a proxy for Lao royalty.

# STATUES AND MUSEUMS

I N an earlier section on the Kaysone cult I noted the erection of busts and statues of Kaysone all over the country and discussed how the creation of cults of secular individuals is problematic in Southeast Asian cultures compared with East Asian cultures. Among the Lao in the past the only statues that were built were those of deities—of buddhas and *thevadas*—not of mortal men, not even of semi-divine kings. In fact, buddhas were stylized so as not to look like mortals. The first public statue of a king to be erected in Laos was that of Setthatirath who now sits jauntily in front of his creation, the That Luang. This statue was only erected in 1957, and even then it was to commemorate the twenty-five hundredth year of Buddhism.[1] In fact, the first public statue of a mortal was created by the French, that is, people inhabiting another cultural universe. The statue was of the famous French explorer, Auguste Pavie, being offered flowers by a young Lao male and female, and was first situated in front of the Ho Phra Keo. The statue of Pavie himself was transferred to the Pavie Square in 1947, and then moved to its

---

1. A tourist booklet, *Guide to Vientiane Municipality* (1995), produced by a mixed state-private enterprise company, Inter-Lao Tourism, lists the date as 1962. This appears to be a case of simple incompetence rather than any tampering with the historical record. Another explanation for the confusion may be that the bronze statue now standing was completed a few years after the original statue of cement, in 1959.

present site inside the French embassy when the Lane Xang Hotel was built on the square in 1961.[2] This is a significant fact because it corresponds to the situation in India discussed by Robin Jeffrey (1980), who points out that before the coming of the British there were no statues of mortals: "the notion of making an effigy of a leader who had no claim to super-natural powers was a foreign one" (1980:485). Of course, Theravadin kings could make some claims to supernatural powers, but even so statues were not made of them until the modern period.

The making of statues, therefore, has broader cultural and historical significance. These effigies, which are somehow mid-points between deities and human beings, signify not only shifts in the cosmology of modern polities, but also the changing scale and changing relations between deities and human beings—the decreasing distance between them.[3] Jeffrey comments:

> . . . when religious and familial authority weakens, when the power and responsibilities of a state broaden, and when, therefore, it becomes necessary to win acceptance of the state from numbers far beyond the face-to-face kin and clan—then statues seem to flourish. Their appearance indicate that politics are becoming more secular and competitive. Yet because the statue is of the same genre as supernatural idols, the aims of statue-

2. The two young Lao were left in front of the Ho Phra Keo, and their flower offerings were then reinterpreted as being offered to the Buddha.

3. I came across a surprising instance of statue building in Luang Prabang in early 1996. It was a statue of the leading monk at Vat Saen. Made in 1994, it was totally realist in execution. What was so surprising about this statue was that this monk is still alive and in the temple. It has, of course, now become relatively common in Thailand for statues to be made of deceased monks. For example, a statue has been made of the Lao Phra Sangharat who fled to Thailand in 1977 and died there in 1984. It now stands in Vat Phone Phanao in Nong Khai. But statues of still living monks are also common in Thailand, and they seem to suggest a secularizing process at work in the heart of Buddhism, similar to that taking place in the society at large.

raising and idol-making are perhaps the same: to deify
certain qualities and make men and women behave with
awe. (1980:501)

Statues have flourished in communist states which have
gone further than any other modernizing states in deifying
their leaders. The Kaysone statues represent the most
intensive episode of statue building ever in Lao history. If the
flourishing of statues suggests the devaluing of deities then it
is not surprising that in regimes which have generally been
hostile towards religion, such as most communist regimes,
that we should find statue building megalomania. It is also,
perhaps, not surprising that the first symbolic targets of the
crowds during the collapse of communism in Europe were
the ubiquitous statues of either Lenin or Stalin, or any other
leader.

The most imposing statue in Vientiane is that of King
Sisavang Vong standing in front of Vat Si Muang, which
houses the *lak muang* of the city. This statue of the king
granting the constitution to the people, written on traditional
*bay lan*, was donated by the Soviet Union following King
Sisavang Vatthana's visit to the USSR in 1972. It was erected
in 1974. In communist revolutions (or revolutions against
communism) statues of old regime figures have often been
torn down, symbolizing as they do, the old regime. In what
must count as one of the nicer ironies of Lao history, the
statue of King Sisavang Vong could not be torn down because
it had been donated by the "fraternal" Soviets.[4] Indeed, a
second identical statue, had been made for Luang Prabang
and was installed inside the old palace grounds in 1977! The
only other extant large statue of King Sisavang Vong was one

4. A photo of Sisavang Vong in the Vientiane Revolutionary Museum
captioned: "King Sisavang Vong shakes hands with the American
Imperialists," still remains on display. The "fraternal" Soviet connection
may also explain why the palace museum in Luang Prabang continues to
display large portraits of King Sisavang Vatthana, his wife, and the crown
prince, Vong Savang. These were painted by Soviet artist Ilya Glazrov in
the 1960s, and they are the only publicly displayed portraits of the former
king and his family in the whole of Laos.

made in the years just prior to 1975 by a metallurgist who specialized in making buddhas in Vat That Luang Dai in Vientiane. He made a large statue of the king in ceremonial military garb out of war materiel. It was, however, never erected because King Sisavang Vatthana thought it was a poor likeness of his father. Thus this statue lay on its back under a tin roof inside the grounds of the temple for the next twenty years (see photo). Suddenly in 1994 officials from the Ministry of Information and Culture from the Vientiane municipality came to the temple and carried the statue away. Where to remains a mystery. But what is significant is that this statue was removed at the same time pressure came on the Villa de la Princesse in Luang Prabang to change its name along with the Wang Sadet in Vientiane, and other moves against royal references. According to one informant there was talk at the same time of removing the statue in front of Vat Si Muang but it was not carried out because it would have caused a popular outcry.[5]

Other statues erected during the old regime were not so lucky. The statue of the former king of Bassac, Khamsouk (1863-1900), was erected in Champassak by Boun Oum at the same time as the statue of Setthatirath in Vientiane. After the revolution Pathet Lao soldiers tore it off its pedestal and

5.   There is one other rather bizarre instance of statue building in Laos and that is at Vat Xieng Khouan, situated about 24 kilometers from Vientiane. Begun in 1958, it is in fact not a real temple but a park beside the Mekong River containing a large number of effigies drawn from Buddhist and Hindu religions, and from folklore. It was built by Luang Phu (Venerable Grandfather), a man who preached a syncretic religious philosophy. The statues were built with donations from his following in Laos, which, judging by the dedications written on the statues, included many high-ranking individuals in the RLG. The syncretism is interesting because it too is a symptom of rapid cultural change (one is reminded of the syncretism of the Cao Dai millenial sect in neighboring Vietnam), and to my eye the style of many of the statues, and their combinations, recall a Hollywood vision of "the East." What is also relevant here is that not only gods are depicted, but also statues of mortal RLG soldiers. However, because this episode of statue building was not a state activity, it does not fall strictly within the purview of this essay. Luang Phu left for Nong Khai, Thailand, around the time of the revolution in 1975, and in 1978 established a similar park there.

smashed the explanatory plaque. They were intent on throwing it in the Mekong River but the townspeople pleaded to be able to place it in Vat Thong, where it now stands in a corner beside the main altar for the Buddha. It does not take much imagination to realize that when the people pay their respects to the Buddha, they are also making them to the former king. The other statue pulled down in the south was a large one of Katay Don Sasorith (1904-1959) which stood in a garden opposite Vat Luang out of which his tall stupa still looms. The statue of this implacable opponent of the Pathet Lao was erected in 1969 and came down immediately after the revolution. Many people in Pakse believe it was then thrown in the Sedone River, but the *chao muang* of Pakse assured me that it had been stored away. Relatives of Katay were allowed to see it in 1994, he said. This was later confirmed in Vientiane where some of Katay's sons and daughters reside. One of these, who owns a hotel in Vientiane, is hoping to finally install the statue in the garden of the hotel.

In Savannakhet, however, to my surprise I found one other statue which had been recently erected in 1995—that of Kou Voravong (1914-1954). He was minister of defense in Prince Souvanna Phouma's first government in 1954 and favored negotiations with the Pathet Lao. His assassination in September led to the collapse of Souvanna Phouma's government and of the negotiations under the government now led by Katay. In the early 1960s Kou's two younger brothers, along with his brother-in-law, the right-wing general Phoumi Nosavan, sponsored the casting of a statue of Kou in Thailand. In the mid-1960s, however, Phoumi was forced to flee to Thailand and so the statue was never erected. Confident in the changing line of the state, the Voravong family in 1989 petitioned the LPRP leadership for permission to erect the statue, citing Kou's resistance to the Japanese in World War II (but no doubt leaving out his resistance to the formation of the Issara government), and his conciliatory line towards the Pathet Lao in 1954. In 1994 they finally received permission from the party and in 1995 the statue was brought across from Thailand and ceremoniously erected on a plot of private land (which happens to be just opposite Kaysone's natal home). The erection of this dainty, well-crafted little statue of Kou dressed in a traditional gentleman's *sampot*, is extremely significant in the midst of Kaysone statue-building mania. It is the first step back onto the historical stage of a non-Pathet Lao figure from the past and registers, I think, part of a play by major families in Laos to have their roles in history recognized too. Speaking with Kou's relatives who live opposite from the statue's square, they said that they had heard a rumor that Katay's statue may be erected again. Although this seems far-fetched in the present climate, a few days later a monk in Pakse also intimated that Katay's statue would be restored "when the time is right."

Modern nationalist regimes are also monument builders. The most imposing monument in Laos is in Vientiane—the *Anousavaly* (literally "monument")—built on a hill at the top of the Lane Xang Avenue Boulevard, looking down towards the Presidental Palace, and providing a "gateway" to That Luang. This structure was commissioned in 1957, around the same time that the city's avenues (such as Lane Xang Avenue) were widened to give Vientiane "at least the aspect of a modern city" (Dommen 1971:288). The combination of the remodeling of a traditional city's layout with the placement of monuments within it can be seen in the history of modern Europe (Agulhon 1978) and of neighboring Bangkok at the turn of this century (Askew 1994). "The Monument," however, with its mixture of architectural styles is engagingly ambiguous. Foreign journalists and others often refer to it as the "Arch de Triomphe" because of its obvious borrowings from its Parisian counterpart, but it is equally in debt to monuments in India, and to aspects of traditional Lao architecture. It was in fact built to commemorate the war dead on the RLG side in the civil war, and indeed was called the "Monument to the Unknown Soldier," as was the stupa built at That Luang by the new regime after 1975.[6] The term

6. Ben Anderson has pointed out that it is only modern nationalism that builds tombs to the unknown soldier, and for this reason he argues:

*anousavaly* has tended to neutralize this old regime connotation.[7]

This ambiguity continued until 22 May 1995 when the Ministry of Information and Culture declared that the *Anousavaly* was a "national hierloom" which from that time onwards should be known as the *Patou Say* or the "Victory Arch." Explaining this attempted appropriation of the monument the LPDR argued that many nations have such victory monuments (and so why not Laos?), and that during the "uprising" in Vientiane on 23 August 1975 people gathered there to demonstrate. In 1996 the monument's facade received a face-lift (or perhaps face-erasure is more accurate), as reported in *Vientiane Times* (May 10—16, 1996): "The Head of the Ministry of Information and Culture's office, Mr Boualiene Sikansay, said the facade used to depict the Lao symbol, Dockchan. But the new face depicts the mythological figure, Kinnaly. He said the facade was changed because the old one no longer had any significant meaning. It

---

"Nationalism is more properly assimilated to religion than political ideologies because most of the deepest symbols of nations are symbols of death. This is not the type of imagining that one sees, for example, in Marxism, Liberalism or even conservatism. You won't find a tomb to the unknown Conservative anywhere in London, or a cenotaph for fallen liberals. This concern with death and with immortality, if you like, makes me think that nationalism supplants, or is aligned with, religion." *Imagined Communities,* directed by M. Millman, Bandung Films, Ltd., Channel Four (UK), 1991.

7. Since before 1975 the monument has also jokingly been called "the vertical runway" because, according to modern folklore, the concrete used in its construction was originally donated by USAID to build a runway. This perhaps apocryphal story of its diversion into the monument is meant to underline the weaknesses of the RLG, and perhaps echoes themes of beating swords into ploughshares which would have appealed to anti-war journalists at the time. A recent publication by one of the figures responsible for its construction does not help clarify this, though it does suggest that the financing of the project was not all that it should have been. Former colonel Tham Saiyasitsena (1995:20-21) says that because the project was financed by government and private sources there was some "confusion" about where the money was coming from and where it was going to, which was also an outcome of the desire of private contractors to make a profit.

120

symbolized, he said, fighting between the armed forces during the colonial era." Just what the "colonial era" means, however, is confusing for the same article claims the monument "was built 38 [sic] years ago during the French era," i.e. four years after Lao independence from France! This account, therefore, verges on surreal history.

In spite of the efforts of the government, few people use *Patou Say,* and the meaning of the monument remains ambiguous and mutely contested. This is most apparent in a booklet produced by one of the persons in charge of the monument's construction, former colonel Tham Saiyasitsena (1995), which provides brief explanations of the decisions to build the monument, its symbolism and its uses. Tham, now in his eighties, was a member of the Lao Issara, and after that he was an important figure in the RLG army who backed Souvanna Phouma. He retired just before 1975 (thereby escaping "reeducation"), and is now a respected elder in Vientiane. Tham's booklet, which uses the new name for the monument, *Patou Say,*[8] studiously avoids referring to the old regime by name throughout (although he does at one point refer to the *labob lasatipatai,* i.e. constitutional monarchy), yet the booklet provides background which shows that the monument was originally built to honor national heroes and war dead, and that the monument was an important rallying point under the old regime (he discretely writes *nai samai nan,* "in those times"). "Since 1976 parades have changed their location to the That Luang parade ground in front of the *new* monument to the unknown soldier which our party and government built" (1995:25. My emphasis). And he notes that since then the monument has simply become a place for tourists. But the booklet, which opens with a description of the arrival of Thai tourists at the monument and the importance of explaining to them its past, would appear to also be an argument for the restoration of the symbolic importance of the monument by having it once again

8. He would have no choice about this as he, like anyone else, has to seek permission from the Ministry of Information and Culture before publishing a book or pamphlet.

represent national heroes, and once again perform its previous role as a focal point of national parades for which it was designed. The monument, therefore, remains in competition with the stupa to the unknown soldier built by the new regime, and as noted earlier, the latter is largely ignored by the populace. Clearly the new regime cannot abandon the new symbolic spaces it staked out after 1975 in favor of those constructed by the old regime. But short of destroying the latter, it can only attempt to incorporate and de-politicize these spaces, to date only with mixed success.

Like statues and monuments, museums are also a product of the modern nationalist imagination and a repository of its memory. In the past, palaces were centers of sacred power and were therefore a kind of de-facto museum because they were places for the gathering of treasures, tribute and ritual and magical objects, such as white elephants. Writing about a traditional polity that operated according to similar principles, Anderson (1990:27) says: "it was an old tradition in Java that the ruler should concentrate around him any objects or persons held to have or contain unusual Power. His palace would be filled not only with the traditional array of *pusaka* (heirlooms), such as krisses, spears, sacred musical instruments, carriages, and the like, but also various types of extraordinary beings, such as albinos, clowns, dwarves, and fortune-tellers. Being in the palace, their Power was absorbed by, and further added to the ruler's own." Tambiah (1985) also talks of the importance of regalia for royal legitimacy in Thailand, and like them traditionally kings in Laos would be offered any white elephants found in the kingdom—but what to do with white elephants when there are no kings? Responding to an ingrained cultural code which said that white elephants at least flow towards the seat of power, the Champassak provincial government in 1989 offered a white elephant that had been caught to the central government. They called it "Lady White Elephant Golden Auspicious Ornament of Laos" (ນາງພະຍາຊ້າງເຜືອກຄຳແກ້ວມີ່ງເມືອງລາວ), and so it was after this gift that the "tradition" of the white elephant procession returned to the That Luang parade in 1992. Here we should also recall "the people" giving elephant tusks, valuable buddhas, and other "regalia" to Kaysone, and indeed an article on Kaysone in late 1996 carries of photo of him feeding the white elephant (*VT* 14-17/12/96).

Thus the transformation of the Luang Prabang Palace into a museum has a certain historical logic. But palaces were never consciously designed as such. Museums, whose special preoccupation is with the past, are a product of a modern consciousness which is acutely aware of change—social, cultural and historical—and of ongoing change. It is this which explains the obsession around the world with the preservation of "heritage," and this "heritage" in some cases may only be a few decades old.[9] The increasingly shallow depth of the idea of heritage is itself an index of the speed of social and cultural change in which people feel that their "heritage" is disappearing before their eyes. The shift in consciousness which comes with modernity is still palpable in Laos where expatriates swoon over what is left of French colonial architecture, or traditional Lao wooden houses, while the Lao themselves dream only of the new concrete houses designed for the Thai *nouveaux riches*. One hears tales (horrifying to modern ears) of villagers using their new-found access to outside commodities to buy tins of bright new paint which they use to paint over old—and to their eyes, ugly—frescoes in their temples.

The state itself, however, has a museum imagination, and the importance of "heritage" for foreign tourists has cultivated it further. The museum imagination of the modern Lao state has its origins in the practice of the French colonial state. The École Française d'Extrême Orient was established in Saigon in 1898, and was soon followed by the foundation of a Directorate of Museums and Historical Monuments of Indochina. These institutions gathered together an impressive group of scholars who played a central role in beginning the restoration of ancient monuments throughout Indochina (Malleret 1969). When they established their headquarters in

9. For an excellent case study of the "heritage industry" in England, see Fowler (1992).

Vientiane it was the French who began the process of reconstructing the Lao "national emblem," That Luang and other temples and stupas in Vientiane city, and of course elsewhere in Laos (Malleret 1969:62).[10] These "sacred sites" then became incorporated into the iconography of the colonies—anything associated with Cambodia, for example, became instantly recognizable by its association with the iconographic large stone faces of Jayavaraman V from the Bayon at Angkor, or Laos with the That Luang. Subsequently, inside Laos a similar iconographic mapping has occurred: Vat Xieng Thong for Luang Prabang, the Plain of Jars for Xieng Khouang, That Inghang for Savannakhet, and Vat Phu for Pakse, while That Luang in this mapping represents Vientiane, although in this context it is sometimes replaced by the *Anousavaly*. These abstract "heritage" icons which then find their way onto banknotes and stamps, among other things, are therefore powerful images for constructing an abstract, or imagined, idea of the Lao nation among its citizens. This is particularly apparent in RLG banknotes which picture King Sisavang Vatthana alongside key temples and stupas from across the nation. The Liberation Kip issued by the Pathet Lao and which was legal tender in Laos after December 1975 (until it was withdrawn in 1977) had a small That Luang motif, but until 1990 when the That Luang reappeared on the 1000-kip note, the revolutionaries attempted to substitute a new iconography of national reconstruction. This attempt to establish a new national iconography of toiling workers and peasants immediately after 1975 has gradually given way to the nationalist iconography already popularized by the RLG. Serially one can see this most clearly in stamps which in the immediate aftermath of the revolution contained mainly revolutionary and national reconstruction motifs, as well as references to

10. The importance of the French in encouraging an interest in historical monuments and their restoration cannot be stressed too much. See, for example, Jean Cuisinier's impassioned plea for preservation in Laos: "La grande pitie des Buddhas au Laos," *Revue Indochinoise Illustree*, Numero 25, Juillet 1928.

"fraternal" socialist countries, or to the anniversary of Ho Chi Minh's birthday. These have subsequently yielded to stamps featuring the icons prominent during the RLG, including Buddha images and so on. Originally I thought that one innovation to be found in the iconography of the new regime compared with the old regime was its inclusion of a new icon signifying minorities, most commonly a female dressed as a white Hmong. But stamps featuring minorities are also among those of the RLG.

Lao themselves first became actively involved in museology in the 1930s when Prince Souvanna Phouma was placed in charge of the restoration of the Vat Phra Keo, begun in 1936, upon his return to Vientiane from his engineering studies in France. In 1937, after outlining the assistance from the French, the prince wrote: "The Laotians themselves did not lack in their contribution, although according to their lesser means, to the restoration of one of the most ancient religious monuments of their country" (1970:6). Writing some thirty years later while reintroducing his original article, the French assistance is elided: "The Ho Phra Keo was in effect reconstructed by the Lao people themselves, and it is no small matter of pride for me to have had the honor of being placed at the head of my compatriots for the realization of this modest but initial task of National Reconstruction" (1970:3). Of course for post-colonial nationalists it became *de rigeur* to de-emphasize connections between their project and that of the colonial state, but as Benedict Anderson (1991) has argued, the relationship was strong and profound—an observation that applies equally to both communist and non-communist post-colonial states. After independence the RLG embarked on its own program of monument restoration, partly spurred on by the coming of the celebration of twenty-five hundred years of Buddhism in 1957. Despite the growing civil war some restoration work continued.[11] After 1975 much of this work came to a halt as the country threw itself into "socialist construction," but the 1980s saw a new concern

11. See, for example, the booklet published by the Ministry of Religious Affairs (ກະຊວງທັມມະການ 1974) which provides a periodization for many of the

with monuments as the regime began its shift towards a more conventional nationalist discourse, and this accelerated in the 1990s.[12] An account of the history of the That Luang and its restoration was published in 1985, but like other books published on temples or other monuments since then, it makes no mention of work done by the RLG. By definition, the "despised" old regime could have done nothing edifying and so their contribution is exorcised from historical narratives.

In 1980 the Lao Museum of the Revolution was established in a large building on Samsaenthai Road in Vientiane which formerly housed the office of Prince Souvanna Phouma. The narrative of the museum's display is a simple one of the heroic struggle of the LPRP and its path to power, and a much shorter section on socialist reconstruction. The exhibition has changed slowly over the years according to political imperatives. Since 1990 the "Lenin Room" contributed by the USSR has been closed. There is less emphasis on fraternal socialist countries, and an exhibition attacking the Thais following the border skirmishes in the late 1980s had, by the mid-1990s, come down. Few Lao go to this museum voluntarily. School children are trooped through, and no doubt young party members. The most enthusiastic tourists who come are the Thai who are apparently fascinated in a vicarious way with the Lao "other," the communists about whom they have heard so much propaganda over the years. To this extent the museum succeeds vis-à-vis the Thai

---

key monuments and the restorations which have occurred, including under the French and under the RLG. Pierre Marie Gagneux (1976) also provides a good account of what historical and archaeological research had been done up to 1975, and reflecting the mood of the times, was somewhat optimistic about what would be accomplished under the LPDR.

12. The key decrees were No. 1375, passed in June 1978, for the protection of archaeological and religious monuments; No. 139, passed in March 1990, with Ministry of Information and Culture asserting national responsibility for the national patrimony; and a following decree, No. 834, passed in September 1993, declaring that all Lao historical buildings, including those from the colonial period, were part of the national patrimony and therefore protected.

in establishing Lao difference and "national integrity"—while the temples that the Thai visit all confirm cultural similarity. In early 1997 the name of the museum, Lao Museum of the Revolution, was changed to the Lao National Museum.

In 1994 an attempt was made to establish a kind of ethnic museum, of the sort that one can see now in China, Taiwan, Vietnam and Java. Set up near the new Friendship Bridge by the Ministry of Information and Culture in cooperation with the military's Highland Development Co., it is called the National Ethnic Cultural Garden (ສວນວັດທະນະ຤ິນວັນຄາຜ່າແທ່ງສາດ) and was to be a "gathering site for the preservation, conservation, promotion and dissemination of the traditional cultures and fine customs of the ethnic groups of Laos." As it has evolved, however, it has become more of an amusement and picnic park for Lao and Thai tourists. On one side it is a zoo, and on the other it has several houses built to typify a so-called "Lao Soung House," a "Lao Theung House" and a traditional ethnic Lao house. Despite original claims that the "construction materials used in this garden will reflect the valuable arts, skills and techniques" of the ethnic groups, the two minority houses are in fact concrete artifacts, and only the Lao house is in anyway genuine. The ethnic minority houses are, therefore, really only signs pointing towards Laos's much trumpeted multi-ethnicity.[13] Otherwise the gardens have a Disneyland quality, the center of which is dominated by several enormous replicas of dinosaurs (these refer to the discovery of dinosaur bones in Savannakhet). Of course, the gathering of dinosaurs, zoo animals and ethnic minority exhibits in one place confirms a deeper prejudice that these people are primitive and backward.

The largest project of museumization, however, came in 1995 when Luang Prabang city was declared a world heritage city by UNESCO. Various features were cited in defense of its

13. At least here we do not have the ethnic zoos such as I have visited in China (in Shenzhen and in Kunming) where young minority people have been dragooned into sitting in their "typical" minority houses all day, bored witless, acting out their ethnicity. At the end of the day they rush to discard their traditional clothes and head for the nearest karaoke lounge.

preservation, such as the beauty of its temples and their number, the beauty and uniqueness of its buddhas, and the fact that it still retained some of the ambience of a traditional Lao (Southeast Asian) city. What is most interesting in the Lao Ministry of Information and Culture's submission (1994:7) is its reference to the important role the old King Sisavang Vong played in its restoration after the ravages of the nineteenth century. While this reference is only brief, it points to a major problem for the Lao government, which is how to exclude or marginalize the role of the monarchy in its narrative about Luang Prabang. A guidebook (in Lao) to Luang Prabang of necessity makes one or two neutral references to the former Kings Sisavang Vong or Sisavang Vatthana, but they remain only ghostly presences in the new discourse of "national patrimony."

Their shadowy attendance was felt during Lao New Year 1996 when Prime Minister Khamtay Siphandone made a special visit to Luang Prabang in honor of its world heritage nomination. He was joined by the Vietnamese prime minister, Vo Van Kiet, making a recreational visit at the former's invitation. The main parade which took place on 14 April filed past the two prime minister's and their wives and various dignitaries, some pausing to bow in their direction. What was intriguing, however, was the position of the viewing stand. It stood immediately opposite the gates of the old palace. The former king would have viewed the parade from within the palace grounds. Despite their conscious intentions, no doubt, the positioning of the viewing stand ensured that the "new kings" drew on the aura of the kings of old.

# CUSTOMIZING
# TRADITION

MUCH of the concern with "heritage" is driven by the
demands of Laos's developing tourist industry, and
thus it is something which is increasingly driven by
the needs of private enterprise as well. It is one of the
paradoxes of international tourism that on the one hand it is
sometimes seen to bring "cultural pollution" or cultural
degeneration, while on the other hand it has also stimulated
both genuine as well as theatrical cultural revivals (Evans
1993:369-77). In the latter both tourist and performer join
hands in a world of make-believe, with natives dressing in
"traditional" garb and performing, say, a "traditional" dance
for tourists, after which the latter return to their five star hotels
and the former exchange their costumes for jeans and go
home, or to a disco, on motorbikes. Leaving aside the purely
commercial aspects, the ubiquity of such performances
suggests that a key function of tourism, or tourist theater in all
its guises, is the ritual display of cultural difference in an
increasingly "globalized" world. On the other hand, revivals,
or sustenance of traditional practices can occur, and in Laos it
is most evident in weaving handicrafts that have boomed due
to tourism.

While they remain closed, communist states can entertain
"tourists of the revolution" (Enzensberger 1976) who are
happy to be treated to displays of revolutionary theater acting
out a fantasy of the present and the future. This may take the

form of the romance of rural cooperation during a tour of what is probably a cooperative in name only (*sahagorn hoop hang* as some Lao farmers referred to them), or in displays which are pure theater, performed by revolutionary dance troupes. The market for this kind of tourism, however, was always small. The gradual opening up of Laos from the mid-1980s onwards demanded the creation of tourist displays, sites and activities which conformed to the expectations of the international tourist industry. This inevitably meant that the Lao had to reach back into the cultural past and revive it, albeit selectively, because so much of that traditional past was permeated by the old regime, the so-called *sakdina* system. Information has had to be produced for tourist consumption and for this, old-regime books and pamphlets have been cannibalized, taking care to excise wherever possible references to the monarchy or any positive references to the RLG. As mentioned earlier, a close reading of the booklet produced in 1995 (Editions du *Vientiane Times*) on That Luang reveals the great care taken to suppress the memory of this particular past. One small surprise, however, appears on page 53 where an old-regime five-kip banknote with the That Luang motif on it appears. This has been carefully chosen because the old one hundred-kip note has King Sisavang Vatthana alongside the That Luang, whereas the five-kip note simply features an elephant beside the stupa. According to one of the producers of the book the censor in the Ministry of Information and Culture at first objected to its inclusion: "Do you know what's on the back of this note?" he asked. "No", came the reply. "I should stop this," the censor said, "but you can go ahead." This exchange is a textbook example of the process of memory and forgetting encouraged by authoritarian regimes, which use their power to create a world of pretence and dissembling where, in this case, both sides choose not to speak the unmentionable fact that the old king's head is on the other side of the note.

Tourism, however, with its insatiable demand for memorabilia has brought the old-regime notes out of hiding and they are freely on sale in markets and shops around Laos, along with other souvenirs from the old regime: stamps, medals, and even some old posters of King Sisavang Vong. Cynics might argue that the tourist market will finally remove all traces of the old regime from the country more thoroughly than all the repression exercised by the new regime. But for the moment, this memorabilia has brought the old regime back into the public eye in a way not seen since its downfall.

The rediscovery of tradition in Laos seemed to reach a climax with the celebration of the new year in 1996, focusing on the special celebrations in Luang Prabang. All over the country it is claimed that Lao are now celebrating various events in their "traditional way," such as, for example, the Buddhist festival at the old Khmer ruins at Vat Phu in Pakse,[1] held in February. The emphasis on tradition and customary practices in the official media has become almost obsessional. Beginning in the early 1990s some old regime publications which had gone out of print, such as those giving instructions for the holding of particular rituals, have been republished with suitable modifications (e.g. Phra Ajaan Sali 1991, in Lao), and an edition in Lao called "Ancient Lao Culture" was published in 1994. This is all symptomatic of the LPDR's move to relegitimize itself in terms of national symbols while claiming it is the defender of "Lao tradition."

This rediscovery, however, is also a product of something more profound and that is Lao society's awareness that it is in a process of rapid change. This became particularly apparent around the time of the opening of the Friendship Bridge to Thailand in 1994. Although there has been continuous contact between Laos and Thailand for aeons, the popular imagery built up around this event was the "opening up of Laos to the world," and speculation about all the changes that would come rushing across the bridge. I spoke with Phoumi

---

1. Vat Phu, built by the Khmer Empire in the eleventh century, is considered a Lao national icon, but there is always an element of disquiet about this because it is clearly a Khmer creation. Discussions of this "traditional" festival also fail to mention the absence of its "high priest," the prince of Champassak.

Vongvichit shortly before his death, and while he saw the bridge as a sign of modernization, he also saw it as a conduit for bad cultural influences and for AIDS. At the time I recall a young, drunk, off-duty soldier asking me for advice for friends who obviously had VD but were too scared to seek help because it might be AIDS. Like most people in Laos they did not know what AIDS was, only that it was coming along with other baleful influences. One man showed me a list of improbable herbal remedies for AIDS which had come to a woman in her dreams. "It's worth trying. It might work," he said hopefully. Thus did the bridge and the accompanying specter of AIDS emerge as a metaphor for cultural change in Laos.

The flip-side of modernity is nostalgia. Everywhere people lament that things are not as they were in the "old days" and lament the differences between generations. It seems to be true that everywhere people experience social change, especially rapid social change, as a loss, despite the fact that people may simultaneously remember hardships in the past.[2] This is primarily because social and cultural practices which actually constituted the individual fall into disuse, or are suppressed, and the discontinuity is experienced as loss and a denial of self. Thus societies, especially village-based societies, make concerted attempts to construct a sense of continuity. Brian Moeran's study of a Japanese pottery village shows how people there try to construct a sense of continuity by reference to "the past" (*mukashi*), but its content differs from one person to the next:

> For Shigeki now, the past means ten years ago; for his sister-in-law, Isae, it is twenty years; for Haruzo, it is the period after the war . . . for his father now aged ninety-three, it is the second and third decades of this century. Chuzo and Shigeki are in fact talking about completely different concepts of the "community" when they refer to *mukashi*. The word alone is enough to make them think

2. No doubt this partly explains the fashion/nostalgia for "Cultural Revolution days" in China today even among those who experienced it.

they are on common ground. It gives them a shared
identity with which to try to come to terms with the
present and to plan for the future . . . [it] is born out of
recognition of continuity, not of change. (1984:232-3)

People in Laos now use the term *papeni* (customary) in
much the same way, but they also have a melancholy
consciousness of their discontinuous "past."

Revolutions, by definition, are deliberately discontinuous,
and obviously traumatic for groups directly affected by them,
such as old ruling classes. But communist revolutions are
globally traumatic because of their intentions not only to
attempt to carry out political and economic transformations,
but also social and cultural transformations of people's
private lives.

Most modernizing societies experience profound changes
in the organization of time, which is increasingly structured
by industrial rather than rural time. This accounts for the
severe contraction of official holidays under the LPDR whose
"modernizing rationality" excluded many previously
recognized religious holidays and events (Evans 1988:20-21).
This is just one aspect of a general process of secularization
that occurs with the growth of modern states. But it was
accelerated by the new regime in Laos whose rituals were
secularized both at the level of state pomp and ceremony, and
in everyday rituals in offices and schools. As we indicated
earlier with reference to the *baci-sou khouan* ceremony, many
of these started to creep back into everyday practice from the
early 1980s onwards. But despite the grandiose claims now
being made concerning the continuity of Lao "ancient"
(*bohan*) traditions, either through deliberate political
intervention, or through cultural attrition in the context of
economic and social change, many things have either been
lost or considerably modified. And so, what people now
remember as "tradition" differs generationally, although a
surprising number of younger people will tell you that in the
old regime they carried out the "traditions" properly, thereby
conveying an understanding that something has been lost.

To illustrate this process of continuity and discontinuity we will look briefly at the New Year ceremony in Luang Prabang in 1996, trumpeted by *KPL* (18/4/96) as being "most renowned in the country due to its observance of centuries-old tradition." The New Year, not surprisingly, is a rite of renewal preceeded by rites of purification, which includes the well-known dousing of each other with water as a blessing (*hort nam*). At the same time people visit the temples where they pour water over Buddha images, placed in a small *phasat* on the porch of the *sim* for this purpose. These basic practices have continued every year, at least for normal people, since 1975.

For New Year in Luang Prabang there are some problems in deciding exactly what is "traditional" practice. One thing is certain—*traditionally* it revolved around the king, and *traditionally* it went on for almost two weeks, not the three official days now allocated to it on 13, 14 and 15 April. Thus, one of the most important parts of the traditional and current celebration, the parading of the Prabang Buddha from the old palace to Vat May on 16 April, and back again on the eighteenth, actually falls outside the official holiday period. This means that the main public event which falls within the official period is that of the parade of *nang sangkhan*, and other beauties, on 14 and 15 April.

*Traditionally* the rites began on a day fixed by the Lao lunar calendar, and commenced with the royal elephants engaging in a rite of purification of the city, as described by Deydier in 1952: "The rites began. Seven enormous royal elephants arrived at Ban Na Luang, ridden by kha guards dressed in a classical red costume with a yellow border and wearing a curious bonnet which recalled the hats of the mongolian armies, and headed towards the Vat May temple." Here a shaman recited a sacred spell into the ear of the elephants, telling them that "they are the protectors [of the kingdom] and must expel the bad spirits. After the termination of this ritual, the cortege followed the main road, to go to Vat Xieng Thon [Thong] where the rite will be repeated. It will then be repeated again when, after having traveled along the shore of the Nam Khan, these weighty protectors of the kingdom come to Vat Vixoun" (1954:137). Four days later they are joined by the protector spirits of Luang Prabang, Phou Ngeu Nya Ngeu, whose masks are brought to life by a shaman and they too go to Vat Vixoun and dance before the assembled crowds before joining in the purification rites. Following a *baci* in the palace, the king and his retinue would join the rites of purification by spending several days visiting the *vat*s of Vixoun, Xieng Thong, Mai and Sanghalok for the aspersion of the Buddha images there, thus enacting a north-south cosmic journey which symbolically reconstituted the kingdom. A few days later the crown prince traveled by boat to the fabled Pak Ou Caves where he would pay homage to the Buddha images massed there and stayed overnight before returning to the capital. The central ritual of carrying the palladium of the kingdom, the Prabang, down from the palace and in a cortege to Vat May for aspersion is then enacted, followed by the king:

> H.R.H. the King Sisavang Vong appeared up on the grand steps of the palace, dressed in ceremonial sampot, a grand sash of the Million Elephants across his white tunic and sporting the cross of the Legion d'honneur. He was wearing a white hat with a golden point, a vestige of the ceremonial attire worn before the arrival of the French. He was supported by a cane, and walked slowly, his rheumatism making him suffer continuously. He was aided in his descent, and was placed in a palaquin carried by eight kha guards which followed the same itinerary as the statue, and headed towards Vat May for the aspersion of the Pra Bang. At the entrance to the temple he was welcomed by the president of the royal Council, the prime minister, and all the members of the government. All the monks assembled there began to chant and their sacred words broke the silence. (Deydier 1954:157)

During the New Year period the palace also sponsored

performances of the Ramayana. Other rituals recognizable today, such as the building of sand stupas on the opposite side of the river as blessings also took place. The festival that Deydier witnessed in the early 1950s, however, saw an important innovation. "The Crown Prince has decided to make a great artisanal exhibition. All the provinces of Laos will participate and be represented there. . . . It is on the large esplanade of the That Luang pagoda, which normally is a place for sport, that will be the place for this exhibition" (Deydier 1954:136). Thus did the old rituals of Luang Prabang attempt to draw the rest of the country into its orbit now that the monarchy encompassed the whole of Laos.

Changes continued to be added to the New Year ceremonies, and the *nang sangkhan* parade, which is now given such prominence, apparently first began in Luang Prabang in 1968 (it is not mentioned in any of the earlier descriptions).[3] Its rationale is based on the legend of Phanya Kabilaphom, the details of which need not detain us here, but it is one that calls for the parading of this god's head once a year by of one of his seven daughters in order to avoid chaos in the world and to ensure prosperity. "That is why," writes the *Vientiane Times* (5-11/4/96), "*each year* at Pimai, you will see a four-faced head being carried by one pretty girl representing one of Phanya Kabilaphom's daughters sitting with her six other sisters in a decorated chariot" (emphasis added). Apparently the beauty pageant element of the parade was first incorporated into the New Year celebrations in tourist conscious Thailand, and it was the *chao muang* of Luang Prabang in 1968 who brought the changes back there following a visit to Thailand. After 1975 the whole New Year celebration cycle in Luang Prabang was drastically reduced, and according to one informant, the *nang sangkhan* parade disappeared, and was only revived again in 1992 (compared with the *Vientiane Times* claim above that it

3. As far as I can work out a *nang sangkhan* beauty parade began in Vientiane the following year, 1969, but since 1975 it has disappeared completely. The actual history of the integration of *nang sangkhan* into New Year ceremonies, and its earlier non-beauty-pageant form, is also unclear to me. But for an explanation of the beliefs surrounding *nang sangkhan* and some of the earlier practices, see Vo Thu Tinh (1971).

can be seen "each year"), with the content of it being increasingly focused on the beauty pageant—i.e. something intelligible to people who know nothing of the legend (like tourists), and indeed it was only when *nang sangkhan* drove past the viewing stand for dignitaries that the Vietnamese prime minister and his wife came to life and waved. A beauty pageant was something they understood. Unlike the past, when the young women were selected by temples, they are now selected by villages, which according to one informant, was in order to allow minority young women to participate (more on this below).

Reconstructing all the historical transformations that have occurred in the New Year rituals fall outside of my aim here, although it is clear that they were in a slow process of amalgamation and change.[4] What we are mainly interested in is the direction of the change. Purification rites of the city previously conducted by parades of the king's elephants have disappeared, as have rites connected with minorities (see below). But nothing has taken their place. Thus the direction of change is towards simplification and secularization of the ritual process through the highlighting of the beauty pageant element. The suppression of the role of the king in the ritual was the cause of a rapid and dramatic simplification and secularization of the ritual process. As one official at Luang Prabang Tourism said: "Because we don't have a king now the ceremony is much smaller." But one *KPL* journalist watching the parade told me blithely, "it is all the same as before." "But it is without the king," I quipped. "Ah," he replied, "he has been gone so long now they don't remember him." This process of simplification applies equally to the legendary ancestors of Luang Prabang, Phou Ngeu Nya Ngeu, and their adopted child the tiger, Singkheo Singkham, who previously played a much more central and elaborate

---

4. It is clear that in various rites the role of the king was changing, if only because of King Sisavang Vong's enfeeblement. Thus, for example, a retreat he had previously made for seven days during the Festival of the Stupa, was reduced to three days, and then to one, and finally he was represented by a family member. It seems that this change then became the fixed procedure for the ritual. (See Archaimbault 1973:49.)

role in the purification ritual. They are now becoming an exotic adjunct to the *nang sangkhan* parade.[5] Indeed, in February 1997, they became an adjunct of the Fifth National Games when they were held in Luang Prabang, for as the correspondent for the *Vientiane Times* noted, they "usually come out of their trunks only once a year" (12-14/2/97).[6]

The parade of the Prabang from the old palace to Vat May remains one of the central religious activities of the New Year in Luang Prabang. This holy relic, the palladium of the former kingdom, after appropriate rituals by leading members of the sangha, is carried down the steps by museum attendants (not by monks, as described by Deydier 1954:156), and placed in its palanquin, at which point scores of tourists with their cameras converge on the statue to photograph it, while older Luang Prabangese in traditional dress watch the spectacle non-plussed. Just before the descent of the Prabang, the foreign minister, Lengsavad and the *chao khouang* of Luang Prabang line up on the steps of the palace, also dressed in traditional *sampots*. Previously it would have been the king who followed the Prabang to Vat May, and begun its purification. Now a high official in the LPDR fills his shoes.

Over the next few days almost every family in Luang Prabang has as least one person go to pour water over the

5. Readers are strongly recommended to compare the above account with the more detailed one offered by Ing-Britt Trankell, "Royal Relics: Ritual and Social Memory in Luang Prabang," in *Lao Culture and Society*, edited by Grant Evans (to be published in 1999 by Silkworm Books). We carried out our research separately and were intrigued by the discrepancies which emerged in the information and explanations we gathered. While our interpretations of events are substantially similar, we have made no attempt to iron out the individual discrepancies as these themselves are registers of the problems of social memory, and of ethnographic practice.

6. The parade at the games was a full mish-mash of "tradition": "*Nang sangkhan*, the goddess of the year, was also present with her six sisters on an elaborate float. . . . Then came 400 *nang kheo*, those heavenly creatures wearing tiaras and long brocaded *sinh*. Characters from *Phralak Phralam*, the Lao Ramayana, with a horde of young monkeys dressed in purple, under the command of their king, Hanuman, dressed in white and gold. . . . Then came a huge replica of a *Baci* plate accompanied by dignitaries . . . while dancers dressed in *Lao Soung* and *Lao Theung* costumes—400 of each—walked by" (*VT* 12-14/2/97).

Prabang, despite the fact that the official New Year celebrations are over, and on the final night there is a veritable orgy of merit-making. But at the side of the temple a traditional orchestra strains to be heard over taped music, and attempts at traditional singing founder, to the disappointment of one older Luang Prabang man who lamented that older styles of singing rounds between men and women were being lost. The Prabang is then returned to the old palace on 18 April. Just inside the grounds, a new resting place for the Prabang, begun under the old regime, is being built with its main sponsor being the Lao government and business.

Around this time of year in Luang Prabang a story has circulated every year since the disappearance of King Sisavang Vatthana, and one can hear it further afield. The story speculates about whether the Prabang today is real or just a copy. Rumor has it that the communist government removed the real one and placed it in a vault somewhere. I have heard this story many times, and this time in Luang Prabang one person assured me she had heard it from an official in the Ministry of Information and Culture in Luang Prabang, and therefore it had to be correct. Perhaps even more astonishingly, during an interview with me in May 1996, the vice president of the Lao sangha said, yes the Prabang in Luang Prabang is a fake. He claimed that in 1976 Sali Vongkhamsao, then attached to Prime Minister Kaysone's office, went to Luang Prabang with an entourage and brought the Prabang back to Vientiane, the seat of government. This story was obviously formed around the assumptions of traditional cosmology which assumed that now that the communists had taken over they were the heirs

7. For good measure, during this same interview he also claimed that the Emerald Buddha on display in Bangkok is also a fake. The real object is kept in an antechamber to the Thai king's bedroom. To add to such Emerald Buddha stories, in the south of Laos I came across one story which claimed that the real Emerald Buddha is hidden at the old Khmer temple of Vat Phu, the former ritual center of the Champassak royal line. That one can so easily collect such stories on the recent wanderings of major Buddhist palladia points to a profound sense of ambivalence about the loss of royal centers of power in Laos.

of its powers.[7] Of course, I have no way of confirming the rumors one way or another.[8] But what is important about this story from an anthropological point of view is that it suggests that people somehow feel that the ritual since 1975 has become debased and is even "fake," too. The fact that the person telling you the story of the Prabang being a fake will go and pay homage to the Prabang during the New Year ritual confirms this interpretation, showing that the rumor reflects on the ritual as a whole rather than the object itself. It is also a comment on the collapse of the monarchy, on the pressure that Buddhism came under in the early years of the revolution, and perhaps even a comment on the illegitimacy of the Lao government. For possession of the Prabang historically has been an objectification of the legitimacy of the Lao monarchy. The idea of it being a fake therefore withdraws this legitimacy from the communist regime.[9]

8. It is my hunch that the story is wrong. There is a copy of the Prabang on display on the Vat Phra Keo in Vientiane; it is made of wood and painted gold and is not solid gold like the Prabang. One ritual detail which may add credence to this rumor is the fact that the Prabang is carried outside by museum attendants and not monks as previously. I have shown photos of this sequence to some Lao and they have been shocked to see the attendants carrying the Prabang down the palace steps.

9. S. J. Tambiah (1984:241) writes on "the possession of *palladia* and *regalia*, which are enduring sedimentations or objectifications of power and virtue. Possession of them is a guarantee of legitimacy. But these sedimentations of virtue and power will remain with the possessor for as long as he is virtuous and deserving. They cannot be removed from their locations against their consent; and their travels are evidence of their changing hands and their passage from one deserving ruler to another. For us, anthropologists and historians, the travels of a Buddha statue, such as those of the Sinhala Buddha (or the Emerald Buddha Jewel)[or the Prabang] provide us with a chain or 'genealogy' of kingdoms and polities that these statues have legitimated . . ." It is of interest to note that all of the Lao I know who have visited Bangkok have gone to see the Emerald Buddha Jewel in the Thai king's palace. It is a point of fascination partly because they know it was once housed in Vat Phra Keo in Vientiane. Given its fame, and given its association with Laos's much bigger neighbor, some people have expressed surprise that it is so small and appear to wonder, "how can something so small be so powerful?" Some have said it is more beautiful than the Prabang, which I have interpreted as being a statement of the relative powers of the two palladia.

# THE MINORITIES
# IN STATE RITUAL

I T has become commonplace among writers on Laos to mention the attitudes of superiority that many lowland Lao, especially perhaps those in the capital Vientiane, express towards the ethnic minorities which make up around 40 percent of the population. It is also common for writers to draw our attention to the word *kha* often still used during the RLG period to refer to the Austroasiatic and Mon-Khmer groups, and glossed in English as "slave." They are now usually called Lao Theung or Lao Gang—referring to their assumed common location at mid-range in the mountains. Previously, the Hmong in Laos were called *Meo*, a word still used in Thailand, derived from the Chinese *Miao*, and having connotations of "savage" or "barbarian." But now they are more consistently called Hmong in Laos, although they are more often referred to as Lao Soung and grouped with Yao, Goh (Akha) and others—indicating their common location in high mountain ranges. These etymological shifts are elements of the symbolic topography of nationalist politics in Laos. In this respect one could say that despite the gross simplifications of Lao Theung and Lao Soung, the terms at least acknowledge these groups as part of the Lao nation.[1] Use of specific ethnic nomenclature, such as Hmong, Khamu, Yao, Loven, etc. is rare.

1. But keep in mind the rejection of this idea by the Hmong participant in the Internet debate discussed in the opening pages of this book.

It has also often been argued that the Lao communists were more successful at formulating a relatively modern and consistent ideology of Lao nationalism, compared with many of the parties and factions associated with the RLG, because they explicitly, or more consistently, incorporated the minorities into their conception of the Lao nation. The historical coordinates of this were: first, the location of the Pathet Lao in the mountainous areas demanded a more inclusivist policy because they depended on minorities for soldiers and sustenance; second, there was the influence of international communist nationalities policy, mediated by the Vietnamese communists, on the Lao communists. In contrast, and keeping in mind that there were many contradictory political currents within the RLG, at times producing bizarre alliances, we can broadly say that the right wing in Laos was strongly influenced by the nationalism being promoted by the military dictatorships in Thailand at the time, and this ideology gave little or no place to minorities. Indeed, as some analysts of modern Theravada Buddhist societies have suggested, because of their equation of religion and citizenship (e.g. to be a Thai is to be a Buddhist) they can produce an ethnic intolerance and missionizing zeal towards minority groups (Keyes 1971; Tambiah 1976:520). "Generally speaking," writes Halpern (1964:91) "the various royal governments of the post-World War II period have conceived of the tribal problem in traditional, i.e. administrative and charitable, terms rather than attempting to work out a positive ideology or an equal or potentially equal relationship." The broad aim was assimilation. Some Hmong rose to high positions in the RLG, such as Touby Lyfong who was *chao khoueng* of Xieng Khouang in the 1960s, or Colonel Vang Pao in the army, but minority representation in high positions was rare. In this respect the LPDR has done better, though not as well they would like to claim (Ireson and Ireson 1991). Indeed, it would be easy to make an argument that LPDR policy, like RLG policy, is still one of assimilation. One clear outcome of the relocation of the communist movement's headquarters from the mountains to the traditional lowland

142

seats of power is that they have become less dependent on the minorities for support or sustenance, and furthermore, the collapse of communism has weakened even the ideological commitment to Marxist-Leninist minorities policies. The outcome has been the reproduction of a social and political structure which is strikingly similar to that of the former RLG—with one important exception, the absence of the Lao king.

We need to be cognizant of the fact that the rituals belonging to Lao royalty, in contrast to those surrounding the Chakri dynasty in Bangkok, were distinctive because in Laos minorities played an important role in their symbolic world. Thus, we need to doubleback and reexamine, for example, the term *kha* which has for modern writers somehow become an icon representing the RLG and previous Lao states' alleged poor relations with the minorities. As indicated above, the term is often glossed as "slave." This term, however, as anthropologists have come to discover is extremely problematic (Evans 1993:218-20). It can signify situations in which there is an almost complete loss of rights and serious abuse through to situations where individuals or groups are virtually members of the families to whom they are supposedly enslaved. These variations in degrees of liberty are obscured by the term "slave" which is based, in most cases, on historically bound assumptions of individual liberty, democracy, and so on, associated with the modern world. The *sakdina* system (glossed as "feudalism") in Laos prior to the French was one where the king theoretically had absolute rights, and his subjects had discrete and subordinate rights, including the *kha*. Both the Lao peasantry and *kha* were obliged to render to the king and his *chao muang* goods in kind or labor. With the coming of the French, "slavery" was formally abolished, although many of the rights of the king and his *chao muang* vis-à-vis their subjects continued. The French in fact initiated a long and slow transition from a concept of the discrete rights of subjects to the universal rights of citizens, which paralleled the monarchy's transition from real power to symbolic power discussed earlier. Similarly the term *kha* changes in meaning over this time, from indicating the discrete rights of a particular group to the modern connotation of "slave," and this has also entailed a slow and complex refiguration of the symbolic world.

If we survey the key ritual events of the kingdom of Laos we find that the *kha* play a central and visible role, and we can see that through ritual, anterior rights of these *kha* to the land are acknowledged. If we look back to the beginning of this century, to the time when Sisavang Vong was placed on the throne in 1904, we can see a dramatic illustration of the fundamental symbiosis between the kingdom and the *kha*:

> The chief of the Khas Khasak[2] approaches the King of Luang Prabang and, taking him by the hand, . . . conducts him to his golden throne covered by its nine-tiered white umbrella.
>
> Thus are the rites carried out. It is the ancient possessors of the soil themselves who place the *Chao Sivit*, master of their existence, on the throne. Not only do they enthrone the successor of those who invaded their territory, but they must also rid him of all evil. The King takes a bowl of sticky rice similar to that used for warding off *Phi* and throws it over the chief of the Khas who then runs out of the room. He is followed by the other members of the tribe, he runs out of the palace, then out of the town and only stops when he is far away, in the mountains where he will have taken with him all the calamities which have menaced the King. (Raquez 1905:1806)

The next phase of the ceremony takes place in the presence of monks, court dignitaries and officials, and concludes with all the king's subjects coming to pay homage, including finally the *kha*: "Deeply moved by the ceremony, the half-naked natives (les sauvages) who had held themselves at a distance now crept up to the feet of the King;

---

2. The historical name for Khamu in the region of Luang Prabang.

we could see them trembling at being so close to the king, not even daring to take his hand, but the young monarch encouraged them on and helped them to complete the rites" (Raquez 1905:1807). What is so striking about these rites of purification and installation is not only the visibility of the *kha*, but the almost intimate way they participate in the ritual. They are not despised heathens but are loyal, and respected, subjects. I use the term "respected" advisedly, and mean by it that in a context where there is no assumption of universal equality, and where if people act according to their "station in life," then one can have a system of mutual respect and reciprocity even though inequality is intrinsic to the system (see Dumont 1983; Moore 1978).[3]

In an inspired and subtle essay, Goran Aijmer has explored the myths and ceremonies associated with traditional kingship in Laos. He notes how forms of ritual kinship were invoked in the rites and myths to establish a connection between Lao royalty and the *kha:*

> In this ritual situation the Kha seem to operate not as subordinate representatives of a conquered minority group stripped of their rights by an intruding and mighty foe usurping political control; rather they act as masters of the land and representatives of the locality . . . in dealing with divine forces; in doing so they express their ultimate and exclusive rights to land as well as their continuing right to allocate these terrestrial rights to the Luang Prabang king. (Aijmer 1978:741)

At New Year, during boat races, and at other rituals, this relationship was also enacted. Following the dedication ceremonies for the French-sponsored new palace in Luang Prabang early this century, a *kha* had to enter the royal palace first because he was more familiar with the local spirits and was protected against their powers (Halpern 1964:110). These

3. For this theoretical reason I will continue to use the controversial term *kha* in the following discussion in order to stress the very different cultural assumptions underlying these rituals.

rituals primarily involved Austroasiatic groups because it is said that they pre-date the Lao-Tai who came later. Among the Black Tai similar rituals were enacted on a smaller scale, and indeed Black Tai villagers in Houaphan still conduct small village-based rituals which acknowledge the prior rites of the Austroasiatic natives (Evans 1992). Groups like the Hmong only migrated into Laos in the last two hundred years, moving into the unoccupied high mountain ranges and therefore they do not feature in these rituals, although they were gradually encompassed by the administrative apparatus of the Lao state.

The basic structure of these rituals remained intact in both the north and the south of Laos up until the overthrow of the monarchy. For example, during the Lao New Year in Luang Prabang in the early 1950s the *kha* played a central role in the transportation of the Prabang, symbol of the unity of Buddhism and royalty, from the palace to Vat May for the traditional rites of purification. Deydier describes the scene:

> Their prayers over, the monks leave the palace. Two of them carry the golden statue and march down to deposit it on a wooden *prasat* at the foot of the stairs. The *khas* lift up the edicule and carry it on their shoulders. Within the grand avenue of the palace, they are preceded by the *kha* guards who advance slowly while keeping time with the rhythm of the drums. The national army in white tunics and red kepi, sloped arms, escort the porters. The monks follow. Everyone is gathered in the main street. The cortège makes its way towards Vat May. (1954:156)

Once again, however, we must not romanticize these rituals by dehistoricizing them. With the definitive passing of the *sakdina* system following the founding of the constitutional monarchy, many of the rituals surrounding the monarchy were in a process of evolution and change, and this includes those related to the *kha*. In an essay on the Kassak Amphay, Dore (1981:186), for example, reports on the decline of a divinatory ritual which bound the Lao and Kassak: "When we made contact with Kassak culture in 1965, we were struck by the sorrow they expressed through complaints, punctuated by sounds improvised on the *khene*, whose theme was the forgetting of ancient rites and the indifference affected by their younger Lao brothers towards their older brothers, the Kassak. According to the latter, the decay was an ineluctable consequence of the ongoing war." [4]

With abolition of the monarchy the rituals fell into disarray. Without the king the prior rights of the *kha* to the land could not be acknowledged, and without the king they had no obvious part to play in, for example, the New Year rituals.

As we have seen, after 1975 in Luang Prabang the very elaborate traditional New Year rituals contracted drastically. Significantly, this occurred during the term of a Hmong governor who retired in the 1980s, who now tends to be blamed for the excessive rigidity of communist policy in Luang Prabang. The deposed king could play no role in the rituals, and as far as I can ascertain from informants, the *kha* lost their role. Only after 1989 when the government began to open its doors widely to foreign capital and tourism was there an attempt to revive some of the pomp of the traditional New Year rituals. The traditional uniforms of the porters of the Prabang (described by Deydier above) were revived, but it was Lao wearing them, not *kha*. There is in the parade one group dressed in blue farmers' tunics and wearing (untraditional) trilby hats, playing musical instruments of bamboo, who supposedly represent minority participation (simply described as a *kabouan son pao* in the *Pasason* 22/4/96

---

4. It is hard to agree with Halpern's (1964:115) exaggerated claim (for which he provides little evidence) that "political and economic innovations have, however, virtually destroyed the symbiotic substructure" between royalty and the minorities. His main evidence is the fact that at the time the Pathet Lao were most active in provinces with large ethnic minorities, and his judgement is colored by his correct perception of the indifference of the lowland political elite towards minority concerns. This, however, does not bear on the practice nor potential of traditional political symbolism.

account of the parade), but when I talked with them, they were in fact a group of Lao. Members of this group agreed that the Khamu played an important role in the past when there was a king, but now they were in the parade because it requires some "country people." According to an official at Luang Prabang Tourism the new regime no longer privileged one group, like the "*pi nong* of the king of Kassak" (the Khamu), but wanted to present the "solidarity" between the different ethnic groups. Thus in 1996, along with the Lao beauties (mentioned earlier), the parade included for the first time a "beauty" from several ethnic groups—Khamu, Hmong, Black Tai, and Yao. But the latter are marginal to the main beauty contest, the *nang sangkhan*, because the latter involves Buddhist rituals from which they are excluded. For example, when *nang sangkhan* and her "sisters" reached Vat Xieng Thong and entered the temple to be received by the monks there, the young minority beauties simply mounted the steps but did not enter the temple. Therefore, if they ever wish to win the beauty contest they will have to become Lao.

The term *kha* gradually fell into disrepute during the life of the RLG. In the 1950s the communists started popularizing the terms Lao Theung and Lao Soung, thereby trying to emphasize a concept of citizenship of a nation-state rather than the idea of a king with subjects. This notion was also taken up by some people on the RLG side. Indeed, documentary footage from the mid-1950s onwards shows the RLG to have been more sensitive to these issues than assumed. The various minorities are referred to as "part of the Lao family," and a tour of Saravane and Attopeu by the king shows these minorities arrayed under their individual names of Lawae, Alak, etc. The older concept of *kha* acquired pejorative connotations because of its association with a system of institutionalized hierarchy, and after 1975 was systematically replaced by Lao Theung, an equally general category ethnically, but with more neutral social connotations. In the traditional, non-nationalist structure, ethnicity was not the most salient category, as it has become in modern nation-states, especially in communist ones which attempt to construct systematic lists of ethnic categories. While many people in the main cities of Laos remain ignorant of the specific names of the various ethnic groups there is perhaps a greater awareness of ethnic diversity in the LPDR compared with the RLG, and more frequent if somewhat banal treatment of it in its mass media. But Laos now shares this feature, and this problem, with all other societies in the modern world.

The reconceptualization of minorities in Laos conformed to ideas about ethnic categorization first introduced by the colonial state (Anderson 1987), and to ideas concerning the equality of citizens propounded by modern democracies— which, of course, did not mean that these states were necessarily democratic. It was simply a prerequisite for the conceptualization of the modern nation which had "hard edges" rather than the soft ones of traditional states in the region. In the historical narrative of "the nation" produced by the LPRP minorities have been given a place, especially the leaders of minority revolts against the French. Yet there is a tendency to de-emphasize the minority aspect of these revolts and to stress the idea that they were part of some more general "Lao resistance" to colonialism. Similarly, narratives about the "war against the Americans" (i.e. the civil war with the RLG), stress the solidarity between the different ethnic groups in the struggle, but no key minority figures stand out in this narrative like, for example, the early twentieth century Loven leader in the south, Ong Khommadan, or the leader of what anthropologists would call the millenarian Hmong revolt of the 1920s led by Batchai, who loom large in the "struggle against French colonialism." The idea that the minorities may have participated in the armed struggle for their own peculiar reasons is not entertained. Within the optic of national solidarity any minority revolts against the LPDR, such as the one among the Hmong after 1975 (Evans 1983: Chapter 2), which also contained a strong millenarian component, can only be conceived as being caused by outside interference. For a time after 1975 the minorities political profile remained relatively high while government propaganda still dwelled on armed struggle and the need for military preparedness. This, however, has given way to a new emphasis on economic and social development in which the minorities are increasingly conceptualized as "backward" (*la lang*) and problematic compared with the Lao who dominate the modern sector of the economy. Sadly, some minorities in the south who suffered greatly from the war, still treasure the memory of struggle and during their spectacular buffalo sacrifice rituals older men wear their war medals as badges of their warrior spirit. They believe their war participation still has some wider value. But Lao officials watching the occasion laugh and tell them to forget about the war. "That was twenty years ago."[5] The latter are in charge of a massive government program to resettle all the minorities on the plains by the year 2000.[6]

The LPRP, it seems, also has a program for rewriting the history of Laos which overturns the narrative contained in the old royal rituals. At a seminar at Dong Dok College for historians and geographers in April 1996 Sisana Sisane, former minister of culture and former head of the Committee for Social Sciences in Laos, questioned previous inter- pretations of ancient Lao history that suggested that the Lao had migrated into Laos and taken over the territory of the Lao Theung. "This is not true," he said. "The Lao have been here for as long as the Lao Theung." Whatever the actual facts of the case (and they are still far from clear), what this reconceptualization attempts to do is to definitively undermine the older narrative, and by doing so deny the Lao Theung prior rights. If this view is accepted, it produces a new academic problem, namely why the older rituals and

5. For these observations I thank Yves Goudineau.

6. In this respect the *policies* of the RLG and the LPDR are not all that different. The Lao prime minister in 1960, Prince Somsanith, stated that the goal of his government was "to establish the mountain people on the plains so that their standard of living, which up to now has been extremely low, can be raised" (cited by Halpern 1964:91). The main difference in this regard between the two regimes has been the LPDR's determination to carry this out, and its willingness to use force.

myths took the form that they did. More importantly, this shift in perspective elevates the historical position of the Lao vis-à-vis the minorities. Although at this seminar Sisana said it was important for historians to search for Lao Theung ancient "heroes"—"like Khun Bulom is for the Lao," the new interpretation of Lao history will inevitably strengthen the already established bias towards lowland Lao history.[7]

The now defunct rituals which gave prominence to the *kha* and which suggested a profound kinship relationship between them and the Lao have not been replaced by any rituals of equivalent depth. Minorities today in Laos, while legally equal, find themselves in a position similar to minorities in many other Asian countries—they simply provide ethnic flavor for the tourist industry. Furthermore, this works for only some "colorful" minorities like the Hmong. The Khamu, however, who played such a crucial role in the rituals of Luang Prabang do not have this color and therefore they are likely to drop completely out of sight. It must also be said, however, that tourism has created a demand for information about minorities in Laos and an interest in their culture which is rarely evident among the lowland Lao. Minority figures, usually the easily identifiable Hmong, are featured in the state dancing troupe which performs on major state occasions, either posing in revolutionary opera style, or adopting the classical dancing gestures of the Lao. Their presence simply registers difference, while their gestures suggest they have been tamed by the dominant culture. The purely theatrical nature of this is underlined by the fact that these dancers are usually Lao dressed as minorities. This is also obvious in a government-produced picture book which contains photos of Lao women

7. At least Sisana Sisane acknowledges the existence of the Lao Theung. In a series of articles in *Vientiane Mai* by Phongsavat Boupha on the "Lao State" written to "inform Lao who do not know much about their history," he speaks of Tai-Lao migrations into Laos (in this respect he follows the older historical narrative), but fails to mention that there was anyone already in the areas they migrated to. It is as if no one was there. (*VM*, 4/5/95)

standing in front of the Lane Xang Hotel in Vientiane posing as minorities, and now in the That Luang parade young Lao (under instruction from the NLSS) dress up as minorities to add "color" to the proceedings. In 1992 Lao teachers and students from the School of Fine Arts were directed to put on a show of Lao Theung (they dressed as Lavae from the Attopeu) as they may have paraded before the king. Thus a fanciful version of the older ritual was made into tourist theater.

Writing about minorities in China, Dru Gladney (1994) asked himself why in communist states in particular, but in modern states in general, does one always find minorities dressed up dancing (always dancing!), especially on major state occasions. He suggests that one of the functions of this display of ethnic difference is to confirm or reinforce a sense of commonality amongst the culturally dominant group (which is perhaps regionally divided), and indeed to reinforce the dominant culture which stage-manages these occasions. He writes: "the objectified portrayal of minorities as exoticized, and even eroticized, is essential to the construction of the Han Chinese majority, the very formulation of the Chinese 'nation' itself. In other words, the representation of the minorities in such colorful, romanticized fashion has more to do with constructing a majority discourse, than it does with the minorities themselves." (1994:96) In Laos where the relative sway of the dominant ethnic group, the Lao, is comparatively much weaker and therefore the specter of ethnic division more real, the continual displays of ethnic "solidarity" also help to reproduce the solidarity of the dominant Lao—temporarily taking their minds off the vexed question of who the Lao are culturally vis-à-vis the Thai.

# ROTE MEMORIES: SCHOOLS OF THE REVOLUTION

E DUCATION for the masses and the nationalist state have marched hand in hand throughout the modern period. Indeed, compulsory formal schooling has been one of the main mechanisms for constructing a consciousness of the nation, for propagating a national language and for passing on the memory of the nation and its people.

Education is now recognized as a right belonging to all citizens of the "democratic" state, so much so that it is everywhere one of the key indices of "development" and "progress." Pre-modern and colonial states (which are un-democratic by nature) are measured against this index and always found wanting. Post-colonial and revolutionary states have, therefore, always thrown a great deal of effort into expanding education.[1] The motivation, at least initially however, is more political than educational and develop-mental, especially in communist revolutions. Kaysone Phomvihane made this clear when he said: "Education of children and youths must be considered a significant tool of

---

1. A striking exception is the Khmer Rouge in Cambodia. Significantly it was also the Maoist Cultural Revolution which launched a massive assault on education, especially higher education. These reactions, perhaps, are attributable to what Woodside (1991:191) sees as the inherently conservative nature of schools. "As long as the village school has even the vaguest association with the notion of training and choosing talent for a limited number of high status positions, it may be that it will have, in structure and in form, a certain irreducible conservatism."

proletarian dictatorship to build a new generation, new men and the country" (cited in Stuart-Fox 1986:148).

In the past in Laos, and in the neighboring Theravada Buddhist countries, the teaching of much cultural lore and reading and writing took place in the temples and was only available to men. These were literate societies and it is inaccurate, as Tambiah (1968) has noted, to refer to villagers as "illiterate," as those steeped in developmentalist fervor are wont to do. But, he goes on, "there was of course no mass literacy, but a literacy of specialists who were in touch with the higher learning of Buddhism, with gods, with codified curative knowledge, and in more recent times with the government" (Tambiah:1968:120). It is unclear just how many literate people this temple education produced, i.e. people who could read and write Lao, the sacred language *tham*, or classical languages like Pali. By and large, it seems, these skills were only learned by those men who remained in the temples for a considerable period of time or for life, and these people constituted the society's sages and literati.[2] For most people who worked as farmers, literacy was not necessary, nor was it highly valued as a source of social mobility as it was in neighboring Confucian societies, although learned monks were highly respected. Literacy was found among the aristocracy and members of the small state apparatus, and also among urban merchants, although the latter were often Chinese or Vietnamese. A rich oral tradition passed on folkloric history and moral tales, and dance and shadow puppet theater performed during religious festivals, were bearers of cultural memory. This was a perfectly workable and acceptable arrangement within traditional Lao society.

---

2. In his study of a Lao village outside of Udorn, Tambiah (1968:97) provides the following quantitative assessment: "In 1961-2, a sample of 106 households out of a total of 182 families produced the following figures: a little over half the family heads had served as monks, about a third as novices and nearly a fifth as both. We can safely assume that from the point of view of literacy it is the fifth who served as both novice and monk who constituted the pool from which the literates emerged." No similar study of traditional literacy has been done in Laos, but there is little reason to believe that it would be radically different.

The expansion of European colonialism, however, called all such traditional arrangements into question. As the advance guard of an emerging global industrial capitalism (which was only partially democratic at home and where education was still not universal), the colonial state initiated modern education in those countries it conquered, or compelled those that remained unconquered, like Thailand, to take defensive counter-measures and introduce their own reforms. Thus in 1898 King Chulalongkorn, surrounded by a group of foreign-educated modernizing aristocrats like himself, promulgated the first decree on state-sponsored popular education and launched a centralized modern curriculum to be taught to all pupils throughout the kingdom. In 1921 basic state-sponsored education became compulsory for all Thai children, thereby placing the Thai system in the forefront of modern education in Southeast Asia, along with the Philippines.

The French introduced modern education into Laos, and initially their attention fell upon the aristocratic class through whom they would rule. Thus Sisavang Vong was quickly sent off to France to train in the *École Coloniale*, and he was soon followed by Prince Phetsarath, and others. A school already existed in the palace for teaching Lao and Pali to the young princes and princesses. In late 1896, according to the account of Phetsarath (1978:7), the French opened a school catering to young aristocrats with one French and one Lao teacher. For higher education many of them would go on to Saigon or Hanoi, and some finally to Paris. This training of aristocrats in European style modern education followed a path taken some decades earlier in Thailand, except here it was directly under the aegis of the colonial power.

In 1902 one saw the beginnings of public education with the opening of an elementary school in Luang Prabang and another in Vientiane. Then, similar to Thailand at the time, the state from 1907 onwards encouraged a mixed system which attempted to integrate the schools which already existed in the temples into the evolving state system. This integration became official in 1911, and remained so up until the late 1950s. The association of schools physically with temples, and through having monks as teachers has continued up to today, but as Taillard remarks, by the 1970s the relationship had become tenuous: "Not only had the monks lost their teaching function but the school had moved out of the pagoda. In the whole of Laos only 9% of establishments were still situated within the Vat. . . . As for the region of Vientiane this evolution was even more advanced since the percentage did not even reach 4%. The school and the Vat were geographically dissociated" (1974:150).

This is not the place to provide a history of colonial education in Laos (see Clergerie 1954), but needless to say by the mid-1940s it fell far short of the needs of the emerging modern Lao state. As moves were made towards full independence from France, educational development began to accelerate (see Tay 1959; and Mauger 1959), and this continued after independence. "Between school year 1953/54 and 1969/70 enrollment grew by 10 percent a year. In 1969/ 70 there were about 200,000 elementary pupils in Royal Lao Government schools compared with fewer than 35,000 in 1953/54. . . . An additional 25,751 pupils were enrolled in private schools" (Whitaker 1972:76). A 1968 study "concluded that the rate of literacy—defined as the fourth-grade reading level—among men between fourteen and forty-five years old was 50 to 60 percent. The rate among women between fourteen and thirty-five years old was about 25 percent. In the youngest age group surveyed, those from fourteen to twenty-four years old, the literacy rate was 75 percent for men and about 29 percent for women" (Whitaker 1972:77). Higher education was limited to the Upper School of Pedagogy, the Royal School of Medicine, and the Royal Institute of Administration, all of which were brought together as the Sisavang Vong University in the early 1970s. Up until then higher education had relied on overseas teachers and on the French language (partly a product of the fact that few modern textbooks are written in Lao—a problem that continues today), although the RLG had initiated a plan to replace French, and teacher training and secondary texts in Lao were beginning to appear.[3] The curriculum emphasized a nationalism which focused on the king, the Buddhist religion, and the home and community.

Then came the revolution.

All commentators on Lao education remark on the rapid quantitative growth in pupils and schools after 1975 (Chagnon and Rumpf 1982; Ng 1991; ADB 1993), but they all also comment on the dramatic fall in the quality of education.[4] The government was determined to place a primary school in every village, and a rapid expansion in the number of secondary schools occurred as well. This, of course, meant the establishment of many "skeleton schools" (much as there would later be "skeleton cooperatives") in order to fulfill the commands which came from above. Many of these schools were flimsy bamboo structures with a (usually young girl) "teacher" who had had a few years of primary education. Facilities, not surprisingly, were worst in the countryside and in mountain areas among the minorities.[5] This expansion of education was not only limited by the lack of money for capital equipment, such as buildings and books, it was also severely hampered by the lack of qualified

3. While much commentary dwells on the so-called neo-colonial elements of continuing French influence in higher education in particular, few writers remark on the strong influence of Vietnamese educational philosophy and instructors in Pathet Lao zones, or on the fact that all higher education for pupils from the PL zones had to take place in "foreign" Vietnamese institutions of higher learning, and in Vietnamese.

4. The significance of this quantitative growth is partly a statistical illusion after one amalgamates the numbers of children in schools in both zones before 1975, and then takes into account natural population growth. But this is not the place to engage in a critique of the use and abuse of statistics by the government and other commentators on education in the LPDR.

5. Most commentators blithely assume that "the minorities" are illiterate. In fact, among the Yao, Hmong and Goh there is an autonomous religious scriptural tradition derived from Chinese. In Yao villages I have seen recently completed histories of the Yao written using Chinese characters. And I have also observed many Hmong in post offices in the north of Laos who are writing to their relatives overseas in an alphabetic script created for them by missionaries. Just how widespread this literacy is I do not know, but as a form of "traditional" literacy it is significant.

teachers. Indeed, one consequence of the revolution was that Laos "lost up to 90 per cent of its already miniscule educated population as refugees" (Ng 1991:182). One reason why teachers fled, of course, was because they had been one of the main instruments for imparting the values and views of the RLG to the younger generation. Part of the "hidden curriculum" of schools everywhere is the inculcation of the dominant values and views of the society. Therefore, teachers feared that they would be singled out by the new regime for "reeducation."

The new regime's primary concern in its first years was political, and the main purpose of education and the spread of literacy was so that the population could learn the policies and line of the LPRP. Political education became an important part of the curriculum in schools and teachers' colleges, as well as in every other government institution throughout the society. This primarily entailed a form of rote learning of the latest party directive or resolution of the party. The leading cadre at whatever level—the school or the ministry—would read out the resolution to the assembled individuals and responses to questions would entail an attempted word-for-word repetition of the appropriate passage in the state-supplied documents. The main message communicated in such sessions was, of course, obedience and conformity to the wishes and views of the state. The content of such sessions included attacks on the old "neo-colonial" regime, on American imperialism, celebrations of the patriotic struggle for independence, the need to defend the country against "traitors," and the need to build socialism.

Books for primary schools were the first to appear, no doubt because they were the easiest to produce. In these books, of course, no reference was made to the king as one would have found in RLG primary texts (or in Thailand today), nor is there any reference to Buddhism. There are, however, many stories about the war. Stories of "American imperialists" bombing Laos or of victorious battles conducted by PL soldiers, and stories of patriotic soldiers. The violence and aggression presented in these stories was one of the things that upset teachers, and I recall interviewing teachers from Luang Prabang in a refugee camp in Chiang Rai, northern Thailand, in 1979 who complained bitterly about having to teach tiny children about such things. These teachers were also upset about having to teach the "history of the victors" which obliterated all memory of the struggle which took place on the RLG side. All of these books are illustrated, and in one of them (ຄຸນສົມບັດ "Behavior" for level five) one finds an interesting attempt to foreground the stupa for the unknown soldier, leaving the That Luang in the distant background. (In fact in these early illustrations we find few of the familiar icons of Laos). A small group of school children gather around a wreath which they are clearly about to place at the base of the stupa, and the story begins by saying that without the loss of life and blood by "revolutionary martyrs" in the past we would not be able to "study in the new style of school and receive education about the new culture." In these books young people are also encouraged to join the revolutionary youth organization of the NLHS where they can learn to "love the nation, love the Lao People's Revolutionary Party, and love all of the leaders." The importance of these youth organizations to the state had been underlined by Kaysone: "If one is able to attract and control the youths, this means that one is able to control a great strength for realising one's own objectives. Hitler controlled the Nazi youths to carry out his scheme of aggression; and Mao Zedong controlled the Red Guard youths to oppose the revolution. . . . In short, youths have a very significant strategic role to play" (*SWB* 21/12/85). The only reference made in these textbooks to an individual political leader is one reference to Souphanouvong. The reader for level five published in 1984 (ຫັດອ່ານ) reproduces a letter Souphanouvong sent to "the Lao people" on 12 October 1966 on the occasion of "Freedom from the French" Day.

These textbooks also try to teach about the virtues of socialism as against capitalism. In the third grade reader for primary school, for example, we can find a story entitled "Who will be the People Responsible for the Nation in the

Future."[6] These people will "have to be people with a high level of knowledge about politics, be resolute, patient, knowledgeable, and have technical and scientific ability, and understand the new culture. Above all, they must struggle against individualistic thinking, . . . to build new socialist people whose hearts are clean and pure." Other stories feature solidarity work teams and cooperative enterprises, and celebrate the virtues of hard work and of hardworking peasants and workers.

While it was relatively easy to produce simple textbooks for primary schools it was much harder to produce material suitable for secondary education, where expansion in fact had been most rapid. The Asian Development Bank study (1993:18) remarked that "Even though most schools are located in built-up or urban areas, they are poorly equipped with regard to libraries, laboratories, learning materials and school furniture. Overcrowding in many upper secondary schools reflects the low level of infrastructure development as well as the rapid increase in enrollment." It was not until 1984 that a politically acceptable short history of Laos was available for teaching in schools and even then few students ever laid hands on one. It would be read to them by their teachers and they were expected to copy it down word for word. Examinations would later require a word-for-word reproduction of answers from this text. In 1989 a much fuller history appeared, *Lao History from 1893 to the Present*, and this was to be used by teachers and for students at post-secondary level.[7] The last section deals with the building of socialism in Laos since 1975. It is perhaps needless to say that this book is a standard propagandistic text in which the modern history of Laos is rendered simply as a struggle for independence led by the LPRP and its claimed forbears against imperialist aggressors and their local puppets, with the inevitable victory of the former. No other books were available to students. Most

6.    Published as ຫັດອ່ານ "Reading Practice" by the Ministry of Education, Sports and Religion in 1979.

7.    This is the third volume of a 3-volume history of Laos. The other two volumes have not yet appeared.

books from the old regime had been destroyed and foreign books were no longer available.

After the breaking up of the Sisavang Vong University some students could continue with their tertiary education in Laos at Dong Dok Teachers' College or at the Medical University. Those with the right political connections up until 1990 would travel abroad to one of the Eastern bloc countries to study, while a significant number of students continued to go to Vietnam. The results of this seem to have been a mixed blessing in every way. Linguistically, returning students were a socialist bloc analogue of the Tower of Babel, speaking Hungarian, Bulgarian, Polish, German, Russian, Czech, Vietnamese and other languages. A friend of mine who had been a Columbo Plan student in Australia and returned to work in a state mining company after 1975 spoke in a typically lighthearted Lao way about how he and others would sit around a table pouring over dictionaries trying to find a common technical language given that each had trained in a different country. But it was chaos. With the departure of the French, Americans and others from the institutes of higher learning in Laos, professors from the socialist bloc were imported to deliver their lectures in whatever language they spoke and these would be translated (often imperfectly) into Lao. In secret some people began to think wistfully of RLG times when Lao had to wrestle with only French or English, both of which at least gave access to a wider world.

While most were sent abroad for technical training, others studied Marxism-Leninism. Yet, for those sent to Eastern Europe, they were learning it in societies which were increasingly not only cynical about the claims of the ruling communist parties, but openly hostile. This was less true for students who went to Vietnam. Few returned, as it was hoped they would, singing praises of the socialist system. If anything it imbued them with the spirit of reform, and when socialism collapsed in the countries which had trained them they added their voices to the calls for faster reform in Laos. While travel abroad for these young Lao was something of an adventure, in retrospect many now feel as though they wasted their time learning a language (like Czech or Bulgarian) which is useless to them now, and learning many skills which are obsolete, compared with students who can travel to Australia, France or Thailand in the 1990s. Among educated Lao in their thirties one finds a pool of cynicism about the claims of socialism.

This too has made it increasingly imperative for the LPDR to clothe itself in a retraditionalized nationalism. Thus the collapse of communism in Europe has also seen a rapid reorientation within Lao education and a reassessment of its achievements to date. For a start, the achievements of the new regime were shown to be much less than the initial rosy statements of its first years. The first issue of a new magazine *The New Education* (ສຶກສາໃໝ່) writes about how teacher training at all levels remains low, and the magazine reports that 38 percent of primary teachers have had no training, while retention rates at the primary level are also low: "on average throughout the country, of the students who enter the first grade only 27% reach the fifth grade, in places which are richer such as in the Vientiane municipality, students who entered first grade in 1987-88 numbered 23,664 of whom only 11,223 reached fifth grade in 1991-92, that is 47%." It goes on: "the number of people who cannot read nor write has grown, and according to surveys around 40% of people between 15 and 40 years are illiterate." If we compare this with the figures for literacy in the RLG given earlier then there has been little improvement in literacy in twenty years! Perhaps awareness of this dismal performance led one writer to claim that 95 percent of people in the old regime were illiterate (*The New Education*, 3/96:18). In the early 1980s LPDR officials, it seems, were prepared to concede literacy rates under the old regime of approximately 40 percent (see Chagnon and Rumpf 1982:168), and placed against the exaggerated claims of the new regime that it had, by 1984, completely wiped out illiteracy in Laos, 40 percent did not look so good.

Another article in *The New Education* (3/96) entitled, "What rights does the new constitution give to the Lao population concerning education?" shadow-boxes with often unstated complaints concerning how the new regime is little different from the old regime in the field of education. The writer says some people "say. . . during the time of 'the Lao Kingdom' we also had a constitution which had sections which spoke about education" (3/96:18), and he sets out to show that even though the LPDR did not have a constitution for fifteen years it still was much better in the field of education than the RLG. What is of interest about this article, of course, is that a writer in 1996 feels he has to defend the educational achievements of the new regime against the memory of education under the old regime. And, indeed, I have had it said to me privately many times that "the quality of people educated under the old regime is much higher than now."

The collapse of communism in Europe triggered off a crisis of higher education in Laos because it was no longer possible to send students on to higher education there. This was a crisis that affected the Lao elite especially, and it responded through the party by reforming education in such a way that it became easier for students to attend universities and colleges in Australia, Thailand, and other capitalist countries. But this in itself highlighted the low standard of Lao high school graduates, leading in the early 1990s to the state allowing the setting up of private schools in Laos, which have quickly become stratified according to the cost of education, with the new elite and those with wealth being able to send their children to the best schools. This is a source of considerable discontent in the main cities where these schools can be found, and indeed *The New Education* article cited above also feels the need to rebut those who say "education is only for those people who have money" (3/96:20), and here too he is shadow-boxing not very convincingly with the implicit question: "how is this different from the old regime?"[8]

---

8. In mid-1997 the three private high schools in Vientiane were closed, allegedly because of their low teaching quality and failure to follow the curriculum. This, however, simply caused overcrowding in the state high schools. Private schools remain open at the primary and junior high school level. Private tutoring will no doubt absorb some of the stresses and strains in the system.

Reform of the curriculum has accompanied these changes with a reorientation of language training towards English and French rather than Russian, and a rewriting of all textbooks. The large *History of Laos Since 1893* is being revised to tone down the more strident rhetoric about "American imperialism and its puppets," as well as toning down the rhetoric about socialism. Since 1994 new primary school texts have begun to appear and these exhibit important shifts in presentation and in subject matter. If, for example, we take the third grade reader (issued in 1996) and compare it with the 1979 reader referred to earlier, the most striking difference is that there is not a single story about the so-called "American War" (and this is true too of all the other new readers which have appeared). There is one story, however, about "The Hero Si Thong" who has been captured and tortured with electric prods by "foreign imperialists"—who remain unnamed, but are obviously French—because after his escape Si Thong is given a medal on Army Day in 1956 (though no doubt this dating would mean little to primary school students). Nor are there any stories relating to the building of "socialist man." There is one dealing with National Day which celebrates the creation of the "democratic regime" (no mention of socialism), but there are no other stories with obvious political content.

A further contrast is the presence of Buddhism in a story on Boun Pavet illustrated by a drawing of Phanya Pavet and his wife and two children. The story is a simple description of the preparation of the *boun* (festival), and then of the reading of the story of *Phanya* Pavet by the monks to the congregation the next day. Another story, "Village Birthplace," also suggests the centrality of Buddhism with its illustration of a *vat* in the central place of this obviously lowland Lao village. This is explicit in a story in the second grade reader published in 1995 in a story "My Village Temple" where the temple is not only described as central to the village but as a "holy place" where Buddhism has been practiced for a long time. The new fifth grade reader produced in 1994 has a story on *Boun* That Luang which provides a rather populist rendering of the building of the stupa: "It was King

Saysetthatirath who led the people of Vientiane in the building of it in 1566," and That Luang, which historically had the meaning "royal stupa," in the story is rendered as "big stupa." The story is largely a description of the *boun* which it explains simply is the "festival for paying hommage to the Pha That Louang." This reader also contains a story about sending young volunteers off to the army and features a description and illustration of a *baci*. In fact the illustration is the same as one which appeared in the 1984 reader, but the early story is headed "Going to be People's Revolutionary Soldiers," while the latest version simply talks of them as voluntary soldiers. The later story also provides much more information on the details of the ritual, compared with the more overt political message of the earlier story.

There are also two political stories, one simply called "Government" which is a general description of how all countries must have governments whose task is to protect and build the country, without specifying what kind of government, and one called "The Lao People's Army" which speaks of its founding in 1949, and very briefly of its role in the "national revolutionary struggle," but with an emphasis on its peacetime role of "serving the people." Finally we can contrast a story on "The Monument to the Unknown Soldier" in the 1995 grade two reader with the story from the 1970s book *Behavior* for grade five. In the latter the sacrifices of the soldiers in the war are an inspiration for youth to build the country and the revolution. In the 1995 reader there is none of this activist emphasis, and indeed celebrations at the stupa are marked as something the leaders do on special days. Otherwise, it is explicitly assimilated to traditional architecture: "The appearance of the monument is very like the *that*s we normally see around us, but the one thing that sets it off from other stupas is that it has a star stuck on its tip."

There are also important continuities between the early readers and the later ones. The early ones emphasize the importance of respecting elders and teachers, of being a well behaved family member and a good citizen, and they contain stories on sanitation and health, and stories which feature animals are used to convey moral tales about helping other people, and so on. Similar stories are contained in the new readers, and are expanded at the expense of political and war stories. In this respect the new Lao readers are similar to readers that can be found in Thailand, Indonesia or many other developing countries. Stories of obedience to superiors, patriotism, cleanliness and so on, are not so different from the readers I had in primary school in Australia in the 1950s. What is so striking is the disappearance from their pages of themes which previously legitimized the revolution and the formation of the LPDR.

In September 1996 a new curriculum which had been worked on for several years came into operation throughout Lao education. "The Ministry of Education introduced the new education system," explained the deputy director of the General Education Department, "because the situation in the world has changed, for instance, in terms of technology and science, which have developed rapidly" (*VT* 30/8/96). This new curriculum not only relied on new textbooks, but it also discouraged rote learning. Then on 5 November 1996 the National University of Laos was inaugurated in recognition of the country's need to improve higher education, although the standard of education and facilities there remain very low, and research almost non-existent.[9] Of course, there was no

---

9. In the mid-1980s a Committee for Social Sciences was established in Vientiane, housed in the old USAID compound in Nahaidyao. Its director was Sisana Sisane who held the rank of minister, and who initially was given considerable leeway (freedom to issue research visas, for instance). The committee was modeled on its Hanoi counterpart and was designed to coordinate research on Laos. It contained Institutes of Ethnography, History, Literature, and Geography. Very few people in the committee had higher degrees, and those that did had obtained them in the Eastern bloc. Some RLG-trained intellectuals who had gone through "reeducation" were employed as ordinary researchers. Library resources and training were poor, and during its existence the committee produced little of substance. Foreign researchers, with Lao counterparts, began research in areas of the country previously closed off, but this freedom was soon restricted due to political paranoia. From 1991 until its dissolution in 1993 the committee drifted aimlessly, and the dead hand of political censorship quickly

mention that there was a previous national university, the Sisavang Vong University.

Regardless of all the weaknesses of education in the LPDR it has been through the school system that the majority of young people alive in Laos today have first come in contact with the state, and it has been through the school that they have first participated in the national rituals constructed and propagated by the new regime. For the majority of them school has probably been the place where they first saluted the flag and sang the national anthem, and if they saw pictures of their rulers it was probably in their classrooms at school. However imperfectly, it was at school that they became familar with the iconic map representation of the Lao nation and first learned something about Lao history— although there are few young people that I have questioned who remember very much about these lessons at all. All they are left with is general impressions, but these are enough for them to clearly identify themselves as Lao. In general, they learn little or nothing about the old regime, and only have a vague and general knowledge of the kings of the past. Any knowledge they may have comes from what parents have told them rather than from the schools. For most of them, the current regime is all they know and so far it does not seem to inspire any great faith or allegiance, despite attempts to promote the cult of Kaysone. In one sense, the failure of the new regime to build a robust education system has meant that many Lao remain politically agnostic, but at the cost of considerable political, social and cultural amnesia.

---

dampened the early enthusiasm of the Lao researchers. Sponsored by Kaysone, the committee dissolved not long after his death. At the party which celebrated its end Sisana said that the decision to redistribute the researchers back into institutes under the various ministries was a "wise one." For a very brief moment, therefore, Vientiane felt like it had an intellectual center. It remains to be seen whether the new university will generate such an atmosphere.

# MANDALA MEMORIES

THE state-sponsored "revival of tradition" in Laos today by a post-socialist government in search of legitimacy raises important theoretical questions concerning the nature of change and continuity in Lao culture. It also joins up with more wide-ranging debates about the nature of modernization and cultural change in Southeast Asia. In particular I have in mind those areas whose traditional political cultures bear a family resemblance—Java, Bali, Sulawesi, Cambodia, Laos, Thailand and Burma. This family resemblance is based on what Tambiah called "galactic polities" and the general principles and characteristics associated with such polities (see also Jumsai 1989). These are sacred centers of power with charismatic kings whose legitimation in the mainland states was intimately bound up with Theravada Buddhism, and surrounding these centers were satellite centers of power modeled on the same principles. They all provide an interesting comparative framework for the study of change.

Anthropologists studying these societies have usually been inclined to see profound cultural continuities in them despite colonialism and modernization. Tambiah (1976:525) argues: "Thailand is a conspicuous example of the persistence of traditional features—of historical continuities that modify modernisation—and also of transformations based on tradition." He does, however, "concede that European colonisation of Sri Lanka and Burma has radically affected and perhaps introduced irreversible changes regarding the twin axes of traditional kingship and monastic organization . . ." (ibid) Strangely, he does not consider either Cambodia or Laos where these twin axes of the "galactic polity" remained largely intact during the period of French colonialism, and for almost twenty years after independence. In other words they would also seem to broadly fit the Thai model up until the republican coup in 1970 in Cambodia and the 1975 communist revolution in Laos.

For Tambiah, "continuity in the pivotal institution of kingship in Thailand," despite the 1932 revolution, is fundamental:

> The end result today is that the king does in a real way symbolize the dharma of politics, and with Buddhism the collective identity of the Thai people, while at the same time, and perhaps precisely because of, being removed from the actual arena and practitioners of politics. To reign but not to rule, to enjoy the charisma of legitimating the actual rulers and therefore of also mediating when the times are out of joint—all this connotes a return to some deep-seated aspects of the heritage, in spite of recognized changes. (1976:527)

In acknowledging this we should not forget that for approximately twenty years (roughly 1935-1955) the Thai monarchy was extremely fragile, and as Christine Gray (1991) has argued, the real ascendancy of the monarchy began with Sarit Thanarat "latching onto" its prestige and symbolic power for the purposes of national development. But once ascendant, the autonomy of the monarchy has grown powerfully.

As we have seen, a great deal of popular religious *ideology* based on Buddhism, and a great deal of ritual practice in Laos today, presumes a "galactic polity" with a king at the center. It was proposed earlier in relation to the monarchy under the French, and then after 1947, that ideology does not require that real power be exercised by the king. Instead, he acts like a high priest at national and religious rituals. This too, in essence, is the role of the king in Thailand. I have already suggested how the ritual structure of Lao society spontaneously strains towards the realization of this role. Indeed, in Cambodia, where the monarchy was overthrown, the cultural logic of the new Cambodia after the UN elections there (leaving aside the political complexities) was to reinstall King Sihanouk (Osborne 1994).[1] In Burma, where the monarchy was destroyed by British colonialism, the cultural and political system continually oscillates around the role of Buddhism and the accompanying idea of a righteous king. One need only recall U Nu's Buddhist socialism of the early 1960s in which he only just stopped short of declaring himself the new king and defender of the faith. After his overthrow by a military coup there was a swing towards a secular regime, but the current SLORC regime, desperate for legitimacy, has now swung back and presents itself as the major patron of Buddhism.

Thus the return to "tradition" in Laos by the LPRP is not without its problems because the whole structure of "Lao tradition," its rituals in particular, revolve around certain principles which are continually pointing in the direction of a monarch who is no longer there and who cannot be

1.   President Nouhak of Laos, on 25 November 1993 congratulated Sihanouk on his accession to the throne. In an essay penned in the early 1980s Serge Thion (1993:135) wrote: "The Khmers dream of the advent of a dharmaraja, maybe without the name, but a just and righteous ruler, a messianic figure they call nak mien bon, a source of harmony, a fountain of merit. The only candidate for such a wishful dream would be a king. This is not a matter of any particular person; nobody is looking for another politician. On that level they are all bankrupt. But let us for one moment entertain a sociological dream, and picture the royal palace with a great festival going on for the crowning of a young descendant of Ang Duong, the royal barges on the river, the monks chanting, the villages rejoicing, the dawn of a new era. . ." While Thion at that time may have vaguely entertained the idea of Sihanouk's return to the throne, there is no way he (or anyone else!) could have imagined that in 1996 we would see former communist head of state Heng Samrin being carried in a palaquin dressed in full royal regalia to carry out the first ploughing ceremony on behalf of the king who was out of the country at the time. This is the return of a repressed royalty with a vengeance!

mentioned. Overthrow of the *sakdina* system has been the central *raison d'etre* of the regime up to now, therefore any suggestion of a royal revival would naturally pose the question: "Why the revolution?"[2] For this reason all questions relating to the monarchy remain extremely sensitive. When asked about the fate of the old king by a BBC journalist at a press conference during the regime's twentieth anniversary, the foreign minister, Somsavath Lengsavad, was visibly unnerved and angry.[3] The government, however, attempts to fill this absence by stepping into the kings shoes—structurally that is—on ritual occasions, such as with the foreign minister himself when the Prabang was brought out of the palace during the New Year celebrations in 1996. That the structure is there in people's minds was demonstrated again and again by my enquiries concerning whether Kaysone Phomvihane had ever attended the That Luang festival. In fact there is no

2.   It should be said that resistance to a revival would also be based on the fact that the revolution has been a source of rapid upward social mobility for many of its cadres, and has given them a solid material interest in the regime's maintenance. Besides leading cadres being given houses by the state, others have expropriated the houses and land of old elite members who fled, and in 1996 land-titling exercises carried out in Vientiane (financed by AusAID and the World Bank!), these properties were simply transferred from the old elite to the new one. This exercise, I believe, marks the definitive demise of the revolution in Laos. What we see now in the LPDR is the undisguised use of political power to transfer resources from one elite clique to another. That the final outcome of more than thirty years of civil war and revolution is a grubby "land-grab" is part of the hidden tragedy of modern Laos.

3.   One could interpret this anger as a continuing sign of guilt among the leaders of the new regime. As Walzer has argued in *Regicide and Revolution* (1974:1), subjects of the king believed in his sacredness and inviolability: "The murderers of kings presumably do not share these feelings and beliefs, though we may doubt that they escape them entirely." Walzer argues that the intense debate about whether to execute the king or not after the French Revolution finally came down on the side of public execution because, "Public regicide is an absolutely decisive way of breaking with the myths of the old regime, and it is for this reason, the founding act of the new" (1974:5). This decisive public act of symbolic disenchantment never occurred in Laos, hence the older symbolism remained potent, and this is reflected in the guilty secretiveness with which the new regime has surrounded information about the fate of the old king.

evidence from reportage that he ever did, and furthermore, his long time close friend and biographer, Sisana Sisane, confirmed that he never went. He would celebrate the occasion with rituals at home. Yet person after person, in the government and out of it, including one long-time foreign resident, were sure he had gone to the celebrations, or that they had seen him there. (On closer questioning, however, they were always less sure). The point is, as the most powerful man in Laos while he was alive, Kaysone was expected to be there—just like the king was expected to be before 1975. This cultural structure which now evokes both a sense of absence and of presence also combines with an awareness that such rituals do not have the same grandeur as before. Yet, it is also a structural space able to be filled by Thai royalty from a distance, at least in the imagination.

Having deserted communism and having failed to create potent rituals or symbolic centers of their own, the LPRP leaders have spontaneously gravitated towards older sacred centers of the cultural order. In doing this they have been responding to a deeper cultural program, and in this regard it is important to understand that these leaders (or the majority of them) were brought up to be culturally Lao, imbibing Buddhist ideas from their infancy, and learning to act and speak like Lao. Indeed, with the reforms one cannot help but feel that everyone is more comfortable, and as I remarked when discussing *baci*s for visiting royals, the new Lao elite responded smoothly and joyfully to the protocol. In all this one senses a growing congruence between power and legitimacy. Geertz has argued for "the inherent sacredness of central authority" (1985:33), no matter whether that authority is a king or a party president. He argues that sacred centers "are essentially concentrated loci of serious acts; they consist in the point or points in a society where its leading ideas come together with its leading institutions to create an arena in which the events that most vitally affect its member's lives take place. It is involvement . . . with such arenas and with the momentous events that occur in them that confers charisma. It is a sign, not of popular appeal or inventive craziness, but of being near the heart of things" (1985:14). No doubt this "inherent sacredness" of power partly helps explain the formation of political cults with semi-divine leaders. But the "sacredness" of secular leaders is always fragile as their "majesty" is so clearly made and not born or inherent in the order of things.[4] And no doubt the fact that a cult of Kaysone has been fabricated at a time when he is no longer near the heart of things has helped ensure that the cult is stillborn. But a further problem for Kaysone and for the communist state he led, was that there was a permanent hiatus between the leading ideas of the culture and the leading institutions of the new regime, which ensured that no coherent and potent "loci of serious acts" emerged.

In this light Ernest Gellner has put forward an interesting proposition which argues that while the rationalistic discourse

4. In the light of all the scandals surrounding the British monarchy one may like to dispute this. However, it seems to me that there has been an important symbolic transformation in what the "British royal family" are supposed to symbolize. In an environment which culturally idealizes monogamous nuclear families, the "royal family" should be the ideal family, and princes should not "whore around" like the princes of old. Mere mortals, of course, cannot live up to such expectations, and the extreme media surveillance they are subjected to ensures de-mystification. Interestingly, a number of old upper-class female informants in Laos made a point of remarking on the fact that King Sisavang Vatthana only had one wife, in contrast with the many concubines of his father, and this suggests that in Laos new values were being attached to a modern constitutional king compared with a traditional king. The Thai monarchy has guarded itself from unwanted scrutiny by the law on lese-majeste, but according to Streckfuss: "The dynamics of this law do more damage to the monarchy than its critics could ever hope" (1995:453). Another basic problem is that rules of succession have become more formalized in the modern period, in favor of male primogeniture. Which raises the obvious problem of, what do you do with an unsuitable rightful male successor to the throne? The fact that the two longest reigning monarchs in England in the modern period have been women would suggest that they are on their way to solving this problem by institutionalizing a kind of bilateral system. In Thailand the shift has begun with the appointment of Prathep as Regent in 1987. The ability of the Thai monarchy as an institution to draw on the cultural practice of bilateral kinship in the culture at large and to enhance it at the expense of ideas of male dominance in the public sphere and ideas of male potency remains to be seen.

introduced by the Enlightenment is essential for modern scientific knowledge, it does not provide a basis for rational utopias, as failed Marxist experiments demonstrate. Modern societies need ritual elaborations as much as they need science, and perhaps constitutional monarchies are well equipped to perform the role. It is, he writes:

> a system which retains the ritual symbolism of genuine monarchy, whilst transferring most of the real business of running society to a more technical, secular and unsacralized sphere. On the assumption that ritual theater is needed, but that the "new science" either cannot produce it, or will only produce a disastrous version, the ritual and the real spheres of social life become separated. Ritual now mirrors, not the real situation, but the past or a fictitious distribution of social power. The separation of powers is extended to the institutionalization of the distinction between symbolism and decision-making. Ritual reflects not social reality but social phantasy, but contributes to social stability by not endowing temporary and technical centers of power with any sacred aura, and not imperilling them by linking their legitimacy to doctrines which may be proved false tomorrow. This disconnectedness seems to work rather well. (Gellner 1992:91)

Theravada Buddhist societies would appear to be cultural-ly well equipped to realize this form of state.[5] Indeed, the

5. Coming from an Australian in whose country the prospect of a republic in the near future is real, this endorsement of constitutional monarchy must seem strange. But the monarchy there now only signifies the colonial past and therefore points to the deepest running sore in the Australian national consciousness, the dominant, European-derived society's fraught relationship with the aborginal population. A secular Australian republic will need to search for some transcendent discourse of legitimacy, and it is my guess that an important part of it will come to focus on "nature," "the land," "ecology" and so on. Thus some of the received mythologies of white settlement of the land may be able to be combined with the aboriginal "Dreamtime" and the latter society's historical depth in

174

purely ritual function of the Thai constitutional monarchy, and I have argued above that this ritual aspect became progressively dominant in the Lao monarchy under the French and culminated in the constitutional monarchy in 1947, perhaps can lead us to new thoughts on Geertz's notion of the "theater state" where he argues that the main role of the king, his court and the state in traditional Southeast Asia was to act out, or "to image" the cosmology of the society. Tambiah (1985) and others have criticized Geertz for overstating the court's detachment from the mundane world of "practical" economics and politics associated with lower orders. While this criticism may be true for traditional polities, the idea of the "theater state" seems to fit rather well with constitutional monarchies whose kings' main functions are to "image" the ideas associated with the "galactic polity" through their role as "high priests" in religious and national rituals.[6] This is not to underestimate by any means the power of newly invented modern nationalist symbols in places like Thailand. From the beginning these have been yoked to the monarchy and they have evolved together, so much so that the signifiers and signifieds in the domains of nation-monarchy-religion continually collapse into one another thereby creating a highly potent symbolic order.

A main difference between Laos and its neighbors Thailand and Cambodia, and to a lesser extent Burma, is the ethnic composition of Laos and the fact that a large number of its people lie outside the lowland Buddhist-centered cultural universe. At first glance this would seem to suggest the limited social and cultural efficacy of symbols associated with

---

such a way that a convincing national mythology can be created. Obviously, constitutional monarchies are not a panacea. They are simply one possible political form in places where they are culturally plausible.

6. Juliane Schober has recently argued that the "galactic polity" cultural paradigm is under serious threat from reformist Buddhism in Thailand. However, she still concludes that "it is also unlikely that these new, alternative Buddhist communities will establish the totalizing, exclusivist hegemonic orders they advocate in other than locally circumscribed contexts" (1995:325).

kingship.[7] Yet, as I have already shown, traditional kingship in Laos had elaborated a profound ritual relationship with the surrounding minorities, and as I suggested, this was one aspect which distinguished the Lao monarchy from the Chakri kings in Bangkok. But recent research in Thailand has suggested that there may, neverthless, be important symbolic congruities between "galactic" polities and the upland societies. Thus Deborah Tooker's research on the Akha argues that because upland and lowland systems have historically interacted over a long time they have, therefore, developed "similarities in the *symbolics* of power" (Tooker 1996:342). She sees in Akha practices similar ideas of potency radiating out from a sacred center, of spatial coding of hierarchy, and ideas of the purity of a ruler at the center of this space.[8] Otome Hutheesing has provided a similar view as a result of her observations of Lisu syncretism. "The merger of different religious traditions may also be viewed as a correspondence of similar basic structural ideas between Buddhist theology and village symbolic expressions; similarity is thus detected

7. One may want to argue that the importance of minority support for the Pathet Lao is an indication of their disaffection from the institution of kingship. This, however, is difficult to substantiate given the Pathet Lao's propagandistic support for the monarchy right up until they seized power. Indeed, their abolition of the monarchy took many people by surprise and prompted Phoumi's explanation about the fate of the king in late December 1975. Nevertheless, the long war years restricted travel by the king within the country stopping him from acting like a king who, as Geertz (1985:16) puts it, "journey[s] around the countryside, making appearances, attending fetes, conferring honors, exchanging gifts, or deifying rivals, [to] mark it, like some wolf or tiger spreading his scent through his territory, as almost physically part of them." The Lao king, of course, did this where he could. Pathet Lao areas were off-limits and thus royal influence in them was weak, but this does not add up to opposition, just absence and indifference. Among the Pathet Lao leadership, however, republican sentiment was strong and for some of them it went back to their Issara days. For others it sprang directly from their Marxist-Leninist beliefs. Overall, however, republican sentiment in Laos was weak.

8. Tooker also wishes to contest the degree to which the Akha are "encompassed" by the dominant lowland systems and points to how the Akha also use their symbols to challenge dominant meanings. This, however, is of less interest to us here.

despite different levels of communication competencies" (1990:135). Thus the symbolics of power between these upland systems and the lowland are coherent and translatable. It is of interest, therefore, that in the development of modern kingship in Thailand the current Thai monarch should begin to act as the patron of the "hilltribes" in the north, in particular through his much publicized Royal Project begun in 1970. Nicholas Tapp (1989:74) in his book on the Hmong of northern Thailand says they "respect the Thai King, and reserve their disapprobation in general for his officials and bureaucrats." Furthermore, among the Hmong there "is a strong tendency to envy the Thai for being powerful enough to have a king" (1989:75), which reminds one of the millennial rebellions in Laos by Hmong expressing a desire for their own king. The king in Thailand would seem, therefore, to represent a transcendent source of power and a personalized court of appeal for minorities in their encounters and confrontations with the ethnically Thai–dominated state. This transcendence would appear to arise out of the ability of a constitutional monarch to "image" an older world where kings ruled over subjects and were indifferent to ethnicity, while at the same time also being able to symbolize the modern democratic state's openess to popular influence.

Although Hmong, for example, have some representation in the Lao state, this has not stopped them from feeling alienated from sources of power within the ethnically Lao–dominated state, and from reacting against it. Again, one can only wonder whether a Lao king could have performed a similar role vis-à-vis the minorities as the Thai king. A report on an April 1960 visit of the Lao king and queen to Luang Nam Tha where they "appeared before an immense crowd of mountain peoples who knelt down to greet their sovereign, proving by this gesture that, in spite of the differences in language and customs, they were faithful to the nation and devoted to his Majesty" (cited by Halpern 1964:91), gives us a glimpse of a cultural possibility contained in modern kingship, such as we can see with the Thai, but which was subsequently foregone in Laos.[9] The LPDR now gives considerable publicity to events such as the Hmong New Year, and ensures that photos of leading government officials in attendance at Hmong celebrations are carried on TV and in the press. But these staged and visibly awkward ritual occasions seem to only highlight the cultural differences between the Hmong and the dominant Lao rather than ritually encompassing them. It is perhaps a sobering thought that it has only been in modern nation states, especially communist ones replete with statutes on ethnic equality, that we find "ethnic zoos" such as "minority parks" and staged occasions which mark ethnic difference. By contrast the old rituals in Luang Prabang discussed earlier were not marked ethnically, and they dramatized the encompassment of all within the kingdom. The current Lao government has found no satisfactory ritual substitutes.

Trying to grasp the full cultural and social implications of the destruction of the monarchy by the Lao communists is not easy. That it has been a dramatic instance of cultural discontinuity is indisputable. That its loss has culturally enfeebled the country is certainly arguable. Thus one might suggest that with their reversion to a manifestly incomplete "tradition," the Lao will have greater difficulty differentiating themselves from the Thai. This problem was not as stark while the LPDR remained communist because then a line was drawn sharply in political terms on both sides of the border, and to some extent Vientiane's strong alliance with Hanoi suggested a shift in cultural orientation away from Thailand. The "bamboo curtain," however, has lifted and now the cultural boundary between the two countries has blurred.

"Leach," writes Ohnuki-Tierney (1990:13), "has repeatedly reminded his colleagues that they cannot think of a culture in

9. Dommen (1971:297) reports on a visit of King Sisavang Vatthana to Long Cheng to see Hmong troops where he "moved at ease among his tribal subjects . . ." One informant who accompanied Souphanouvong on a visit to the Loven minority on the Boloven Plateau in the south after 1975, told me about how these people flocked to see him. One wonders whether they were responding to his royal charisma which elevated him above the Lao officials with whom they normally have difficult relations.

the same sense as they think of a society, which is a bounded political unit. Culture, in contrast to society, is never bounded." In the Thai-Lao case this is most apparent with reference to Buddhism, whose sacred topography as defined by pilgrims does not conform to political topography (Keyes 1975). The opening of the Thai-Lao border once again to Buddhist pilgrims has revived the cultural bonds between the two countries. Lao make pilgrimages to Wat Doi Suthep in Chiang Mai or to the Emerald Buddha in Bangkok, and they once again participate in the long-established rituals of Lao Buddhism associated with Phra That Phanom in the Thai northeast. Meanwhile Thai make pilgrimages to That Inghang, or That Luang, or to the former royal temples of Luang Prabang. In the modern world it has been kings as "high priests" who have symbolically mediated between the sacred topography of Buddhism and the political topography charted by the state. In this way modern monarchs have served to anchor their subjects allegiance to the nation-state despite cultural blurring. The disappearance of the Lao monarch, however, has also led to a blurring of the symbolism of the Thai monarchy in Laos. Hence all over Laos we find images of Thai royalty where once we would have found images of Lao royalty, and it suggests that at least in some respects the Lao have been drawn into the orbit of the Thai realm.

Modern nationalist states like to imagine that culture is bounded and they attempt in various ways to symbolize this, as we have seen throughout this book. The LPDR today is desperately trying to invoke "culture" as the main basis of a separate Lao nation. Yet because culture does not respect political boundaries they are finding this task to be extremely problematic. The discourse quickly becomes entangled in all kinds of convoluted thinking about cultural similarities and differences between Thai and Lao, which ends finally with a simplistic primordial definition of Lao as those people who eat sticky rice and fish paste (*gin khao niao gap pa daek*). When Thai delegations visit Laos or Lao delegations visit Thailand, they mutually celebrate their cultural similarities. Yet each is determined to mark their differences. The Thai have a much easier job of this, not only because they have a more developed corpus of nationalist ideology, but also because they can point to their monarch. Thus one wonders whether the Lao, by destroying their constitutional monarchy, have lost an important institution which could have simultaneously symbolized its cultural similarity but separateness from the Thai more effectively than the current "democratic" regime. Significantly, while there was a Lao monarch, his separate domain (of course, subordinate in the Thai view) was acknowledged, signaled by the fact that the Thai monarch never trespassed on it. Furthermore, I would suggest that the intense interest in the historical figure of Chao Anou among intellectuals in Laos today springs not only from the obvious fact that Chao Anou's ill-fated uprising against the Siamese over 1827-8 can easily be used to symbolize the Lao determination to be independent from the Thai. More profoundly, it springs from the unconscious cultural recognition that it is the figure of a king which most effectively symbolizes this desire,[10] something which cannot be expressed explicitly.

Of course, other parts of Southeast Asia have either lost their monarchies during the colonial period, or abolished them themselves, and survived, though often not as nations. In them an array of everyday social practices continue to reproduce cultural ideas of a sacred center in the absence of a king. Shelly Errington (1989), in her study of south Sulawesi, shows how people there act as if the old nobility with its principality was still intact. They do this through their conceptions of persons, etiquette, ritual, organization of

10. A seminar on Chao Anou which attracted more than one hundred people was held at the National University over 21-23 January 1997. Previous seminars I have attended have also discussed Chao Anou with uncharacteristic vigor. We look forward to Drs. Pheuiphanh and Mayoury Ngaosyvathn's long awaited historical account of Chao Anou which will be published by Cornell University Press in 1997. "Chao Anou is just a man like any other, with his passions and his weaknesses," Pheuiphanh told me in January 1996. At a seminar in Dong Dok in April 1996 he pointedly remarked that he can only publish his views outside the country.

space, marriage strategies and so on.[11] But while there is considerable evidence for the endurance of deep cultural structures, other "cultural revivals" in former communist countries are often partial and superficial. When looking at cultural revival, therefore, it is important to consider the points of transmission from the past. Many of these social synapses may have been destroyed, or damaged. On the other hand, they may have remained intact for reasons which are not immediately apparent.

The partialness of any cultural revival can have straightforward demographic coordinates. Several generations of people in the USSR only knew communism; this is also true for at least two generations in China and northern Vietnam, and at least one generation in southern Vietnam, and in Laos. The world the average Soviet citizen lived in at the time of the collapse of the USSR in 1990 was fundamentally different from that of a 1917 peasant due to economic and social changes, and not least terror and politically directed changes. In these conditions cultural attrition from one generation to the next was considerable.[12] Even the Islamic revivals on the periphery of the former USSR today are in part a reaction to these transformations, rather than some simple efflorescence of the past, although practices in traditional family structures kept alive much of what had been suppressed in the public sphere. Family structures have also been important for the

11. It is important to grasp this aspect of the argument. I am well aware that the cult of the king in Thailand has been strongly promoted by conservative forces, but it has been an easy task given the cultural receptiveness of the population. Conservatives may attempt to manipulate the symbols of monarchy, but so do poor farmers or students when they demonstrate in Bangkok holding aloft pictures of the king.

12. A recent study in the former USSR shows the amnesia which developed in family histories. One informant told of how in joint photographs of his grandfather and grandmother, his grandfather's image had been cut: "So his image was cut away from all the pictures, . . . but actually I can say nothing about it, because this issue was never discussed in our family. The civil war mixed people up and people were not ashamed of their relatives, they were simply afraid that . . . memories about them would cause troubles for the rest of the family. They were very afraid of it, and it was never discussed at home . . ." (Pahl and Thompson 1994:139).

persistence of many basic practices in China, especially in rural areas. Nevertheless, much cultural reversion there has been partial (Siu 1989), despite the ostentatious rebuilding of lineage halls and temples. The population of China is now on the verge of being predominantly urban for the first time in history, and this is already having far-reaching cultural consequences. Similar observations could be made about northern Vietnam. In Cambodia, while the period of communism was short, war, political terror and famine literally destroyed many agents of cultural transmission and demographically skewed the population. On the other hand, for southern Vietnam and Laos, although one whole generation has grown up under the new regime, their parents did not. Furthermore, orthodox communist policies in both lasted less than ten years. Thus many of the points of social and cultural transmission in both countries remain intact. Yet one should not underestimate the profound cultural damage caused by the fleeing of the culturally learned cadres of the old regime, from monks to ministers.

Of course, in RLG days cultural changes were occurring in Laos and even if it had not experienced revolution the country would have undergone important cultural changes over the past years. It is difficult to speculate on what those changes may have been or the direction they may have taken—although developments in Thailand provide some clue. But in restrospect the changes could not have been worse than what actually happened, and most likely they would have been better. Judged from the perspective of 1997 the Lao socialist revolution was an enormous waste of lives and energy. It avoided the enormous tragedy that was inflicted on Cambodia, but that can hardly be counted as an achievement. Attempts to build socialism in Laos achieved nothing economically, and wrecked a fledgling modern education system. Economic, social and cultural development only began to occur after the LPDR, step by step, put back in place capitalist policies and practices which were already in action under the RLG. And with each step the LPRP further dramatized the pointlessness of the revolution. Not everything has been reinstated, however. A parliamentary system of government (however imperfect) has not been reinstalled, nor have the freedoms enjoyed by civil society. Furthermore, some of the central cultural institutions of Laos (such as the monarchy) have been completely destroyed.

As I have said elsewhere (Evans 1990a:42-3), revolution in Laos did not occur as a result of internal social changes, but because the war in Vietnam allowed larger countries to manipulate Lao factions for their broader interests, and thus the Lao lost control of their destiny. Yet there can never be a simple return to the past. Attempts at armed counter-revolution were crushed in the late 1970s, despite sporadic small-arms engagements since then.[13] Dreams of forcefully restoring the monarchy hatched in France by exiles surrounding a son of the former king were dashed, and moreover, have little meaning for the sons and daughters of these exiles. Not surprisingly, it would be dangerous to express any strong desires for the return of the monarchy in Laos today, and hence one does not hear such sentiments. Instead, Lao appear to be fatalistically content with their current ersatz solution of having the Thai monarchy fill this imaginary space. Meanwhile, however, the surprising restoration of Sihanouk to the throne in Cambodia gives food for future thought.

Cultural continuity and discontinuity are both felt acutely in countries like Laos which are being drawn into the vortex of global capitalism at a speed unknown by the older centers of capitalism. I recall sitting in a Black Tai village in Houaphan province listening to the story a young Mig jet pilot was telling to his family and friends about his exploits during the border fighting between Thailand and Laos in 1988. His audience of highland farmers understood the warrior idiom of his tale, but the technology and education (which had taken him to the USSR for training) that he was now familiar with was light years away from the people gathered around

---

13. Vietnamese troops played a crucial role in these engagements and were vital to the security and survival of the new regime in its early years.

him. Yet the warrior idiom was a bridge between the worlds, and all were certain that the young pilot would marry according to customary rituals, and return to bury his parents according to custom. Thus do ordinary people find points of contact, while at other points experiencing radical disjunctures.

What is now clear is that some transitions into the modern world are more destructive of customary practices than others. Besides the corrosive forces of capitalism we have already alluded to, the destruction may be a product of colonialism (though the extent to which colonialism was destructive varies widely, and is often exaggerated), or a product of internecine war. But it would seem in retrospect that some of the most culturally and socially destructive regimes of the twentieth century have been communist ones, precisely because of their totalitarian/millennial aims. The reversion to capitalism on the part of these regimes and the vigorous attempts of the people within them to revive older practices stand witness to this. That it offered only culturally impoverished innovations is shown by the fact that none of the rituals initiated by communism appear to have survived intact.

This can be seen in Laos where, for example, National Day has retreated indoors in the face of the massive popularity of the That Luang festival. Or during May Day 1996, which for people outside the government passed without notice (except that it was a holiday), whereas in 1977, for instance, there was a rally of 100,000 people in Vientiane. Otherwise, most of the rituals in which "everyday life is envisaged as a structure of exemplary recurrence" (Connerton 1989:65) have returned in Laos, itself an outcome of the fact that the high communist phase there lasted such a short time and ensured that a repository of social memory could be drawn on. Nevertheless, the country has had to forgo the opportunity to crown this cultural resurgence with a constitutional monarch who, as we have suggested, is better able than other cultural institutions at present to symbolize the "eternal" Lao-ness that the Lao are striving for.

# LAO SOUVENIRS

I T is in the awareness of time, of history, that we have witnessed one of the more profound and long-term cultural changes in Southeast Asia. This shift in consciousness came to Laos in the late nineteenth century when French colonialism introduced the idea of "the history of the nation." The change had already begun among the elite in neighboring Siam where the encounter with occidental imperialism had already led them to reflect on the problem of their "backwardness" and the reforms needed to overcome it. As in Siam, the transformation in consciousness began first among the Lao royal elite. In the late 1890s Sisavang Vong had gone to study at the colonial college in Paris, and was crowned on his return. Later Prince Phetsarath would also go to Paris to study, followed by the crown prince, Sisavang Vatthana, and others. A colonial education system was established in the main cities, and sons of merchants as well as the traditional elite attended these. Higher education was obtained in Hanoi and Saigon, and some went from there to France. In these schools they studied European history, and the triumphal history of the French revolution. It should be remembered, however, that history as an object of education in Europe had only arisen in the nineteenth century, and it was yoked to the cause of nationalism. The program outlined for the study of history in the classic *Histoire de France* by its director Ernest Lavisse in the first decade of this century was this: "To historical education falls the glorious duty of making our fatherland loved and understood. . . . If the schoolboy does not carry away with him the living memory of our national glories, if he does not know that our ancestors fought on countless battlefields for noble causes, . . . if he does not become a citizen imbued with his duties and a soldier who loves his flag, the teacher will have wasted his time" (cited in Le Goff 1992:152). This sentiment would fit easily into contemporary LPDR introductory history texts, and of course it was precisely this nationalist lesson that Lao learned in the French system; they simply had to transpose it into their own history.

Anthropologists in particular, but also historians, have argued among themselves about the nature of "time" in pre-modern societies, some appearing to attribute a timeless consciousness to these societies, others only a consciousness of circular time.[1] Much of the confusion appears to have arisen from a tendency to generalize the conception of time expressed in one domain, say ritual, to the whole of society, and it perhaps also reflects a failure to specify the culturally hegemonic idea of time which coexists with other contemporaneous concepts. What is apparent is that states and elites in Southeast Asia, and great religious traditions such as Theravada Buddhism, have different preoccupations from peasant farmers concerning the nature of time. Therefore, it is perhaps best to say that these societies had differential temporalities, and that sometimes these differential temporalities coincided to produce great occasions, like a That Luang festival. For purposes of legitimation, kings produced annals of dynasties, and for purposes of claims to power and marriage strategies elites were conscious of genealogies, while Buddhism produced a concept of eras (Buddhasakaraj, "Buddhist Era;" Mahasakaraj, "The Great Era;" Tiunlasakaraj, "The Little Era"). But these apparently linear ideas of time in Laos, and neighboring countries, were subordinate to a general circular concept of time built into the Lao calendar in

1.  For the details of these debates, see Gell (1992).

which "Mount Meru (of the earth) is considered as a fixed point constituting the rotation center of all the Stars" (Phetsarath 1959:106). Although in the temples one may be taught "the history of the travels of the Buddha," the leitmotif of Buddhist cosmology was life's "endless cycle" of rebirths, with its hoped-for final dissolution in a timeless nirvana. It was the temples which provided ordinary peasants with "historical" narratives, most of which were themselves legends, and these were then combined with folk legends. The peasants' main preoccupation with larger time was with seasonal time, and this too had a circular or recurrent motif. Outside of their own existential awareness of growing old (although this too attracts a circular narrative in the idea of old people becoming like children), peasants had little reason to reflect on "history." Furthermore, Lao peasants show little interest in genealogy (unlike traditional Chinese who attempt to model their family histories on those of dynastic great families)[2] and this is demonstrated by the absence of surnames until their imposition by the state in 1943,[3] although this does not necessarily imply a lack of interest in ancestors, or at least ancestor spirits (Cohen and Wije-yewardene 1984).

It was only the coming of the modern state and national-ism (via French colonialism) that saw the creation of a different sense of time among the elite, and the emergence of a concept of linear history of the nation, which after independence was increasingly communicated to the masses

2.  Here I simply allude to a complex debate about whether traditional Chinese culture exhibits a stronger sense of history than others. It has been argued that traditional Chinese historical writings simply have "a ritual, sacred, magic function. They are a means of communication with the divine powers. They are written down 'so that the gods may observe them,' so that in this way they may become efficacious in an eternal present" (Le Goff 1992:138).

3.  In one of his many modernizing moves King Vajiravudh issued a decree on surnames in 1913, though it was for a long time basically ignored in the villages. (See Vella 1978:128-136.) In Laos today one can still find people without surnames. For a discussion of time in the northern Thai context, see Davis (1984:85-96).

through education, propaganda and ritual. But the weakness of the Lao state both under the RLG and the LPDR has meant that this new consciousness has remained relatively weak and slippage between legend and the modern idea of history is pervasive.

Benedict Anderson has suggested that because nations are modern inventions and yet imagine themselves as ancient, their process of constructing a history of the unified nation, or the teleology of the national essence, must be one of simultaneous remembering and forgetting. Thus, for example, Laos must both remember and forget that the kingdom of Lane Xang included much of northeast Thailand. Or they are asked to remember the exploits of Lao kings, but not of the last king. In a strange way national histories also require continual reminders of past internecine bloodletting, "the reassurance of fratricide" as Anderson calls it, while simultaneously being asked to forget them in the interest of national unity. The passage by Katay Don Sasorith cited in the opening pages of this book is a classic of this genre. To cite him again briefly: "It is clear, therefore, that even when *Muong* Luang Prabang, *Muong* Vientiane, and *Muong* Champassak had each a separate existence, *Muong* Lao nonetheless remained *Muong* Lao." This passage also contains a typical elision between the traditional concept of *muong* with its indefinite, pulsating, galactic structure and the modern concept of nation. For during the period Katay is writing about there was no concept of the Lao nation. It is a projection back in time by Lao nationalists who embody a radical change in historical consciousness. But as Anderson (1991:204) writes: "All profound changes in consciousness, by their very nature, bring with them characteristic amnesias. Out of such oblivions, in specific historical circumstances, spring narratives."

Laos today is still in search of a convincing national narrative, because "fratricide" there was not only in the distant past but very recent—and it is still not "reassuring." The civil war lasting from the late 1950s until 1975 has to be remembered for it is the process by which the new regime came to power, but it also has to be forgotten as a period of disunity. The LPDR tries to accomplish this through several devices. The first is to characterize opposition figures as somehow non-Lao, "traitors" who were the tool (*luuk meu*) of foreign powers. Secondly, to simply ignore the reality of Lao independence in 1954 and characterize the old regime as the period of "new colonialism" (compared with the "old colonialism" of the French). Thirdly, to write lobotomized histories wherein, for example, Prince Phetsarath may appear as the leader of the Lao Issara in 1945, and then simply disappear from view altogether, or wherein the intervention of America on the side of the RLG is emphasized, whereas the intervention of large numbers of Vietnamese troops on the Pathet Lao side is ignored, or glossed as "solidarity."

In the modern world, however, such state-scripted histories can be sustained ultimately only by force. Modern bureaucratic states with their commitment to "rationality" and their need for statistics and enumerated data, find that history writing (or anthropology, etc.) becomes subject to the same rational and empirical logic, and state-officialdom becomes uncomfortably aware of their hypocrisy in suppressing non-official narratives, and an uneasy sense of illegitimacy grows. Of course, historians have their own axes to grind, but left to themselves, history becomes contested ground rather than an official single narrative. States can simply suppress what is known, but in the end this only produces widespread cynicism, rather than legitimacy. Recall my earlier discussion of the seminar on the role of politics and history at Dong Dok College in April 1996 where voices were being heard for writing histories which are not subject to the dictates of the party. And more and more frequently, Lao intellectuals are in contact with foreign analysts of Laos—historians, anthropologists, sociologists, political scientists, economists—who cannot be silenced by the Lao state. Furthermore, there remains a pool of counter-memory to the LPRP both inside and outside Laos which will increasingly demand to be heard, as we saw in the strikingly visible reassertion of Kou Voravong as an actor in Lao history or indeed in Tham's booklet about the *Anousavaly*. So, in Laos shared memories remain illusive.

On the pessimistic side, however, rapid change in the modern world may mean that people have shorter and shorter memories, as the quote from Hobsbawm at the front of this book suggests, allowing for the possibility of crude manipulation by the state. For example, Lao people are now exhorted to only remember that Kaysone Phomvihane introduced the new economic policies. Not that he also introduced the old economic policies after the revolution and presided over one of the most repressive political periods in modern Lao history. Similarly, Lao people are not allowed to say publicly that, for example, the LPRP tried to suppress the use of the *nop* after 1975. In the new revival of "custom" and "tradition" such memories of relatively recent events are suppressed.

Yet one senses a strong desire among Lao people to go along with this. The invocation of "tradition" at all levels is an attempt to construct a sense of continuity where people have for many years felt a sense of discontinuity. We saw how members of a Japanese village invoked "the past" (*mukashi*) in a gesture at solidarity, although each person's memory of that past was different. At a general level, similar processes are at work in Laos today. In ordinary conversations people are often evasive about the immediate "socialist" past, and I believe no longer for purely political reasons. They simply prefer to say, "But we now have a democratic regime" (*labop pasatipatai*), by which they mean not a politically democratic regime but one which allows them to make money, set up their own business or work where they like, to live where they like, to travel internally and overseas, and to be able to watch Thai TV. Things are better than before, their manner suggests, so why dwell on yesterday which may be divisive? Better to invoke it as a hazy, "we are all Lao who all share the same traditions as we always have done." To this extent, the regime's relegitimization project is working.

Perhaps the dominant consciousness among ordinary Lao about their society today is its "backwardness," a consciousness which has sprung from the LPDR's endless promotion of the importance of "development," and in more recent times through the growing exposure of Lao to the outside world which draws attention to how "backward" Laos is. Out of this arises a very contradictory configuration: awareness of backwardness produces a future-oriented desire to modernize, but this occurs in a context where the state is promoting tradition and where the unanticipated consequences of social change induce widespread traditionalist nostalgia. In this respect one feels a deep and growing sense of disorientation in Lao society.

It was Marx who coined the evocative phrase, "all that's solid melts into air," to characterize the massive cultural and social changes brought into being by capitalism. Its restless spirit moves through serial time leaving in its wake yesterday's fashions in clothing, speech, manners, housing, transportation and metaphysical beliefs. Nothing appears to be invulnerable. Yet if this is a fundamental reality of the late twentieth century, it also seems equally true that human societies cannot tolerate such ephemeralness. Rituals—reinvigorated, revived or invented—are one of the ways humans cope with these incessant changes. They are "facades erected to screen off the full implications of this vast world-wide clearing operation" (Connerton 1989:64). Rituals draw participants into another time dimension, often sacred, of eternal recurrence, rather than eternal discontinuity. This, no doubt, partly explains the vigor with which the Lao have thrown themselves into reviving "tradition," regardless of the state's prompting and the commercial demands of international tourism. In this context too, the national festival of That Luang reveals its full significance, as the nation takes leave of profane time and revolves around a still point, its own Mount Meru.

# GLOSSARY

There is still no standardized way of spelling Lao words in English. Over the years many variations have appeared. Thus, the spellings used here may differ slightly from variants used elsewhere, but the terms should still remain recognizeable.

| | |
|---|---|
| *anisong* | reward of merit |
| *anousavaly* | monument |
| *baci* | soul-calling ceremony or blessing |
| *baan* | village |
| *bay lan* | palm leaf manuscripts |
| *bok* | to expel |
| *boun* | accumulated merit; also festival |
| *boun kong bouat* | ceremonies to induct monks into the monkhood |
| *caw / chao* | lord, an honorific |
| *chao khoueng* | provincial governor |
| *chao muang / mouang* | district head |
| *chao poh* | godfather (mafia) |
| *hong haem* | hotel |
| *kabouan son pao* | procession of minorities |
| *kathin* | robes given to monks at the end of lent |
| *kha* | slave or subject |

| | |
|---|---|
| *khene* | pan pipe |
| *lak muang* | territorial pillar |
| *lam* | didactic style of singing with regional and ethnic variations |
| *Maha* | senior honorific in the monkhood |
| *mat kaen* | tying of cotton threads around wrists during a *baci* |
| *moh cham / tiam* | spirit medium |
| *moh lam* | singer of *lam* |
| *moh phone* | officiant at a *baci* |
| *muang / muong* | principality, district, country |
| *nang sangkhan* | mythical figure who has been incorporated into the Lao New Year festivities |
| *nang tiam* | female spirit medium |
| *nat* | spirit, in Burmese |
| *nop* | gesture of respect |
| *ouparat* | second king |
| *phanya* | honorific for non-noble officials under the monarchy |
| *Phanya* **Pavet** | figure in a Buddhist moral tale |
| *pathan* | president |
| *pathan khoueng* | province president |
| *pathan song* | president of the monkhood |
| *pattikan* | reactionary |
| *pha khouan / phakuan* | central flower arrangement for a *baci* |
| *pha gaew pheuk* | white jewel buddha |
| *phasat / prasat* | object representing Mt. Meru |
| *phi* | spirit or ghost |
| *phra sangkarat* | head of the monkhood |
| *pi nong* | relatives, kin |
| *sahagorn hoop hang* | skeleton cooperative |
| *sakdina* | feudal |
| *saksit* | metaphysically powerful |
| *sala* | meeting hall in the temple |
| *samloh* | three-wheeled pedicab |
| *sampot* | the traditional courtly style dress for men |
| *sangha* | the organization of the monkhood |
| *sangkhan bai* | the day of the passing of the old year |

| | |
|---|---|
| *sangkhan keun* | the first day of the new year |
| *sim* | sanctuary of the buddha images in a temple |
| *sinh* | the traditional Lao skirt |
| *sou khouan* | spirit calling ceremony or blessing |
| *tham* | traditional religious script |
| *that* | stupa |
| *thevada* | angel |
| *vat / wat* | temple |
| *vinya* | Buddhist code of commentary and judgment |

# REFERENCES

ADB—Asian Development Bank

*BEFEO—Bulletin de l'Ecole Française d'Extrême Orient.*

BSSR—Bureau of Social Science Research

*KPL—Khao San Pathet Lao*

*SWB—BBC Summary of World Broadcasts—Far East.*

ULBA—United Lao Buddhist Association

*VT—Vientiane Times*


ABHAY, Thao Nhouy. 1959. The That Luang festivities; The baci; Marriage rites; Buddhism in Laos. All in *Kingdom of Laos: The land of the million elephants and the white parasol,* edited by Rene de Berval. Saigon: France-Asie.

AGULHON, Maurice. 1978. La "statuomanie" et l'histoire. *Ethnologie Française,* 145-172.

AIJMER, Goran. 1978. Reconciling power with authority: An aspect of statecraft in traditional Laos. *Man,* vol. 14.

———. 1996. Political ritual: Aspects of the Mao cult during the Cultural "Revolution." *China Information,* vol. 11, nos. 2/3.

ANAGNOST, A.S. 1987. Politics and magic in contemporary China. *Modern China,* vol. 13, no. 1.

ANDERSON, Benedict. 1987. Introduction to *Southeast Asian tribal groups and ethnic minorities.* Cultural Survival Report 22, Cambridge, MA: Cultural Survival, Inc.

_____. 1990. The idea of power in Javanese culture [1972]. In *Language and power: Exploring political cultures in Indonesia*. Ithaca, NY: Cornell University Press.

_____. 1991. *Imagined communities: Reflections on the origin and spread of nationalism*. London: Verso.

ARCHAIMBAULT, C. 1964. Religious structures in Laos. *Journal of the Siam Society*, vol. 52.

_____. 1971. *The New Year ceremony at Basak (South Laos)*. Data paper number 78, Southeast Asia Program. Ithaca, NY: Cornell University Press.

_____ 1973. *Structures religieuses Lao (rites et mythes)*. Vientiane: Vithagna.

ASIAN DEVELOPMENT BANK. 1993. *Lao People's Democratic Republic*. Education in Asia Series 1. Manila, Philippines: Asian Development Bank.

ASKEW, Marc. 1994. Bangkok: Transformation of the Thai city. In *Cultural identity and urban change in Southeast Asia: Interpretative essays*, edited by Marc Askew and William S. Logan. Geelong, Victoria: Deakin University Press.

BALZER, M. M. 1990. *Shamanism: Soviet studies of traditional religion in Siberia and Central Asia*. London: M.E. Sharp.

BARBER, Martin. 1974. An urban village in Vientiane. In *Sangkhom khady san*. Vientiane: Pakpasack Press.

BOUTSAVAT, V. and G. Chapelier. 1973. Lao popular Buddhism and community development. *Journal of the Siam Society*, vol. 69, no. 2.

BROWNELL, Susan E. 1993. Qing dynasty grand sacrifice and communist national sports games: Rituals of the Chinese state? *Journal of Ritual Studies*. vol. 7, no. 1.

_____. 1995. *Training the body for China: Sports in the moral order of the People's Republic*. Chicago: University of Chicago Press.

BUDDHADASA Bhikkhu. 1986. *Dhammic socialism*. Edited by Donald K. Swearer. Bangkok: Thai Inter-Religious Commission for Development.

BUREAU OF SOCIAL SCIENCE RESEARCH. September 1959. *Information and attitudes in Laos*. Raymond Fink, study director. Bureau of Social Science Research, Inc., 2017 Connecticut Avenue, N.W. Washington D.C.

Canla TANBUALI, Maha. 1977. The state of Buddhist religion in the Lao People's Democratic Republic. Bangkok: Khana Sasanikachon. (A translation from the Thai).

CHAGNON, Jackie and Roger Rumpf. 1982. Education: The prerequisite to change in Laos. In *Contemporary Laos*, edited by Martin Stuart-Fox. St. Lucia, Queensland: University of Queensland Press.

CHANDLER, David. 1996. *Facing the Cambodian past*. Chiang Mai, Thailand: Silkworm Books.

Chatthip, NARTSUPA. 1984. The ideology of holy men revolts in northeast Thailand. In *History and peasant consciousness in Southeast Asia*, edited by Andrew Turton and Shigeharu Tanabe, *Senri Ethnological Studies*, no. 13, Osaka.

CLERGERIE, Bernard. 1954. L'oeuvre francaise d'enseignement au Laos. *France-Asie*, nos. 125-7.

COHEN, Paul and Gehan Wijeyewardene, eds. 1984. *Matrilineal spirit cults in northern Thailand*. Special issue of *Mankind*, vol. 14, no. 4.

CONDOMINAS, Georges. 1975. Phi ban cults in rural Laos. In *Change and persistence in Thai society*, edited by G.W. Skinner and T.A Kirsch. Ithaca, NY: Cornell University Press,

CONNERTON, Paul. 1989. *How societies remember*. Cambridge: Cambridge University Press.

DAVIS, Richard. 1984. *Muang metaphysics: A study of northern Thai myth and ritual*. Studies in Thai Anthropology, no. 1. Bangkok: Pandora.

de BERVAL, René, ed. 1959. *Kingdom of Laos: The land of the million elephants and the white parasol*. Saigon: France-Asie.

DEUTSCHER, Isaac. 1969. *Russia after Stalin*. London: Jonathan Cape.

DEUVE, Jean. 1992. *Le Laos 1945-1949, Contribution a l'histoire du mouvement Lao Issala*. Montpellier: Center d'Histoire Militaire et d'Etudes de Defense Nationale, Université Paul Valery.

DEYDIER, Henri. 1954. *Lokapala: Génies, totems et sorciers du nord Laos*. Paris: Librarie Plon.

DOMMEN, Arthur J. 1971. *Conflict in Laos: The politics of neutralization*, Revised edition. New York: Praeger.

_____. 1985. *Laos: The keystone to Indochina*. Boulder, Colorado: Westview Press.

DORE, Amphay. 1981. La chemise divinitoire kassak. *Peninsule,* no. 2, Avril.

DUMONT, Louis. 1983. *Essais sur l'individualisme.* Paris: Editions du Sueil.

EDITIONS VIENTIANE Times. 1995. *Le That Luang de Vientiane: Symbole de la nation Lao.* Vientiane: Editions du Vientiane Times.

ENZENSBERGER, Hans Magus. 1976. Tourists of the revolution, [1973]. In *Raids and reconstructions: Essays on politics, crime and culture.* London: Pluto Press.

ERRINGTON, Shelly. 1989. *Meaning and power in a Southeast Asian realm.* Englewood Cliffs, New Jersey: Princeton University Press.

EVANS, Grant. 1983. *The yellow rainmakers.* London: Verso.

_____. 1985. Goosesteps and flowers for a Lao anniversary. *The Age* (Melbourne) December 3.

_____. 1988 *Agrarian change in communist Laos.* Singapore: Institute of Southeast Asian Studies.

_____. 1990a. *Lao peasants under socialism.* New Haven and London: Yale University Press.

_____. 1990b. Millennial rebels in colonial Laos. *Peasant Studies,* vol. 18, no. 1.

_____. 1991. Reform or revolution in heaven?: Funerals among upland Tai. *Australian Journal of Anthropology,* vol. 2, no. 1.

_____. 1993a. Buddhism and economic action in socialist Laos. In *Socialism: Ideals, ideology and local practice,* edited by C.M. Hann. ASA Monograph 31. London and New York: Routledge.

_____. 1993b. Hierarchy and dominance: Class, status and caste; The global village: Anthropology in the future; both in *Asia's cultural mosaic: An anthropological introduction,* edited by Grant Evans. Singapore: Prentice Hall.

_____. 1994 Lao culture: What is its future? *Vientiane Times,* December 23-29.

_____. 1995. *Lao peasants under socialism and post-socialism.* Chiangmai, Thailand: Silkworm Books.

EVANS, Grant and Kelvin Rowley. 1990. *Red brotherhood at war: Vietnam, Cambodia and Laos since 1975.* London: Verso.

FAR EASTERN ECONOMIC REVIEW. 1976. *Asia 1975 yearbook.* Hong Kong.

FORMOSO, Bernard. 1990. From the humanised body to the humanised space. *Journal of the Siam Society,* vol. 78, part 1.

FOWLER, Peter J. 1992. *The past in contemporary society: Then, now.* London: Routledge.

GAGNEUX, Pierre Marie. 1976. Tendances actuelles de la recherche historique en Republique Democratique Populaire Lao. *Asie du Sud-Est et Monde Insulindien,* vol. 7, no. 4.

GEERTZ, Clifford. 1985. Centers, kings, and charisma: Reflections on the symbolics of power. In *Rites of power: Symbolism, ritual, and politics since the middle ages,* edited by Sean Wilentz. Philadelphia: University of Pennsylvania Press.

GELL, Alfred. 1992. *The anthropology of time: Cultural constructions of temporal maps and images.* Oxford: Berg Publishers.

GELLNER, Ernest. 1994a. *Post-modernism, reason and religion.* London: Routledge.

_____. 1994b. *Conditions of liberty: Civil society and its rivals.* London: Hamish Hamilton.

GLADNEY, Dru. 1994. Representing nationality in China: Refiguring majority/minority identities. *Journal of Asian Studies,* vol. 53, no. 1.

GRAY, Christine E. 1991. Hegemonic images: Language and silence in the royal Thai polity. *Man,* vol. 26, no. 1.

HALPERN, Joel M. 1964. *Government, politics, and social structure in Laos: A study of tradition and innovation.* Monograph series no. 4, Southeast Asia Studies. New Haven: Yale University Press.

HEINZ, Ruth-Ing. 1982. *Tham khwan.* Singapore: Singapore University Press.

HOBSBAWM, Eric. 1994. *The age of extremes: The short twentieth century, 1914-1991.* London: Michael Joseph.

HUTHEESING, Otome Klein. 1990. How does a "Tai" spirit come to be on a Lisu home altar? A note on the merger of lowland and highland cosmologies. *Proceedings of the 4th International Conference on Thai Studies,* 11-13 May. Institute of Southeast Asian Studies, Kunming, China.

IRESON, Carol J. and Randy Ireson. 1991. Ethnicity and development in Laos. *Asian Survey,* vol. 31, no. 10.

IRVINE, Walter. 1984. Decline of village spirit cults and growth of urban spirit mediumship: the persistence of spirit beliefs, the position of women and modernization. *Mankind,* vol. 14, no. 4.

ISHII, Yoneo. 1986. *Sangha, state, and society: Thai Buddhism in history.* Honolulu: University of Hawaii Press.

JACKSON, Peter A. 1989. *Buddhism, legitimation, and conflict: The political functions of urban Thai Buddhism.* Singapore: ISEAS.

JEFFREY, Robin. 1980. What statues tell: The politics of choosing symbols in trivandrum. *Pacific Affairs,* vol. 53, no. 3.

KAPFERER, Bruce. 1988. *Legends of people, myths of state.* Washington, D.C.: Smithsonian Institution Press.

Katay D. SASORITH. 1959. Historical aspects of Laos. In *Kingdom of Laos: The land of the million elephants and the white parasol,* edited by Rene de Berval. Saigon: France-Asie.

Kaysone PHOMVIHANE. 1980. *La révolution lao,* Moscow: Editions du Progrès.

KERTZER, David I. 1988. *Ritual, politics and power.* New Haven: Yale University Press.

KEYES, Charles. 1967. *Isan: Regionalism in northeastern Thailand.* Cornell Thailand Project, Interim Reports Series, no. 10.

_____. 1971. Buddhism and national integration in Thailand. *Journal of Asian Studies,* vol. 30.

_____. 1972. Religious and social change in southern Laos. *Journal of Asian Studies,* vol. 31, no. 3.

_____. 1975. Buddhist pilgrimage centers and the twelve-year cycle: northern Thai moral orders in time and space. *History of Religions,* vol. 15, pp. 71-89.

_____. 1977. Millenialism, Theravada Buddhism, and Thai society. *Journal of Asian Studies,* vol. 36, no. 2.

_____. 1987. From death to birth: Ritual process and Buddhist meanings in northern Thailand. *Folk,* vol. 29, pp. 181-206.

_____. 1991. The proposed world of the school: Thai villagers' entry into the bureaucratic state system. In *Reshaping local worlds,* edited by Charles F. Keyes. Monograph 36, New Haven: Yale Southeast Asia Studies, Yale Center for International and Area Studies.

_____. 1993. A princess in a peoples' republic: A new phase in the construction of the Lao nation. Paper presented at the International Thai Studies Conference, SOAS, June 1993.

KREMMER, Christopher. 1997. *Stalking the elephant kings: In search of Lao.* ChiangMai: Silkworm Books.

LAFONT, P-B. 1982. Buddhism in contemporary Laos. In *Contemporary Laos,* edited by Martin Stuart-Fox. St. Lucia: University of Queensland Press.

LANDSBERGER, Stefan R. 1996. Mao as the kitchen god: Religious aspects of the Mao cult during the Cultural Revolution. *China Information*, vol. 11, nos. 2/3.

LATEGUY, Jean. 1967. *The bronze drums*. London: Mayflower Paperbacks.

Le GOFF, Jacques. 1992. *History and memory*. New York: Columbia University Press.

LEE, Begonia. 1996. Houses of the holy. *Far Eastern Economic Review*, June 6.

LIND, Elisabeth & Gotz Hagmuller. 1991. *The Royal Palace Museum of Luang Prabang: General condition, conservation and restoration needs*, 1991. NIAS, Report 6, Copenhagen, Denmark.

LOPEZ, Donald S. 1995. *Curators of the Buddha: The study of Buddhism under colonialism*. Chicago and London: University of Chicago Press.

MALLERET, Louis. 1969. Histoire abregee de l'archeologie Indochinoise Jusqu'a 1950. *Asian Perspectives*, vol. 12, pp. 43-68.

MARTIN, Helmut. 1982. *Cult and canon: The origins and development of state Maoism*. New York and London: M. E. Sharpe, Inc.

MAUGER, Marc. 1959. Secondary education. In *Kingdom of Laos: The land of the million elephants and the white parasol*, edited by Rene de Berval. Saigon: France-Asie.

MILLS, Mary Beth. 1995. Attack of the widow ghosts: Gender, death, and modernity in northeast Thailand. In *Bewitching women, pious men: gender and body politics in Southeast Asia*, edited by Aihwa Ong and Michael G. Peletz. Berkeley: University of California Press.

MINISTERE DE L'INFORMATION ET DE LA CULTURE, LPDR. 1994. Nomination au patrimoine mondial de l'UNESCO: Ville de Luang Prabang, Vientiane. Septembre.

MOERAN, Brian. 1984. *Lost innocence: Folk craft potters of Onta, Japan*. Berkeley: University of California Press.

MOORE, Barrington. 1978. *Injustice: The social bases of obedience and revolt*. London: Macmillan.

NG Shui Meng. 1991. Social development in the People's Democratic Republic: Problems and prospects. In *Laos: Beyond the revolution*, edited by Joseph J. Zasloff and Leonard Unger. London: Macmillan.

NGAOSYVATHN, Mayoury. 1990. Individual soul, national identity: The baci-sou khuan of the Lao. *Sojourn*, vol. 5, no. 2.

_____. 1995. Buddhism, merit making and gender in Laos. In *"Male" and "female" in developing Southeast Asia*, edited by Wazir Jahan Karim. Oxford: Berg Publishers.

NGAOSYVATHN, Mayoury and Pheuiphanh. 1994. *Kith and kin politics: The relation between Laos and Thailand*. Manila, Philippines and Wollongong, Australia: Journal of Contemporary Asia Publishers.

OHNUKI-TIERNEY, Emiko. 1990. Introduction: The Historicization of Anthropology. In *Culture through time: Anthropological approaches*, edited by Emiko Ohnuki-Tierney. Stanford, CA: Stanford University Press.

OSBORNE, Milton. 1994. *Sihanouk: Prince of light, prince of darkness*. Sydney: Allen & Unwin.

PAHL, Ray and Paul Thompson. 1994. Meanings, myths and mystifications: The social construction of life stories in Russia. In *When history accelerates: Essays on rapid social change, complexity and creativity*, edited by C.M. Hann. London: Athlone Press.

Pathoumxad KROUNG. 1959. Organization of the sangha. In *Kingdom of Laos: The land of the million elephants and the white parasol*, edited by Rene de Berval. Saigon: France-Asie.

PEACHEY, Titus and Linda. 1983. Religion in socialist Laos. *Southeast Asian Chronicle*, issue 91.

PHETSARATH, Tiao Maha Oupahat. 1959. The Laotian Calendar. In *Kingdom of Laos: The land of the million elephants and the white parasol*, edited by Rene de Berval. Saigon: France-Asie.

_____.("3349"). 1978. *Iron man of Laos: Prince Phetsarath Ratanavongsa*. Translated by John B. Murdoch and edited by David K. Wyatt. Data Paper no. 10, Southeast Asia Program, Cornell University, New York.

RAQUEZ, A. 1902. *Pages laotiennes*, Hanoi: EFEO, F-H Schneider.

_____. 1905. Au Laos. *Revue Indochinoise*. Nouvelle Série, deuxieme semestre.

Rattanavong HOUMPHANH. 1995. The rapid Siamisation of Lao culture today: A serious cause for concern to the Lao people. In *Culture, development and globalisation*. Proceeedings of a series of symposia held at Nong Khai, Hanoi and Tokyo. Tokyo: The Toyota Foundation.

REYNOLDS, Craig J. 1976. Buddhist cosmography in Thai history, with special reference to nineteenth century culture change. *Journal of Asian Studies*, vol. 35, no. 2.

REYNOLDS, Frank. 1978. The holy emerald jewel: Some aspects of Buddhist symbolism and political legitimation in Thailand and Laos. In *Religion and legitimation of power in Thailand, Laos, and Burma,* edited by Bardwell L. Smith. Singapore: Anima Books.

ROWLEY, C.D. 1960. *The lotus and the dynamo.* Sydney: Angus and Robertson.

Sanitsuda EKACHAI. 1993. Sadet Pho: What lies behind a cult of worship. *Bangkok Post,* August 18, 1993.

Saowarop PANYACHEEWIN. 1992. Chulalongkorn as a divine being. *Bangkok Post,* October 23, 1992.

SCHOBER, Juliane. 1995. The Theravada Buddhist engagement with modernity in Southeast Asia: Whither the social paradigm of the galactic polity? *Journal of Southeast Asian Studies,* vol. 26, no. 2.

SCOTT, James C. 1990. *Domination and the arts of resistance: Hidden transcripts.* New Haven and London: Yale University Press.

SICARD, Marie-Noele & Didier. 1981. *Au nom de Marx et de Bouddha.* Paris: Inter Éditions.

SIU, Helen. 1989. Recycling rituals: Politics and popular culture in contemporary rural China. In *Unofficial China: Popular culture and thought in the People's Republic,* edited by Perry Link, Richard Madsen, and Paul G. Picowicz. Boulder, Colorado: Westview Press.

SMITH, Donald Eugene, 1965. *Religion and politics in Burma.* Englewood, Cliffs, New Jersey: Princeton University Press.

SOUVANNA PHOUMA, Prince. 1970. Restauration du Ho Phra-Keo. *Bulletin des Amis du Royaume Lao,* no. 2.

STEVENSON, Charles A. 1973. *The end of nowhere: American policy toward Laos since 1954.* Boston: Beacon Press.

STRECKFUSS, David. 1995. Kings in the age of nations: The paradox of lesé-majeste as political crime in Thailand. *Comparative Studies in Society and History,* pp. 445-475.

STRENSKI, Ivan. 1983. On generalized exchange and the domestication of the *sangha. Man,* vol. 18, 463-77.

STUART-FOX, Martin. 1986. *Laos: Politics and society.* London: Frances Pinter Publishers.

STUART-FOX, Martin and Rod Bucknell. 1982. Politicization of the Buddhist sangha in Laos. *Journal of Southeast Asian Studies,* vol. 13, no. 1.

Sumet JUMSAI. 1989. *Naga: Cultural origins in Siam and the west Pacific*. Singapore: Oxford University Press.

TAILLARD, Christian. 1973. Essai sur la bipolarisation autour du vat et de l'école des villages Lao de la plaine de Vientiane. *Asie du Sud-est et Monde Insulindien*, vol. 3.

TAMBIAH, S.J. 1968. Literacy in a Buddhist village in north-east Thailand. In *Literacy in traditional societies*, edited by Jack Goody. Cambridge: Cambridge University Press.

———. 1976. *World conqueror and world renouncer*. Cambridge: Cambridge University Press.

———. 1984. *The Buddhist saints of the forest and the cult of amulets*. Cambridge: Cambridge University Press.

———. 1985. A reformulation of Geertz's conception of the theater state. In *Culture, thought and social action: An anthropological perspective*. Cambridge, Mass.: Harvard University Press.

TAY Keoluangkot. 1959. Primary education. In *Kingdom of Laos: The land of the million elephants and the white parasol*, edited by Rene de Berval. Saigon: France-Asie.

THEE Marek. 1973. *Notes of a witness: Laos and the second Indochinese War*. New York: Random House.

THION, Serge. 1993. *Watching Cambodia: Ten paths to enter the Cambodian tangle*. Bangkok: White Lotus.

TOOKER, Deborah E. 1996. Putting the mandala in its place: A practice-based approach to the spatialization of power on the Southeast Asian "periphery"—the case of the Akha. *Journal of Asian Studies*, vol. 55, no. 2.

TUMARKIN, Nina. 1981. Religion, Bolshevism, and the origins of the Lenin cult. *The Russian Review*, vol. 40, no. 1.

TURNER, Victor. 1974. *Dramas, fields, and metaphors: Symbolic action in human society*. Ithaca and London: Cornell University Press.

———. 1977. The ritual process: Structure and anti-structure. Ithaca, New York: Cornell University Press.

van ESTERIK, Penelope. 1980. Royal style in a village context. *Contributions to Asian Studies*, vol. 15.

VELLA, Walter F. 1978. *Chaiyo! King Vajiravadh and the development of Thai nationalism*. Honolulu: University Press of Hawaii.

VO Thu Tinh. 1971. Les divinites tutelaires du nouvel an Lao. *Bulletin des Amis Royaume Lao*, no. 6.

WALZER, Michael. 1974. *Regicide and revolution: Speeches at the trial of Louis XVI*. London: Cambridge University Press.

WATSON, James L. 1985. Standardising the gods: The promotion of T'ien Hou ("Empress of Heaven") along the South China coast, 960-1960. In *Popular culture in late imperial China*, edited by David Johnson, Andrew Nathan, and Evelyn Rawski. Berkeley: University of California Press.

WIJEYEWARDENE, Gehan. 1986. *Place and emotion in northern Thai ritual behavior*. Studies in Thai Anthropology 2. Bangkok: Pandora.

WOODSIDE, Alexander. 1991. The contributions to rural change of modern Vietnamese village schools. In *Reshaping local worlds*, edited by Charles F. Keyes. Monograph 36. New Haven: Yale Southeast Asia Studies, Yale Center for International and Area Studies.

WORSLEY, Peter. 1964. *The Third World*. London: Weidenfeld and Nicholson.

XIN Yuan. 1995. A place in the pantheon: Mao and folk religion. In *The posthumous Mao cult*. Special issue of *Chinese Sociology and Anthropology*, vol. 28, no. 1.

ZAGO, Marcel. 1972. *Rites et ceremonies en milieu Bouddhiste Lao*. Documenta Missionala 6, Rome: Universita Gregoriana, Editrice.

_____. 1976. Buddhism in contemporary Laos. In *Buddhism in the modern world*, edited by Heinrich Dumoulin and John C. Moraldo. New York: Collier Books.

## Lao References by Year (with English translations of author/title):

ກະຊວງທັມມະການ, *ປະຫວັກ ພຣະທາດຈຄີ–ວັກສຳຄັນ ແລະ ພຣະຄຣູຍອດແກ້ວໂພນສະ-ເມັກ*, 1974. (Ministry of Religion. *History and important days of Thats, and of Phra Khru Nyot Gaew Phonsamek.*)

ສິລາ ວິຣະວົງສ໌, *ປະຫວັກທຸງລາວ*, ວຽງຈັນ ຖຸລາ 1975 a. (Sila Viravong. *History of the Lao flag.*)

ສິລາ ວິຣະວົງສ໌, *ປະຫວັກ ວັນທີ 12 ຖຸລາ 1945*, ວຽງຈັນ 1975 b. (Sila Viravong. *History of the 12 October 1945.*)

ກະຊວງສຶກສາແລະກິລາ, ສະຖາບັນຄົ້ນຄວ້າວິທະຍາສາດສັງຄົມ, *ປະຫວັກສາດລາວ ເຫຼັ້ມ 3, 1893 ເຖິງປະຈຸບັນ*, 1989. (Ministry of Education and Sport, Social Science Research Institute. *The history of Laos, vol. 3: 1893 to the present.*)

ຄະນະກຳມະການວິທະຍາສາດສັງຄົມ, ເຈົ້າສຸພານຸວົງ ຜູ້ນຳປະຕິວັກ, ວຽງຈັນ, 1989. *(An autobiography of Prince Souphanouvong).*

ກອງປະຊຸມໃຫຍ່ຜູ້ແທນສ້ງຄົ່ວປະເທດ ຄັ້ງທີ 3, ກຸມພາ, 1989 [ວຽງຈັນ]. *(Congress of sangha representatives from throughout the country, no. 3.)*

ພຣະອາຈາມມະຫາສາລີ ອານຸຈາໂຣ, ໜັງສືເທສນາສະຫລອງງານຕ່າງໆ, 20 ກັນ, ພຣະພຸທະສັງກຣາດ, 1991. (Phra Ajaan Maha Sali Anujalo. *Book of sermons for various celebrations,)*

ພຣະອາຈາມມະຫາບົວຄຳ ວົລະພັກ, ປະຕິທິນລາວ 7 ປີ, ໂຮງພິມປະຊາບໍລິການ, 30/10/93. (Phra Ajaan Bouakham Volaphet. *A seven year Lao calendar.)*

ດວງໄຊ ຫລວງພະສີ, ຜ່ສາວະການລາວ, ຄົນລາວແຜ່ນດິນຂອງລາວ, ຈັດພິມໂດຍ ປະຫານ ຄະນະກຳມະການລາວ, 1995. (Douangsai Louangpasi. *Lao history, Lao people and the Lao territory.)*

ບຸນເຮ້ງ ບົວສີແສງປະເສີດ, ປະຫວັດ ສິລະປະ ແລະສະຖາປັດຕະຍະກຳລາວ ເຫຼັ້ມ 2 ເມືອງຫລວງ ພະບາງ, ວຽງຈັນ, 1995. (Bounheng Bouasi Saengpaset. *History, arts, and architecture of Laos, vol. 2: Muang Luang Prabang.)*

ປະຫານ ໄກສອນ ພົມວິຫານ ວິລະບຸລຸດແຫ່ງຊາດລາວ, ວຽງຈັນ, 1995. *(President Kaysone Phomvihane, Lao national hero.)*

ວັດທະນະທຳໃບຮານລາວ, ວັດໄພນນພຣະເນົາ, ວຽງຈັນ, 1995. *(Ancient Lao culture.)*

ທຳ ໄຊຍະສິດເສມາ, ປະຕູໄຊ: ການກໍ່ສ້າງ, ຄວາມໝາຍ, ກິຕິສັກ, ວຽງຈັນ, 1995. (Tham Sainyasitsana. *Patou Say: Its construction, significance and uses.)*

ຈານ ນອງອິນຫະວົງ, "ຊາວພຸດ ກັບວັດທະນະທຳລາວ" ວຽງຈັນ, 1995. (roneo) (Jan Nong Intavong. *Buddhists and Lao culture.)*

ມະຫາຄຳຕັນ ເທບບົວລີ, "ພະສົງລາວກັບການປະຕິວັດແລະລະບອບປະຊາທິປະໄຕ ປະຊາຊົນ", ວຽງຈັນ, 1995. (roneo) (Maha Khamtan Thepbouali. *The Lao sangha and the people's democratic regime.)*

ມະຫາສີລາວິຣະວົງສ໌, ເຈົ້າມະຫາອຸປຣາດ ເພັດຊະຣາດ, ວຽງຈັນ, 1996. (Maha Sila Viravong. Ouparat *Prince Phetsarath.)*

Thai References:

สมเด็จพระเทพรัตนราชสุดาฯ สยามบรมราชกุมารี (1994) ม่วนชื่นเมืองลาว, มูลนิธิ สมเด็จพระเทพรัตนราชสุดา, กรุงเทพฯ (Princess Maha Chakri Sirindhorn. *Pleasant journey to Laos.)*

# INDEX

*See also* New Year ceremony
RLG. *See* Royal Lao Government
Rocket festival, 58-9
Royal Lao Government (RLG),
  15, 23, 42, 48, 51, 52, 56, 65,
  69, 70, 92, 96, 103, 119, 182,
  188, 189

attitude towards minorities, 142-
  3, 148-9, 150n
centrality of Buddhist ritual to,
  54
education under, 156
iconography of, 124-5
people's memory of, 7
references to, excised, 130
royalty
  and *kha*, 143-6
  rituals of, 143
  Thai, 172
  *See also* monarchy
S
sacredness of power, 171, 172-3,
  174
*sakdina* system, 130, 143, 146, 171
Sali Vongkhamsao, 139
sand stupa building ritual, 136
sangha, 50, 55, 60, 64, 66, 67
  and changes in Buddhism, 62
  "as leader of cultural pride", 63
  as social mobility for poor
    boys, 55
  contact with Thailand, 65
  discipline in, 50, 60-1, 69
  government control of, 52-3,
    57, 63
  in Cambodia, 55
  move towards socialism, 65
  politicization of, 61-2
Saravane, 148
Sarit Thanarat, 92, 169
Savannakhet, 74, 118, 124
Sayabouri, 92
Saysetthatirath, King, 165
Saysomporn Phomvihane, 37-8
school textbooks, 158-166
  socialism in, 159-60
  war in, 158-9

history in, 160
schools
  conditions in, 157-8, 162
Setthatirath, King, x, 39, 41, 42n,
  45, 114, 117
shaman. *See* spirit mediums
Shinawatra, 21
Si Thong, 164
Sihanouk. *See* Norodom
  Sihanouk
Sila Viravong, Maha, xvii, 13n,
  15n, 101-2
Siri Thivaphanh, General, 113
Sirindhorn, Maha Chakri, 44n,
  108-10, 111
  as envoy to Laos, 110
  donations to institutions, 112
Sisana Sisane, 25-6, 40, 150-1,
  166n, 172
Sisavang Vatthana, King, 43, 93,
  94, 95, 98, 102, 103n, 128,
  139, 173, 178n, 185
  abdication of, 99
  balancing role of, 96
  disappearance of, 99-100
  meeting with King Bhumibol,
    111
  photos of, xviii, 109, 116n, 124,
    128, 130
  statues of, xix, 116, 117
Sisavang Vong, King, 89, 92, 93n,
  95, 99, 100, 108n, 109n, 128,
  131, 137, 144
  education of, 155, 185
  funeral rites, 94
  in Prabang parade, 135
  magical powers of, 102
  photos of, 109, 116n, 131
  statues of, 116-7
Sisavang Vong University, 156,
  161, 167
Sisomphone Lovansai, 20n, 28
Sithon Kommadan, 63
slave. See *kha*
socialism, 2, 182
  *See also* post-socialism
socialist ideology
  replaced by Buddhism, 70